AF264276

Belles of the Creek Nation

By: Christopher Hodalee Scott Sewell

Published by Backintyme Publishing

Crofton, Kentucky, U.S.A.

Copyright @ 2015 by Backintyme

ALL RIGHTS RESERVED

Backintyme Publishing

1341 Grapevine Rd.

Crofton, KY 422117

270-985-8568

Website: http://backintyme.biz

Email:backintyme@mehrapublishing.com

Printed in the United States of America

October 2015

ISBN: 9780939479504

Library of Congress Control Number: 2015910822

Cover Art: Pictured here is a drawing rendered from a photo of the Poarch Creek Indian Chief Calvin McGhee of Atmore, Alabama taken in 1967. The photo compliments of Bobby McGhee of Blountstown Florida.

INTRODUCING

THE AMERICAN BRED SERIES;

ODYSSEYS OF THE MIXED BLOOD PIONEER

FAMILY

FROM BACKINTYME PUBLISHING

Belles of the Creek Nation

By Christopher Scott Sewell

Forward by Scott Withrow

"Your blood will mix with ours; and will spread with ours, over this great island...The ultimate point of rest and happiness for (Indians and Americans) is to let our settlements and theirs meet and blend together, to intermix, and become one people." -Excerpted from a letter written by President Thomas Jefferson to United States Indian Agent to the Creek Nation, Benjamin Hawkins, to relay to Creek leaders, February 18 1803

"The past is never dead. It's not even past." -William Faulkner

"What is life? It is the flash of a firefly in the night. It is the breath of a buffalo in the wintertime. It is the little shadow which runs across the grass and loses itself in the sunset." - Crowfoot, Blackfoot warrior and orator

Dedicated to my children Sehoy and Harjo Sewell and to
all my Creek ancestors struggle to carry on our identity
and cultural heritage…
Hesaketamese momekvs komen.

Original artwork by the author Scott Sewell

Contents...ix

Foreword

In the mid-1950s Davy Crockett was the rage, propelled
to fame in a Disney mini-series. It is in this series that many
first learned of Muscogee Creeks and the Creek War. Pictured
as a civil war between the Red Sticks and a more acculturated
faction, it was, in fact, more a war between the Red Sticks and
state militias. Thank goodness some at least have moved past the
stereotypical and Eurocentric Disney version of history to
discover in the Muskogee Creeks "the most sophisticated
political organization north of Mexico."[1] In *Belles of the Creek
Nation*, Scott Sewell adds significantly to understanding Creek
history, from the fresh perspective of one with Creek ancestry.

Sewell takes the reader beyond the standard history
concerned chiefly with the McGillivray's and McIntosh Traders
and the Creek Nation of Alabama, the Creek War and European
heroes. Instead, he centers his narrative on the Indian
Countryman Nimrod Doyle and his Creek daughters, Amanda,
Nancy, and Sarah--the Belles of the Creek Nation (as described
in a newspaper article about their wedding to three soldier
brothers from the Hill family). Subsequently, he follows the
daughters and their families through the Removal Era and
beyond and makes the important point that they lived during one
of the most difficult times in Creek history. True, he does write

---

[1]   "Muscogee Creek Nation History," Muskogee Creek Nation
http://www.muscogeenation-nsn.gov/Pages/History/history.html (accessed
May 23, 2015).

about Lower Creek Chief William McIntosh and his capitalist bent and tendency toward oligarchy. But his purpose is to show the dilemma faced by mixed-blood elites in the Creek War and events leading to Removal. Intertwined are Sewell's insightful understanding of white society and its patronizing attitude toward Indian peoples and all the complexities of that relationship. Throughout, he writes authoritatively of Creek towns, Creek trails, Creek matrilineal society, of race, of genealogy, and the geopolitics of the region. In doing so, he tells a compelling story that covers a wide geographical area— South Carolina, Georgia, Florida, Texas, and Oklahoma, as well as Alabama. I can't say what he handles best—his understanding of migration, of Indian culture, of genealogy, and race is all superb.

The author, foremost, displays his in-depth knowledge of his own people, the Creeks, whom, it is clear, he has not abandoned. It is, in fact, the local emphasis that makes this book so important. Academics often fail the see the importance of state and local history and have little concept of the role of the same in a national or universal context. The author demonstrates not only good research and academic excellence but also down-to-earth knowledge, the "experience of life," so eloquently advocated by the late Jacques Barzun in *Teacher in America*.[2] In this undeniably original treatment of the Creek

---

[2] Jacques Barzun, *Teacher in America* (Indianapolis: Liberty Press, 1985. Jacque Barzun was a French-born American historian who died in 2014 at

Nation we find that academic excellence on one hand and the local and the little known or seemingly obscure, on the other, are not at all incompatible and inconsequential. And like Barzun, Scott Sewell is a storyteller at heart, and one whose approach is academic, without the extremes of academic jargon.

For all of his emphasis on the local, Sewell goes beyond that history and writes of events and people in a regional and national context.   Scott Sewell in *Belles of the Creek Nation* not only tells a good story but he also gives us the gift of authenticity. His is an original work that makes the Creek Nation an integral and visible part of this continent's history. Importantly, throughout and especially in latter chapters, he makes it clear that Native peoples are not a relic of the past, that they have an identity in the modern world.

Scott Withrow, editor of and chapter contributor to *Carolina Genesis: Beyond the Color Line* (Backintyme Publishing, 2010), teaches adjunct history classes at North Greenville University and continuing education classes at Furman University, both in Greenville County, South Carolina.

---

age 104. I don't always agree with Barzun, but, nevertheless, agree on some of his views on writing and education.

FIGURE 1 ARTWORK: ORIGINAL BY AUTHOR, TITLED: INDIAN SEMINOLE GIRL

Original artwork by the author Scott Sewell

For a good part of our lives, my cousin S. Pony Hill and I have investigated the roots of our community, haunted by the stories of our elders of a time and place we would never know. With the names of Oxendine, Jacobs, Hill, Porter, Islands, and McIntosh in our ears we delved into the records available. We passed countless hours indulging that most common and yet treasured of the pastimes of Southerners everywhere, delving into family folklore and legend about our forebears. Some of these roots go deep into the Southeastern soil, indeed, stretching back for thousands of years. Others have only recently arrived from other parts of the globe and their roots are newly planted in the Southern lowlands. After decades of researching the origins and history of the unique Florida community to which our own family as well as many others belong, we have gained some understandings of the journey.

We come from a community that has been known by several names and viewed with some uncertainty as to its "racial purity" by its neighbors during the last two centuries. For the sake of generations to come, I wanted to put pen to paper about the lines of ancestry closest to my heart and experience; the Muscogee Creek Indian ancestors of my grandmother, Voncille Conyers, though she married a man of Catawba ancestry through the Scott family. Families sharing Creek and Catawba ancestry are common in the Florida panhandle and on the Poarch Creek

Indian reservation in neighboring Atmore, Alabama as well. One of the main motivations to do so was for my children, Sehoy and Harjo Sewell, and their descendants in the years to come, that they might know a little of the struggles and triumphs that their ancestors had, in this case those of those of the Muscogee Creek people. I also wanted people from families like my own to hear a story that may well correspond with their own family's journey of generations. It has been several generations now since the hothouse of segregation and institutional racism which was the order of the day was lifted, and our small tribal communities have been severely eroded by modernity.

I also have learned as a researcher and historian that we all somewhat selectively choose which ancestors we look upon among the many in our lines of descent as "more like us". Indeed, each person today has around 1, 024 ancestors[3] alive only a couple hundred years ago, assuming that one's family isn't from the many communities with high degree of intermarriage. My Creek ancestors were from such a heavily intermarried community. A person alive in 1800 could well have many thousands of descendants today, across continents and around the world even. As I look back on twenty years of gathered research on over a thousand individual ancestors which are in my database, I can see the vast crowds of faces from the distant past that have all contributed to the face I see in the

---

[3] Indeed, 400 years ago (or 1600 AD), means that you had as many as 1,048,576 distinct ancestors around the planet!

mirror. Yet like a handful of those from a century ago, I am part of the Creek community, attended the annual Corn Dance at the ceremonial grounds with my grandmother Sallie, and reared my children with the traditional view of our world as understood from the Creek perspective.

Phenotypically, I look much like many other Americans, as most Southerners do, and in light of this book's focus, my face appears like that of the majority of those who are today counted as enrolled citizens of the Creek Nation; of the more than 80,000 enrolled members only two thousand are "full blood" Indian, according to a recent 'State of the Nation' report by the Principal Chief of the Muscogee (Creek) Nation. Few; if any today are "pure blood" Creek. My families' roots like those of most Creek people today share the intertwining of the European in large part and the African to a smaller degree, as well as Indian. As well, like most the majority of the membership of the Muscogee (Creek) Nation today, the majority greater parts of my ancestors are European, and to a lesser degree African and Native American. In today's twenty-first century world, this is what it is to be Creek in a political sense. Even we who are members of the traditional ceremonial grounds, who live a lifestyle closer to the Creek people of centuries ago than do most, must understand that the many centuries of contact with outsiders have impacted the Creek people as a whole greatly, though the Creek people have made out better than many tribes now extinct. The tradition of the institution which lies at the heart of the Creek culture, the ceremonial ground, continues to this day.

Almost since first contact with Europeans, the Creek people have been a constantly changing flux of many peoples, languages, and traditions; different yet united by a connection to the ancient chiefdoms, bloodlines, and customs of the original peoples of the warm humid river bottoms of the Southland from which the name arises, the *Mvskvlke*, people of the lowlands. For we Eastern Creek people who remained in the south after the disaster of the Indian removal of the 1830's, the struggle to maintain ties to our Creek roots has not been without its challenges, each generation facing them as the tide of history and fortunes have ebbed and flowed around and through them. While many of us have understood ourselves to be Native American, to be Creek, at times our neighbors have had other views of us, many still do. Sadly, our homeland is known for its intolerance and history of oppression.

In Florida's panhandle, where my family has lived for generations, there is a uniquely Floridian term for "people like us": Dominicker (Howell, 1972), though less used today once designated the many mixed blood families found across the panhandle, often in the fringe areas deep in the swamps and pine barrens. Although during the Jim Crow era this term denoted someone who while appearing to be "White" to the eye was actually a "Negro" under the one-drop rule, it was applied as often to the many families of Native American descent of Creek, Catawba, and Lumbee origin. Several small settlements of such folks dotted the panhandle and adjoining lower portions of Alabama and Georgia, and the descendants are still present to some degree in those areas even now.

During segregation these families would be legally and socially treated as Negro or Colored as communities to some degree by census takers and outsiders, but on the local level the identity of these people was more nuanced. One avenue was relocation to a new area. Known as a "people of their own" in the surrounding counties to their settlements,, community members who moved away or severed ties to these settlements would lose the status as Colored within a generation or two, and as my and S. Pony Hill's research for our 2010 book "*The Indians of North Florida*" showed, Whites who married into these settlements would themselves come to be classified as Mulatto in some cases! In the several generations since segregation many of the families who were once the residents of these half dozen "Dominicker" settlements have crossed the color line and become fully White, while others since that time have vociferously struggled for a Native American identity and to be acknowledged by state and federal authorities as such.

I have attempted to document the fate of one family who struggled to preserve ties to the heritage of our forebears of survival and accommodation, those who preceded my grandmother Voncille, as a part of this much larger community of Mixed Bloods. I endeavor to illustrate the tangled threads of history, race, and place in creating the cultural heritage and identities we all have inherited today. The infamous removal of the large Indian Nations known as the Trail of Tears from the South during the 1830's didn't end the story of Native people in the Southland. From the late 1950s onwards many thousands of people fought mightily to assert their identity as Creek Indians in the South, including my own.

And this effort wasn't without some limited success, if the acknowledgement by the federal government in the mid 1980's of a couple thousand people as the Poarch Band of Creek Indians (out of thirty thousand claimants to the Indian Claims Commissions monetary settlement of the seizure of the lands held by the "Old Creek Nation" of 1832) is any kind of success. Since that time thousands of people still struggle on, asserting their Creek heritage without acknowledgment of their identity by the authorities but not without a social structure of their own largely unknown by the mainstream.

I have in my own 45 years saw the resurgence of the community's collective will to face our past. The families like my own, who generations ago were centered in Scotts Ferry in Calhoun County, Scotts Church, Woods in Liberty County, and Mount Zion Community in Holmes and Walton Counties, remain today. Many are reasserting that though as a group we are of primarily Eastern Siouan origins among the Cheraw, Lumbee, and Catawba, we like our cousins at the Poarch Creek Indian reservation, who are also of mixed Eastern Siouan and Muscogee Creek stock, deserve to have our story told, our social and political goals acknowledged, and our struggle for continued survival honored by our neighbors.

Introduction

I have elected to begin this story of two centuries of family history, struggle and identity with an interesting event from the crossroads of American history. It is the wedded union of three young Mixed Blood American Indian girls, referred to in historic newspaper articles from the archival documented event as "Belles of the Creek Nation" to three young men of the Hill family of Union County, South Carolina. According to the article in The Cherokee Phoenix from the event, on a spring day in early March of the year 1829, these three Muscogee Creek girls, daughters of noted Indian Countryman Nimrod Doyle by two of his Creek wives, would become the brides of three American soldiers stationed at Fort Mitchell, an American outpost located near several prominent "lower towns" of the Creek Nation. This is probably an event similar to hundreds in that era. Two civilization meet, two families become one, two lives entwine into one, founding a lineage that descendants would recount in future generations.

According to an article from The *Cherokee Phoenix* which documented this event, over one hundred notables from the Native American community would be in attendance, as well as almost two dozen Non-Indian guests. Few of the hundreds in attendance to this luxurious event on this fine spring day could know the specter of change, destruction, and life-changing events that were soon to befall the Creek Nation and her people. Such an event would have been a spectacle to observe with the leaders of tribes visiting and government officials from the fort in their military finery; the bright colored turbans of the warriors, the pomp of distinguished personalities, the rough edges of the frontier. To have seen this moment in time would have likely been a feast for the eyes. It was a quiet moment before the storm though.

The Indian removal would be a defining event in the lives of Nancy Doyle, Sarah Doyle , and Amanda Doyle, the Native American women who inspired this work, as well as an ever-present fact of life for many of their descendants over the generations to come. Like most Creek families, the scars from the uprooting of the Creek Nation would continue to cause dissension for many generations afterward, even until today in some ways. The unions between Nancy Doyle and George Robert Wesley Hill, and Sarah Doyle and Alexander Hill would last the rest of their lives even while Amanda and James's marriage would end within a couple of years.

Being a direct descendent of both Nancy and Sarah, ancestors who remained behind in the south after the removal, I have wondered many times what it would have been like to grow up tribal, in the Creek nation, and to have met old age and life's end with the once mighty Nation being only a memory in the minds of some, Indian names on a map of the state of Georgia and Alabama all that survived of once thriving Creek tribal towns.

The surging tide of manifest destiny and history would carry Amanda westward (along with a new husband she would also soon lose). She would make this trip west along with 20,000 people of the Creek Nation, with her family facing the uncertainties and difficulties of such a journey. The trip would indeed take the life of one husband, even as it led to Amanda finding a new one and rebuilding her life in a new western home. She had already been married three times and was only in her late twenties. The times were harsh and unforgiving as the historic record shows.

That same tide of American manifest destiny that bore Nimrod, Amanda, and others of the Doyle family westward to the Republic of Texas and Creek Nation carried Nancy and Sarah southward to the piney woods of the Georgia-Florida border and communities. This was a wilderness where other

Indians of several tribes and many types of Mixed Bloods would find refuge and isolation in the swamps and forests of the largely unsettled Florida panhandle. The three sisters' children, grandchildren and descendants would live in a swiftly evolving America where the Native American was at best ignored by authorities and at worst denied as even existing. Descendants of these three girls in the east and the west would face the challenges of remaining Native American in a society bent on assimilating them into a mainstream, extinguishing their and other Indian people's identity.

Amazingly, many families of the scattered generations of Creeks (both east and west) to experience the twentieth century would find one another again in the maelstrom of lives disrupted, striving in rebuilding relationships and community connections, and the fabric of the Creek world that was ripped asunder during the bitter days of the Indian Removal would begin to be repaired. Despite the years passed since then and the generations between the removal and now, the struggle in our lives as Creek people to maintain our cultural identity has continued. The proudest days of my life were when my son and daughter were born; the second proudest was when in the presence of my traditional people I received my "War Name" at the Tallahassee Ceremonial Grounds Green Corn Dance in the Muscogee (Creek) Nation in Oklahoma. Receiving my "young man's name" at the small community Green Corn Dance in

Blountstown Florida years previous to receiving my War Name
in Creek Nation for me exemplified in a way the journey of all
Eastern Creeks to reconnect to the root of our current identity,
the Muscogee (Creek) Nation now in Oklahoma. I have
relatives on both sides.

FIGURE 2 PHOTO: THE AUTHOR, BEING NAMED AT THE
ANNUAL GREEN CORN DANCE IN BLOUNTSTOWN, FLORIDA.
APALACHICOLA CEREMONIAL GROUNDS (1997), MEDICINE
MAN DAN PENTON AND DOUG ALDERSON, ERIC JACOBOWSKI
IS TO THE RIGHT.

I used to tell my kids of the naming day in Creek Nation,
when they were still little kids. In the stifling midafternoon
Oklahoma heat Sam Proctor, our Maker of Medicine at
Wakokiye Tallassee Ceremonial Grounds, handed me a
medicine cigarette and intoned the long drawn out cry that is
given when a man's War Name is bestowed.

I was given a name reflective of my Bird Clan ties and my own identity; *"Hotvle Haco,"* the Mad Wind. With this honor I felt that a great circle of seven generations had been completed. As a youngster I went to the ceremonial grounds in Florida, its small number of members and their struggle to hold on to a Creek heritage that had been eroding for generations, a waning fight for self-respect and roots. Being a part of the ceremonial grounds in Creek Nation, among the traditional people there, as many from my family had since the removal, gives me hope for our generations to come. Creek people across the United States, the scattered remnants of a once expansive and powerful nation, are working together to strengthen our language and culture for the generations yet to come. My cousin Jean Hill Chaudri once called the Creek Nation of times past, an "asylum of liberty", and for we who maintain a traditional way of life centered on our ceremonial ground and tribal community, it still is a refuge from the materialism and chaotic of the mainstream American identity.

Figure 3 Artwork: Original by author Scott Sewell
Titled: Electric Chief Indian

Figure 4 Artwork: Circle of Struggle

FIGURE 5 PHOTO: AUTHOR SCOTT SEWELL SPEAKS AT 1996 BLOUNTSTOWN INDIAN COMMUNITY CONFERENCE

FIGURE 6 PHOTO: ANNIE HILL CLAY

FIGURE 7 PHOTO: CLIFFORD SEWELL, VIETNAM 1969

FIGURE 8 PHOTO: SGT. U.S. MARINE CORPS RAYMOND W. KEVER

Chapter 1 Ancestry and Identity

In the last half century, there has been a steadily growing resurgence of interest in Native American ancestry. Indeed both within the American Indian community itself, as well as the American mainstream body of today, a small portion of which is of documentable Native American descent to varying degrees, interest grows. A recent analysis of data from Cornell University's Genetic Ancestry Project said that only a couple percent of the American population have "recent" Native American ancestry, meaning within the last 5 generations[4]. This doesn't mean there aren't millions of Americans with Indian ancestors, because there are; beyond a half dozen generations back though the relationship to any single ancestor is genetically insignificant. The relationship between anyone person and anyone of their ancestors is as much to do with the context of their culture, time and place, and strong attachments to remote ancestors can be found across countless cultures worldwide. The preoccupation with ancestry is well known among southerners and Native American ancestors more than many others are revered. "Proving out" as many predecessors as possible with Indian ancestry has been a major defining factor for the identity of any Creeks east of the Mississippi during the last half century. Tribal roots matter.

---

[4]http://www.slate.com/articles/news_and_politics/explainer/2012/05/elizabet h_warren_says_she_s_1_32nd_native_american_how_many_people_have_th at_heritage_.html

This renewal in the importance of connecting with native roots has grown even as many tribal languages are in decline and tribally mandated blood quantum requirements for enrollment become less stringent or are removed altogether in favor of any descent from an original roll as the member requirement for enrollment instead.

The use of a "descendant roll" is how many of the tribes in Oklahoma today who came from the South such as the Cherokee, Creek, Seminole, Choctaw, and Chickasaw define membership. In general, if one is a descendent of a person of ANY blood quantum who appears on the final Dawes Roll in 1907, one is eligible for membership in many tribes in eastern Oklahoma. There are individuals enrolled in the Five Tribes of Oklahoma with blood quanta of 1/2000or lower now. The vast majority of tribal members, if they took a genetic ancestry test from one of the many available today, would show no Native ancestry, as the quantum would be statistically insignificant.

This phenomenon which is happening often today is known as the "Cherokee paradox" among genetic researchers and social commentators, since it was first noticed among enrolled members of the Cherokee Nation, who would find upon receiving their DNA continental origin test results that NO significant Native American ancestry would show up despite the fact they were enrolled members of the Cherokee Nation. One can imagine easily how little the "blood quantum" system of the last century as used by the federal government, (and the realities for genetic history will match as this phenomenon grows), will be applied as genetic testing becomes more widespread in years to come. While tribal membership grows exponentially the languages, cultures and life ways of tribes everywhere are fighting to survive.

Despite this widespread erosion of native languages and tribally specific cultural practices within native communities, the interest in Indian ancestry by the general public has exploded in recent years. A surge in all things Indian is now happening, along with powwows, 'Indian Clubs', and people boasting Indian forebears proudly and publicly, activities which few would aspire to until fairly recently.

There are several reasons for this 'Indian renaissance' that can be easily identified, while other factors are less apparent. Firstly, the growth in interest in Native American culture and ancestry has paralleled the loosening of once rigid social rules and structures as well as the erosion of majority-imposed definitions of identity across the largest part of American society. In the cultural and social mainstream of this country, the very assimilation sought by the immigrant ancestors of many Americans was felt by their descendants as a loss of origins and a longing for roots, and many turned to genealogy as a tool to answers to that age old question, "where do I come from?" With more free time available in today's modern lifestyles and the availability of countless resources online to peruse in search of ancestors, genealogy has become a major hobby and pastime for many, young and old alike.

A vivid example of the surge of the timeless interest in one's origins that will be remembered by some from decades ago is the premiere of the television miniseries "Roots." This was a multi-generational television mini-series based on a book which followed author Alex Haley's ancestral lines of descent from a man brought from

Africa as a slave, through the generations held in bondage and then Southern social oppression, to the present times. This program was unique and its showing sparked a nation-wide surge in research into not only African American genealogy but led as well to many Americans of all backgrounds inquiring into ancestry. People began talking with family elders, dusting off old family Bibles and venturing into musty record rooms in courthouses and state archives buildings across the country. The premiere of *Roots* was of course in the pre-Internet era and the ease of access to historic records which has increased exponentially since the 1970s has led to a boom in genealogical research.

A recent New York Times article stated that the industry that has grown up surrounding genealogical research is now said to be near 100 million dollars a year with over a million subscribers to various online databases annually paying for the privilege of access to records that formerly one would spend hundreds of hours and travel many miles to access. It is one of the fastest growing and most lucrative web-based businesses, with over 60 million amateur genealogists involved in researching the over 1.8 billion names and related information available from organizations like ancestry.com and others. Today more than ever before people are looking for and finding information about the lives of their ancestors.

Another reason for the growth in interest in "personal identity," familial culture, and family genealogy which has exploded over the last several decades was the loss in the American mainstream family of ties to ancestral communities and culture, that in generations past were a focal point for identity and belonging; a physical, social, and often spiritual space that daily life for most people revolved around, and which often included those persons one had known all their life.

With the end of WW II and the mass movements of populations off the farm and into the rapidly growing cities and suburbs of the post war era, the ties that bound individuals to community were eroded significantly and in many cases lost entirely. The relative ease of life and probable higher standard of living, an indulgence not afforded to many people in the previous generations, allowed for the growing middle class to delve into learning more about their roots, a situation that has increased since that time to become the multi-million dollar industry and favored pastime of that it is now.

One area of genealogical inquiry by many mainstream Americans is research into the possibility of Native American ancestry, often based on oral history and family lore passed down about an ancestor who was said to be an Indian, most often a woman, a Cherokee, and a 'princess' of the tribe. While this situation is most of the time never documented since it is often nothing more than a common family tale, there are indeed millions of Americans of mixed racial ancestry, especially in the American South.

While the majority of the citizens of the United States are still of predominantly and in many cases solely European ancestry, there are certain regions in this country where there was a large amount of intermixture between races during the colonial era. Often there were liaisons that left no 'paper trail' to follow that occurred between Europeans, Native Americans, and (though not as widely known and even less readily acknowledged by the mainstream), African Americans as well. Today the investigation and documenting of these mixed population's origins, histories and modern identities are growing steadily. Thanks to the work of many countless academics who are continuing to search the archives for relevant records and publish them, the many tribal organizations and heritage associations working to synthesize and contextualize them, the many lay researchers everywhere who dedicate untold hours, personal resources, and substantial financial commitment to the task, the true story is emerging.

This hasn't always been the case though, with the historic narrative usually being one of two separate and hostile peoples, African American slaves and Euro-Americans who oppressed them, locked in a social struggle with one another, and Native Americans somewhere far away and largely uninvolved. Indeed, the slow and painful unfolding of the American drama is one in which Native Americans rarely appear except as occasional cameo roles about reservations, forced removals, and warfare soon squashed by the might of the cavalry. The rich and complex synthesis that was the historical reality couldn't have been more different.

The question of who is an Indian has always been a quandary and remains so today, more so even in light of the pressures that economic success has put on some tribes to divide the pie of their resources between less members. I will speak more to the battle of tribal enrollment, and in some cases disenrollment in later chapters. Suffice it to say that Indian identity and tribal membership are without doubt not synonymous terms. Despite its long standing debate and fluid use as a tool in the quest for identity, just who is an Indian and who is not can be viewed in three ways, essentially. Someone can be an Indian severally ways, including racially, politically, or culturally speaking. As well someone can be a combination of two or even all three, of these definitions, understanding these terms cover a vast expanse of complex factors. As my cousin S. Pony Hill recently described, the first two require no small part of "recognition" by societal or political forces that are often beyond the control of the individual, while the third is purely an internal factor, but still quite often impacted by external forces. The interplay of many internal and external forces on the "Indian identity" has changed little from the days of the removal until today; the struggles of Nancy and Sarah Doyle Hill are in some ways my own.

Episodes of Survival: Population Collapse and Indian Removal

To risk simplifying a very complex story, there are generally two sources of the documentable (using federal, state, tribal and county archival sources) Native ancestry that many Southerners in particular share. This Native American heritage among some families from the South is of great importance, for others it means very little. The relationship of tribes in the Colonial era had great impact on the parties to treaties, (and the subsequent assimilations, and removal later by the American's), or having little as with the many tribal communities in the Carolinas had great and lasting effects on those who came later. Indian ancestry among southerners for the largest part originates in two distinct episodes of American history; first the disenfranchisement and collapse of the Eastern Siouan populations of the Carolinas and Virginia in the late 1600s and early1700s, and second the subsequent and notorious 'Indian Removals' of the 1830s. Both these events contributed to the formation of my community and the modern identity of my family. Both these catastrophic events led to massive change in the lives of the survivors, including widespread dissolving of distinct 'tribal' identities, movement to geographical areas of little or no value to most of the settlers flooding into former tribal homelands, and in many cases the establishment of new communities of 'like people.' These refugees, most of whom may have had little, or no tribal ties or biological connections previously, but who find themselves caught in a common trap, found common cause and worked to form new communities, often on the fringes and most marginal areas.

The remnant groups of Eastern Siouan who survived the large mortality events due to diseases and social collapses among many tribes would reorganize into their own communities. Land patents and deeds filed with the colonial administrators in Virginia and the Carolinas from that era show many eastern Siouan ancestors migrating from southern parts of Virginia and northern parts of North Carolina, and areas of South Carolina. In the first federal census the American government executed, the census of 1790, many of these remnant peoples were enumerated on the census as "Free Persons of Color", a term used for many types of non-White people. This catch all statement in some ways could include non-reservation American Indians, people of mixed race between American Indian/European, and mixed race African/European, and others of various ancestries, some of which are only know being known using genetic data from descendent populations. On census from the nineteenth century, labels and terms used for different groups was very local and on the 1800 and 1810 census, many of these mixed blood families were classified as "all other free persons" in the census data (usually on a separate listing after white and black populations). In time these communities of hybridized peoples, sometimes called "little races", would grow into large populations.

One example to have an idea of the extent that some of these eastern Siouan communities had distinct identities is examining Pension records for veterans of the American Revolutionary War. By looking at names of men found in the documentary record who served from Robeson County, one of several strongholds of Eastern Siouan's from the era, a snapshot of the time and events is seen illuminating the new position of these mixed bloods in the changing social environment of post Revolution America. Individuals identified on these records with surnames that would later be associated with the then evolving Lumbee identity, men such as Samuel Bell, Jacob Locklear,

John Brooks, Berry Hunt, Thomas Jacobs, Thomas Cummings, and Michael Revels can tell us about the struggle of these communities and individuals for self-determination in a difficult time.

The social and legal limbo that these individuals, their families and communities navigated through was full of hidden dangers that neither whites nor their slaves would face. Census and court records from the time give countless examples of this balancing act many had to maintain to survive. As an example in 1790, families as Barnes, Bell, Brayboy, Brooks, Bullard, Chavers, Cumbo, Hammonds, Hunt, Jacobs, Locklear, Lowrie, Oxendine, Revels, Strickland, and Wilkins among just some were enumerated as "Free Persons of Color" in the first federal census collected by the government. At this early date these were already well established communities in many cases[5].

The collapse and reorganization of Indian populations in the Carolines and Virginia, and the handfuls of Indians from the larger removed tribes both are the primary sources of the Native American ancestry of many southerners today. Many Indians after the removal of the 1830's who didn't retreat into wilderness strongholds like the Mountains of the eastern Cherokee or the everglades of the Seminole would find a marginal social existence and many would intermarry with whites and blacks and their descendants become part of the

---

[5] U.S. Bureau of the Census, 1790

mainstream populations. The removal and the Eastern Siouan population migrations each shaped the fabric of several tribes including the Poarch Creeks of the Florida panhandle and lower Alabama. Though a Creek tribe, a quarter of its founding population was of Carolina Siouan extraction, individuals who migrated to the area and intermarried with the Creeks who remained in Alabama and Florida under the stipulations of the Treaty of Fort Jackson.

The removal and the Eastern Siouan migrations both have left their mark on remnant Indian families. These two large scale social events are very different, but resulted in the same fate for the majority of the fragmented, often demoralized Indian groups who remained in the Deep South during the nineteenth and early twentieth centuries; abject poverty, social marginalization, and legal disenfranchisement. The strategies and efforts by Native American groups to survive the settling of the eastern half of this country took many forms, some more effective than others, in this period. One of the strategies that developed throughout the fateful colonial era was for smaller tribal groups to join and assimilate into larger stronger ones, or in some cases, to be forcibly incorporated. With disease, slavery, and political maneuvering steadily eroding native populations, the game of survival became one with very different rules than in the pre-contact times.

Ancestry and Identity

In the centuries before removal, many Indian groups joined into larger confederations, efforts which continued through the colonial era and resulted in the evolution of large and powerful groups such as the Creek, Seminole, Cherokee, Choctaw, and Chickasaw 'nations'; polities which vied as equals with the European and early American governments for survival, power, prestige and territory.

Other groups took a different tack and became more mobile, adapting to the increasing numbers of European Americans and their new cultural, religious and judicial presence. In a twist of fate that would later cost them but at the time was fortuitous, many of these small groups never entered into formal agreements with the United States government. Being small and ofttimes very mobile, they were in some cases missed during the genocidal rush by the government to remove the Indians to west of the Mississippi. Almost from the initial contact between the Europeans and Native Americans, we see some Indians changing their social and cultural patterns to survive. While some found alliances and lifestyles that facilitated survival, for many others disease, frequent wars, or being sold into slavery would be their ultimate end. This phenomenon of biological, linguistic, and cultural hybridization was especially pronounced along the Tidewater and Piedmont areas of the East. It is not surprising that this region is the epicenter of remnant Indian communities whose genesis was in the events described earlier.

The colonial records from Virginia and the Carolinas are peppered with accounts of travelers in these areas at the turn of the nineteenth century encountering English-speaking, culturally European Native American groups of phenotypically Indian appearing people all along the frontier of the times.

"A Mixt Crewe"

In the century after the removals, reports of "mixed race groups," many with locally well-known and colorful appellations and accompanying mythologies as to their origins came to be found in the back country, swamps, and marginal areas from Louisiana to Maine. Groups such as the 'so-called' Croatan, Redbones, Brass Ankles, Melungeons, Sabine, Dominicker, Guineas, Wesort, Turks, and Issues, have been the subject of anthropological inquiry for well over a century, yet their places in the social milieu of their local areas during their initial 'formations' most often during colonial times, are yet to be fully understood. These groups almost all share certain distinct attributes where ever they are found. Some things that most of these 'hybrid groups' have in common are frequent self-described claims of Indian ancestry, histories of suspicion, marginalization and exclusion by the mainstream society, and for many the occupancy of the least desirable areas of habitation such as mountains, swamps, pine barrens and other rugged and inaccessible terrain.

Though there were infrequent visits to the settlements of these groups by government officials, academics, and others, most were left to struggle against the oppressive social order of the past until fairly recent times. The latter half of the twentieth century has seen increased anthropological research that has begun to engage this long neglected episode in American history in the Carolinas and Virginia during the colonial era, an episode which birthed the majority of the groups, once known as "tri-racial isolates" and often called hybrid peoples today. The hybridization of 'racial' groups that occurred in these regions, as discussed earlier, would set in motion social struggles by dozens of distinct communities to determine their own identity in the face of institutionalized racism over the next two centuries.

During the 1700s, certain areas in upper and central North Carolina, upper South Carolina, and Virginia saw a process of social hybridization among the various peoples then present. Movements by large numbers of Mixed-Blood Indian families out of these areas in a search for a better life left the Southeast, and scattered with dozens of groups across a half dozen states by the turn of the twentieth century. Some of the populations that emerged from these events in the Carolinas and Virginia were significant by the twentieth century, with estimates in the hundreds of thousands according to the works of anthropologist who visited them. More on this genesis period of these groups can be found in the opening chapter of our book released in 2010, *The Indians of North Florida*. Suffice it to say that these events would play a large role in the shaping of the modern Indian south today. Tribes such as the Lumbee, Saponi, and Tuscarora all find the events of this era as significant sculptures of their modern identity.

On a larger scene, the forced removal in the 1830s of most of the large tribal nations of the Eastern United States, such as the Seminole, Choctaw, Chickasaw, Creek and Cherokee, led to many of the Indians who remained afterwards being subsumed within the larger populations of the White and Black communities. Among the small portion of the remaining Natives in the East who didn't assimilate into the mainstream, the social forces at work led to them 'turning inwards', facilitating the creation of dozens of small, insular, and distinct communities of people of varied phenotypical appearance but cohesive social identity as a group, and in many cases, as Indian, at least in their own eyes, if not their neighbors. The period between the removal era of the 1830's and the outbreak of the Civil war was one of adjustment to a new reality for Indians, while the era after the close of the war would be one of increasing violence and persecution for these populations. The settlements of the many mixed blood Indian groups were reflective of the steady migrations over several generations by some families to new areas. These communities were scattered from the mountains of Tennessee in the West, to the pine barrens of the Florida panhandle in the South, to the rocky coasts of Massachusetts and Maine in the North. Once the iron curtain of racial segregation fell across the South, many of these groups would spend a century in a cocoon of familial and cultural isolation, with life being relatively unchanged from the mid nineteenth to the mid twentieth century.

The winds of social change would begin blowing across all of American society with the end of World War II and would greatly impact the lives of the people of the isolated and insular hybrid communities much as they would all Americans.

Tribal Recognition

With the advent of desegregation in the Southern states, some of these groups passed into the general population, while others began protracted struggles for acknowledgment by state and federal authorities as "Native American" and recognition of their tribal governments. The larger tribal nations, often those with federal acknowledgment, would embark on efforts to recover the severely eroded but cherished sovereignty and self-determination that many had lost. During the second half of the twentieth century many congressional acts would restore various aspects of the tribe's powers to self-govern. Many would begin ventures in economic development, with a few even becoming very successful in that area. Some tribes would successfully recover their status as recognized tribes, either by state or federal authorities. In 2008 over 62 tribes had been recognized by states while 566 had been acknowledged by the federal government, This recognition was often as a result of the process of treaties negotiated setting up reservations in the 19th century

Struggles by groups of Indians in Floridas panhandle for recognition over the last fifty years has been unsuccessful, on a state and federal level. None have achieved recognition by the state due to the Florida Governor's Council on Indian Affairs adopted a policy in 1988 recommending that the state refrain from recognizing any group that does not have federal recognition. The Governor's Council forwarded that if the state government of Florida wished to proceed with recognition, it recommended that "a state action should create a government-to-government relationship between state and tribe, it should set forth an explicit rendering of the state's interpretation of 'recognition,', and additionally be confined only to groups descended from Seminole, Miccosukee, Creek, or a tribe located in Florida prior to May 30, 1830, the date of passage of the US Indian Removal Act."

It also felt that any tribal group the state should entertain recognition of should meet federal criteria for recognition. Out of several groups seeking federal acknowledgement in the second half of the 20th century with ties to north Florida, only the

Poarch Band of Creek Indians would gain federal recognition, and hence state recognition, though the PBCI reservation is in Escambia County Alabama bordering Florida. Half of its population lived in the Pensacola area prior to federal recognition in the mid 1980's though.

Groups seeking acknowledgement by the nearby state of Georgia have been successful, as the Cherokee of Georgia, the Georgia Tribe of Eastern Cherokees, and the Lower Muskogee Creek Tribe have been recognized. In Alabama, the Davis-Strong Act of 1984 established the Alabama Indian Affairs Commission, and empowered it to acknowledge and represent Native American citizens of Alabama. The commission recognized seven tribes that did not have federal recognition. Groups in Alabama who have successfully been recognized by the state besides the Poarch Band include several; the Cher-O-Creek Intra Tribal Indians, the Cherokee Tribe of Northeast Alabama, Echota Cherokee Tribe of Alabama, Ma-Chis Lower Creek Indian Tribe of Alabama, The MOWA Choctaw, the Piqua Shawnee Tribe, the Star Clan of Muscogee Creeks, and the United Cherokee Ani-Yun-Wiya Nation.

FIGURE 9 PHOTO: PONY HILL AND AUTHOR'S SON HARJO

FIGURE 10 PHOTO: INDOOR STOMP

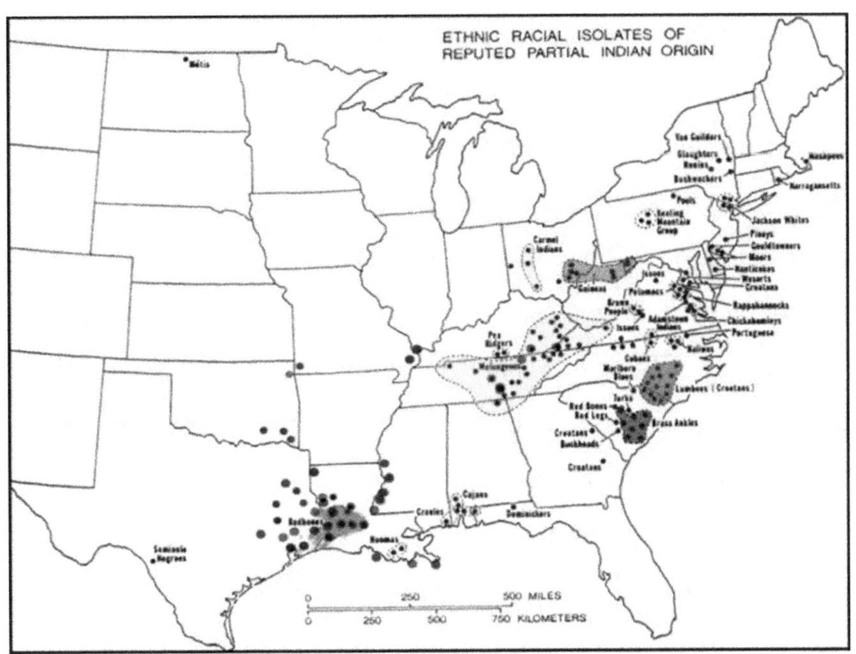

FIGURE 11 MAP: KNOWN MIXED BLOOD TRIBAL GROUPS: VAN GELDERS/GUILDER, SLAUGHTERS, MOSIES, BUSHWACKERS, MASHPEES, NARAGANSETTS, POOLS, KEATING MOUNTAIN GROUP, JACKSON WHITES, PISAYS, GOULDTOWNERS, MOORS, NANTICOCKES, WESORTS, CROATANS, RAPPAHANNOCKS, CHICKABONLAYS, PORTUGUESE, ISSUES, GUINEAS, CARMEL INDIANS, PEA RIDGERS, MELUNGEONS, CUBANS, MARLBORO BLUES, TURKS, ADAMSTOWN INDIANS, BROWN PEOPLE, PATOMACS, CUBANS, LUMBEE, TURKS, REDBONES, RED LEGS, BRASS ANKLES, BUCKHEADS, CROATANS, CAJANS (MOWA), CREOLES, DOMINICKERS, METIS, SEMINOLE NEGROES, HOUMAS, CREOLES, BARATARIANS, FORT "BRIDGERS" (NOT PICTURED) WYOMING, NEZ PERCE (NOT PICTURED) COLEVILLE INDIAN RESERVATION OREGON/WYOMING/IDAHO.

The debate as to who should be recognized has been around for a long time. The American Constitution gives ultimate authority concerning matters affecting the Indian tribes to the United States federal government. Under federal law and regulations, an Indian tribe is defined as a group of Native Americans with self-government authority. This defines those tribes recognized by the federal government. The requirements for tribal recognition by the federal government are much more strenuous than those of the states. According to the National Conference of State Legislatures, only fourteen states recognize tribes at the state level in the opening decade of the century, and this number is growing annually as more groups petition and secure state recognition.

My own family has been involved for generations in efforts to being acknowledgement to both Eastern Creek and Catawba people in Floridas panhandle. Recently the population of Cheraw which many of our ancestors were part of in South Carolina was recognized by the state. Long labeled as "Turks", the fight for recognition as Cheraw Indians has led this tribe, like many others to petition for and receive recognition by the state for its claims to an Indian identity as a people. Today most members of any Indian tribe will most likely have some multi-tribal ancestry, if not multi-racial, and the terms and perspective that outside authorities hold of a community still means a lot in how that community is approached by others. As Chief Oxendine of the Sumter Cheraw made clear to the press on announcement of the state recognition in 2013 approached, "We will be recognized as a real people," Cheraw Chief Ralph Justice

Oxendine told South Carolina Radio Network. "Not a tri-racial people, but one people."

The Indians of Jackson and Calhoun Counties in Florida's panhandle have origins in three groups of Indian people, differing populations of Indians who had migrating families come together and fuse into one people settled in three clustered communities.

The Catawba origins of several founding families of this tribe, especially the Scotts are noted in several historic documents, including an important court case which clearly spoke to the Catawba roots of the family and settlement. On July 10th, 1861, Francis Hill, a "white unmarried male," was charged by the Calhoun County Court with "Fornication with one Eliza Scott a Mulatto woman." This charge was not long-standing, however, as Francis petitioned and provided witnesses who were prepared to testify that, "Eliza Scott is not a Mulatto as named in the indictment but is an Indian of the Catawba tribe, her grandfather Jacob Scott being a headman of that tribe.[6]" The Scott family and its descendants is one of the largest in the community. Other families of Catawba were represented as well, and many of the Catawba families who settled into Florida had the surnames of major early Catawba families, Some of these include Ayers, Brown, Scott, as already stated, and Stephens.

---

[6] 10 July 1861, State of Florida V. Francis Hill, 1860-65 Calhoun Judicial Cases, Calhoun County Courthouse Archives Room 3rd Floor, Blountstown, Florida.

Jacob Scott, Joseph Scott, and Absalom Scott were from the reservation at Rock Hill originally.

These men direct familial connections there, and Isham Scott who was a cousin to the former three had connections to the Catawba-Siouan Indians on the Gingaskin land in Northampton, Virginia as well. Many of the eastern Siouan population overlapped, sharing surnames and ancestral lineages. Richard Jeffries, another founding member of the Florida Catawba community, was the son of Silvia Scott and Andrew 'Drury' Jeffries. He also had ties to the Catawba found in in Northampton. The Jeffreys/Jeffries lineage has been found in many groups and been identified as descended from the Catawba tribe in many different places and times.

Connected to but separate from the Cheraw/ Catawba migrations were several families of Lumbee Indians who journeyed from Robeson County in North Carolina and settled among the Florida people, including the Oxendine, Jacobs, Revels, Bass, and Hunt families, many of whom were settled in the Woods settlement. Ancestral ties between the Carolina Catawba, Lumbee, and Cheraw descendants were many and extensive, even in the smallest of the three settlements in the Apalachicola River area. Daniel Conyers and his wife Elizabeth Moses had migrated from Sumter County, South Carolina, the community mentioned earlier that only recently received state recognition. Elizabeth was the daughter of F.J. Moses who had interestingly had signed a petition of "descendants of David Scott" in Sumter South Carolina in 1830. His signature appeared below that of John Nettles, an Indian identified as a "headman" of the Catawba. The David Scott of the petitions concern was reportedly of Catawba blood. Martha Emma Hill (the daughter of Francis Hill and Elizabeth Scott of Scott's Ferry lived in the Woods settlement along with Mary Brown Kever, the wife of Frank Kever of France and granddaughter of Catawba Jaime Brown and his Pamunkey wife Sarah Mursh. Mary Samantha Blanchard Dasher who was the daughter of John Blanchard and Ellen Scott of Scott's Ferry lived in the small settlement as well. The last group who were a separate but related migration to Florida in the 1800s and who became part of the Indian settlements along the Apalachicola and Chipola Rivers were the Bass, Hunt, Lowry and Oxendine families.

Though the Florida community was dominated by families of Carolina Eastern Siouan extraction, there are several families of Muscogee Creek origins who avoided the removal and found a place in this isolated and rugged settlement, most notably the descendants of Nancy and Sarah Doyle Hill, whom this work focuses on. I will go more in-depth into the lives of these Creek women and their descendants in later chapters. Together these several migrations of differing Indians synthesized into one distinct community, which shares a strong cultural heritage with the Creeks like their nearby neighbors the

Poarch Band even as it had strong genealogical ties to the eastern Siouan's of the Carolinas. The identity of this community, like any other, when examined in-depth is complex.

In our own day there are many ways of being "Native American." There are as discussed earlier , multiple aspects of the Indian identity, and dozens of social, political, and racial terms all associated with describing just who is an "Indian," even while few can agree on any. Persons calling themselves Indians today come in many colors, complexions, phenotypes, and social identities. Many are citizens of federally acknowledged Indian tribes; others are not. A few can proudly display Certificate of Degree of Indian Blood cards with 4/4 quantum Indian "blood"[7] others feel the blood quantum system used by the Bureau of Indian Affairs is a colonial and imposed regimen which is ultimately harmful to Native persons and communities.

Indigenous Decolonization has been characterized by some as a process that Indigenous people whose communities were grossly affected by colonial expansion, genocide and cultural assimilation may go through by recolonizing with other

---

[7] In the early 1990's, a cousin in Creek Nation in Oklahoma, Norma Bible, (a granddaughter of Creek Chief George W. Hill) showed me her degree of Indian blood card which showed her as full blood; the next time I saw her I brought a copy of her grandfather George Hill's enrollment card which documented his blood quantum as a half blood and asked, "how could you be full blood when he was half?." This is one example of several I could cite that documents the endless inconsistencies within the BIA's blood quantum system.

Indigenous frameworks of thought, in understanding the history of their colonization and rediscovering their ancestral traditions and cultural values. My cousin Marcus Briggs-Cloud has worked for many years in the effort to plant seeds of decolonization in the minds and lives of many Indians, striving to liberate the Native American communities and people from the debilitating effects of the loss of genuine identity and naturally balanced ways of life. The debate within many Eastern Indian communities as to the relevance and need for recognition by various powers outside of their community by state, federal and other tribal governments is an ongoing dialogue. For much decolonization is possible only through communities embracing their own languages, cultures and worldviews.

This "decolonization of the mind" as Marcus puts it proceeds escaping the snares of the identity politics prevalent now in dialogues regarding Native identity. The ways many define who and what is Native is no longer taken for granted and calls for the restoration of the importance of native languages and perspectives are now heard throughout Indian Country. The presence of the Bureau of Indian Affairs is constant in the lives of most reservation peoples and the as can be easily perceived on many larger reservations the situation is unacceptable and unsustainable. Alcoholism, tobacco abuse, domestic violence, healthy food options and other issues not "sexy" enough to gain many headlines are at the heart of multiple movements within

Indian country to secure justice for those in need. "The decolonization of the mind for indigenous peoples begins with language acquisition," Marcus said recently "All of our worldviews are encompassed in our respective languages."

With the generation of elders who are the last to have been reared with most Native American languages used as a first language in their homes passing on, the golden moment of preservation of what can be saved is now upon the few who are carrying on the hard work of this unappreciated movement. The efforts within Indian communities to redefine the dialogue concerning the need for resources and effort, often against their own tribal administrations, is one which is gaining ground yearly and is showing results in some tribal settings. The relationship with the federal government and Bureau of Indian Affairs remains troublesome. Increasingly the blood quantum system is being perceived as outdated, indeed flawed from the start in the eyes of many as it imposes a non-Native American perspective into the tribal identity of many communities, excluding many. Not long ago, one of the most controversial actions of the Bureau of Indian Affairs was the late 19th to early 20th century practice of removing Indian children from their homes in the name of bettering them through education.

This program sought to educate Native American children in faraway boarding schools. Government officials with an emphasis on assimilation of these kids into the mainstream often prohibited them from using their tribal languages, living traditional practices, and being a part of their own cultures. It emphasized being educated to European-American culture and finding a place "above" the tribal body that is at the heart of Indian life.

The blood quantum system allowed the tribal body to be dissected and parted out to various denominations, agencies of government, and corrupt tribal leaders. Though changes have happened in the last few generations, the blood quantum system is still a crippling chain on the Native American future.

Some Native American people think it is designed to ultimately eradicate indigenous claims by phasing out the trust relationship between the United States and American Indians by "quantifying" them into extinction. This is a claim made at every point in American history about the "vanishing Redman" by the American mainstream.[8] Yet today, millions of people are claiming Native American identity when a mere fifty years ago the federal census recorded only a few hundred thousand present.[9] In light of the emerging browning of the population, the dynamics of identity become increasingly important. As we witness dramatic changes during our own lifetimes in the dominant population of the planets dominant power, some would have reason for speculation as to their descendants place

---

[8] http://indiancountrytodaymedianetwork.com/2013/05/07/exploring-political-exploitation-blood-quantum-us-149231

[9] From half a million in 1950, the most recent census documents over two million persons self-identified as Native American.

and cause to worry as to their ability to maintain their material wealth and political power.

Indeed as more of America's citizens come from non-European backgrounds, the United States will change its idea of its cultural heritage and the narratives of what defines "us" will change. The pilgrims and the Mayflower staples of past generations are now openly questioned by school age children. The Thanksgiving story is being renegotiated as we watch. Considering the self-centeredness of some whites' behavior toward Native Americans and others in the last few centuries that each have faced one another across the color line, their efforts to strive for social justice today would be more vigorous one would think. America's sins from the past, including removing Indians, enslaving African peoples, the deporting of Chinese, the annexation of the Nation of Hawaii, all these are not "the past" to those who still live with its legacy.

In watching the seemingly growing unrest that has of late gripped some communities, one could say there is cause to worry about race relations in this country, especially with the coming decades when the shoe will be on the other foot. Solutions to stories such as those about police killings of unarmed men of color, of the prison industrial complex, and of income inequality now playing out in the headlines must be addressed, and soon. The rigid duality of race that has long characterized many Americans view of identity must be taken down, and stories such as those of my ancestors should illustrate the need for this.

This work revolved around family, identity, and peoplehood, as well as circumstance, time and place. Through the lives of Nimrod Doyle the Indian countryman, his Mixed Blood daughters, and the family lines they founded, I hear the story of many families, Creek and American, Indian and White. From the beginning the family lineages descended from them, forged in the heat of the dark days of the Indian removal, has had to confront the realities of "choosing" to be Native American or not, as well as impact of being an "American" in our modern era. For some branches of them this meant accommodation, while for others it meant resistance. In telling the story of Nimrod Doyle, his daughters and their descendants, I have searched out the many descendants of this family and their individual tales of survival through the many generations.

My own grandmother, a descendant of Sarah and Nancy Doyle on both sides of her family, was the last of a generation who were born into the social isolation of the old South, a land with deep wounds after decades under Jim Crow segregation. Racial ambiguity was an ever present fact of life for the many communities of Native Americans which eked out survival in the hard scrabble regions economically depressed since the Civil War and socially ignored by the rest of the country for a century. In her lifetime she saw the small, heavily-intermarried, and insular community of the generations since the removal come to an end, and a new struggle for identity in a changed society commence.

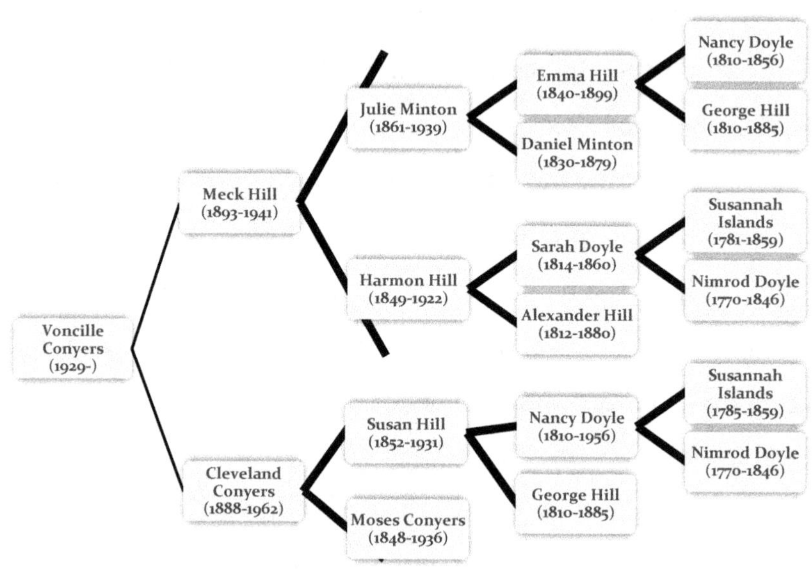

FIGURE 12 PEDIGREE CHART: VONCILLA CONYERS, GRANDMOTHER OF AUTHOR.

The story of my family reaches back through the female line to the ancient Creek Nation, a matriarchal and egalitarian society. Today, we find only a shadow of its former self, culturally, yet in other ways, we can discern a renewed vigor, an expansive perspective, and a determined response to modernity in the last few decades. Eastern Oklahoma is feeling this renewal in the economic development and higher social profile the tribes as well as Individual Indians are portraying. The media and academia are documenting a vibrant and growing cultural milieu among many Nations. I and my family are a part of this resurgence as much as my old ones were part of the twilight of Creek independence in their homeland and the darkness of post removal existence. I am proud to say I am a member of the Bird Clan. Among the Creek the clan one inherits comes from the mother and her mother on back.

Two of Nimrod Doyle's daughters, Nancy and Sarah, were members of the Bird Clan through their mother Susannah Islands, and from her mother Bissie McIntosh. In a direct line of mothers from my own, to my grandmother Voncille Conyers, members of the Bird Clan have flowed from one generation to the next through the ladder of generations; Voncille Conyers to her mother Meck Hill, to her Mother, Julie Minton, to her Mother, Emma Hill, to her Mother Nancy Doyle. The holding of a clan by many citizens of the Muscogee (Creek) Nation and indeed Creek people anywhere is becoming less frequent with each passing generation as rising intermarriage with non-Creeks whittles away those who do have one, as well as the import of having a clan today being considerably less relevant than it once were among Creek people. All this aside to have a direct matrilineal tie to a clan among the Creek is still something to take pride in and celebrate. At the ceremonial grounds it is members of the Bird Clan who do this and I have taken part in this responsibility in the past and been honored to have been asked to do so.

FIGURE 13 PHOTO: SUSAN HILL

Today not all Creek people retain a clan association, though many full blood people do. For a Mixed Blood to have a clan and identify with it is uncommon today. For many of us who follow the traditional way of life this identification with clan and tribal town are still one of the most important parts of our lives, as it always has been known to the for Creek people of past generations. When we go to the overnight stomp dances, I feel that some bit of the energy there is directly from the old people; indeed we have a dance which closes out the night of dancing at daybreak and is known as the "Old Peoples" Dance. As daylight breaks at this point, I often feel the presence of the departed who walked this same path, who lived this same way of life.

On any late Saturday evening during the long, hot, and often muggy summers in the Creek Nation in eastern Oklahoma, there will be a flurry of activity on the dusty back roads that spider web the area. Darkness will fall on the small towns and wide cow pastures of the Sooner state, porch lights will flicker on and the average Oklahomans will settle into their couches for a night of football or sitcoms. In the areas where the first people of this continent predominate, other activities will just be starting up. Carloads of Indians in beat-up late model vehicles can be seen speeding through the gathering dusk. These cars will turn off the back roads into gated tree trail roads through trees that screen the interior from passing eyes. These gates which mark the entranceway to another time and place, though usually closed and locked, will stand open on these special Saturday nights.

Gathering in the deepening gloom will be Indians from a dozen tribes and half dozen states. Keetoowah Cherokee from Vian, Oklahoma, Poarch Creeks from Atmore, Alabama, Houma Indians from southern Louisiana, and Dominicker Indians from the panhandle of Florida will join in with the members of some sixteen other Creek ceremonial grounds scattered across eastern Oklahoma in the evening's gathering and celebration. Some of the participants may have driven for twenty hours to be present for a night's dancing, leaving after daybreak to drive back the thousand miles to their homes. Others present may live only a couple of miles away and leave halfway through the night to go to another dance held at another grounds nearby. On this Saturday night three different ceremonial grounds, one Creek, one Euchee, and one Shawnee, will be dancing as well. The summer nights in Indian Country are often busy, with Indians crisscrossing the region to dance with one another, to share in a camp meal, to fellowship.

In the distance as the cars clear the open gate will be dozens of low-slung open-sided sheds with tables set up full of food around which dozens of people will be gathered. In the central plaza of these many camps will be a large open area bordered by several open sided sheds topped with willow branches, in which the shadowy forms of men sitting on benches can be barely discerned by the faint light cast by a fire burning in the middle of the clean and debris free dance ground. In the lights of the nearby camps can be seen Indian people preparing for the night's dance; women busily strapping on to their legs bulky turtle shell shakers, lean men in vests of patchwork with white crane feathers standing erect in their caps, some sporting eagle-feather adorned Stetsons, long-haired teenage girls adorned with beautiful skirts and finger woven sashes tied around their waists.

Frequent rounds are made among the camps by two designated men carrying canes and announcing in Muskogee Creek the four stipulated warnings that dancing will soon commence. The tension builds and a steadily line of cars streams through the gates. As the midnight hour approaches more and more men will squeeze into the seats within the arbors on three sides of the ceremonial grounds place. Younger men in ball caps, sharp looking patchwork jackets and pressed Levis gather on the front row of seats within the arbors while the elders sit on the back row in their own well-used folding chairs. They watch the night's unfolding events with the ease of having done this every summer for the last three quarters of a century, yet still eagerly looking forward to the night's fellowship and fun. Quietly smoking their pipes and occasionally making comments amongst themselves in Creek and Cherokee, they are a reserved and distinguished group, ready with advice for the curious, and admonitions for those seeking conflict.

With a smile and a handshake they welcome all who come. Frequently leaders from other ceremonial grounds will walk to the arbor that is called *Mekkvlke*, the leaders, and shake hands with those gathered there. These old friends warmly greet their host, the *Mekko* of the grounds, as well as his several *Henehvlke*, or grounds officers who sit to his right and left in the seats reserved for their office.

In several locations on the fringes of the ring dozens of people will cluster in lawn chairs, visitors from nearby ceremonial grounds of the Creek, Cherokee, Shawnee, and Euchee anticipating the fun soon to be had. They come to dance and sing with friends and relatives, knowing that in a few weeks their own grounds will host a similar such stomp dance night and that this grounds' membership will come and support them in turn. Soon the fourth and final call goes out to prepare for the dance and as a full moon rises over the Creek Nation, its light will reveal hundreds of Indians circling a fire, with new arrivals joining in a growing spiral of singing dancers.

Songs centuries old once again drift on the night wind as the communities' many voices lift up as one, the rhythmic shakers keeping time with the human heartbeat, reflecting the turning of earth, mirroring the transit of the stars across the night's sky. As the dawn's first tendrils of light begin to touch the eastern horizon visitors from distant areas begin to make their way home, shaking hands with old friends and sending fond farewells until next time, the next weekend, the next dance, the next chance to really be themselves again. By the time daylight has arrived in full the remaining dancers gather behind an aged yet athletic elder, his stride still strong despite being eighty years old, his voice clear and full as he begins the "Old Peoples' Dance." This final circling of the fire's dying coals closes out a night of fellowship and fun for the people of the grounds.

This night's activities fulfills the hopes of generations past; hopes of tired and sick great-great grandparents walking a thousand mile long tail of tears, hopes of long ago warriors sacrificing their lives on battlefields now seldom-visited state parks in Alabama and Georgia; and the living breathing hopes of any of the faintly smiling elders sitting in the comfort of a well-worn camp chair watching great grandchildren run in the glow of the fires light around the moving mass of dancers, seeking a place to slip into sweating, singing, and happy crowd. It could be 1491, or 2015. Tradition lives on.

Historical Context

The ceremonial ground is the cultural as well as religious center of the Creek culture and identity, as it is for several other tribes who lived in the Southeast at one time. As such it is inextricably linked to the social and political histories of the Muscogee peoples. Until recently, the Sacred Fire[10] that burned at the heart of the ceremonial grounds was the nucleus around which Creek life revolved for each generation, for thousands of years. Today it is still such a living root for many Indians in Oklahoma, Florida, Alabama, and Georgia. For many tribes with

---

[10] Though among "grounds people" this entity is referred to as the "ashes", I will use the term Sacred Fire since it is commonly perceived as the focus of the activities at a ceremonial grounds by visitors and non-traditional Indians.

historic roots in the Southeast such as the Seminoles,[11] Miccosukee, Creek, Euchee, Shawnee, Seneca-Cayuga, Natchez, Catawba and Cherokee, the ceremonial grounds and its annual Corn Dance continue to play an important role in their tribal identity. Additionally many tribes who lost the ties to the ancient southeastern ceremonial grounds culture centuries ago are reviving it and seeking participation with the tribes who have maintained it. Members of far flung Indian settlements from Dulac, Louisiana to Edisto, South Carolina are repairing the threads of identity, weaving again a tapestry of community and tradition.

Tribal groups across Louisiana, Texas, the Carolinas, and other areas are visiting ceremonial grounds in the Muscogee (Creek) Nation and taking back what they learn to their own communities; like a breath of life blowing on faint embers which turn to a flame, the rejuvenation of tribal traditions and Native American identities is taking place across Indian Country as well as in the forgotten corners of the lands once held by tribes but now lost to American states.

What is a southeastern Indian ceremonial ground?[12] In its physicality it is an open plaza surrounded on several sides by

---

[11] The Seminole Tribe of Florida and the Seminole Nation of Oklahoma both have ceremonial grounds today.

[12] The general explanations I am presenting are from a Creek perspective and experience for the most part. Different tribes and various communities within tribes have a broad range of ceremonial architectural and procedural protocols that mark each one as unique even as they share many traditions that all inherited from the pre-Columbian Mississippian Culture.

small open sided cabins or sheds called arbors which contain benches facing inwards. Each arbor has its interior divided into seating areas for differing clans or classes. The roof of these structures is covered annually with cuttings from willows, which when piled high and thick provide protection from the hot summer sun. In the center of this plaza is a built a sacred fire atop the ashes from the sacred fires kindled in the previous years.

A ring of shells, dirt, and debris which is swept from within the ring to clear it is formed in a circle around the sacred precinct's edges. This ring divides the everyday world from that of the ceremonial timelessness within. Within the ring is the specific arbors in which are the designated seats of the men of each clan.[13] On entering the ring, each finds that place of his clan and sits there in quiet contemplation and waiting, a window of reflection and centering engaged in before the start of a night of stomp dancing or during the several days of the Corn Dance.

Scattered around the area outside of this ring are the camps of the women, and in the matriarchal society of the Creek peoples, clan is of paramount importance even yet. Many of the tribes' natives to the Southeast were matriarchal. As a man is

---

[13] Some of the traditional clans of the Muscogee people are now extinct but many still survive including the Bird, Tiger, Alligator, Snake, Raccoon, Deer, Wind, White Potato, Bear, Beaver, Wildcat, Big Town, and others. Among smaller tribal groups who were incorporated into the Creeks historically there were many different clan such as New Earth, Daddy Longlegs, Tobacco, Salt, Eagle, Turtle, and others which some Creek people still have.

born to his mother's clan, he will belong to his mother's camp until he is married, at which time he may still eat at his mother's camp but will have responsibilities for the upkeep and care of his wife's camp. During the hours of the all night stomp dances a spot near the edge of the ring will be a gathering place for the women of a ground, a place where they will converge and set up seats to rest in between episodes of dancing, during which they shake heavy shakers made from turtle shells or milk cans affixed to their legs throughout the night.

These shakers keep the rhythm while the men's call and response singing will stop only long enough to allow another leader to emerge and begin a new round of dancing and singing. With only short breaks for touching medicine or to make announcements about upcoming events or donations of tobacco to the grounds by visitors, the dancing will go on all night unabated. Laughter, songs, conversation, gossip, children's whispers, and babies crying all merge with the unending rounds of song that are the voice of a ceremonial grounds in summer.

Though the grounds is a part of the larger Indian community and will at times host Indian people from many tribes as well as non-Indians from the local area or who are intermarried, it is for the majority of its members the matter-of-fact foundation of their lives and existence. It's not a matter of "being traditional," or even "being Indian..." It is a matter of being human. The way of life of the members of grounds is effortless and without struggle. The ground is a natural outgrowth of their rural and isolated way of life, often lived for the most part in the natural world and integrated to the land. Today the Creek Nation has about 16 ceremonial grounds, not including several Euchee grounds, and the Cherokee have a half dozen as well. The several Shawnee Bands have grounds as well, including Little Axe, where my daughter in law's family has a camp. In isolated Cherokee Communities such as Kenwood ceremonial grounds like Squirrel Ridge carry on the tradition. For years Cherokee elder Boss Cummings and other traditional people of the Rocky Ford and Oaks communities have carried on in the path of the Cherokee nation's roots.

FIGURE 14 PHOTO: NAMING CEREMONY

Rhythms of Ceremonial Grounds Life

Several times annually southeastern Indian people gather at the grounds according to an ancient annual ceremonial cycle that repeats each year to celebrate the natural health that the traditional people believe being a part of the tradition creates in its adherents. The cycle of the ceremonial calendar year begins when the people of a ground[14] first gather in the early spring at their stick ball field which is often located next to the ceremonial grounds, for an all-day session on Sunday of playing the "little brother of war," southeastern Indian stickball. Armed with arm-length rackets carved from hickory wood and bent into a cup on the end, the men will engage in fasting and cleansing ceremonies in preparation for the ball play that initiates the year's commencement of the ceremonial cycle. Well-made stick ball clubs, seasoned over years, are nearly unbreakable and will mature into wood so hard and strong that their surface feels hard as metal.

The game has existed for thousands of years and is another remnant of the ancient southeastern chiefdoms which birthed the Creek, Choctaw, Cherokee, and Seminole tribes of our time, as well as others. The ball game is indeed a game, yet is understood to have a sacred aspect, and its inclusion in the

---

[14] Often the membership of a ceremonial ground is called the "tribal town" by grounds people. Outsiders who hear this term often confuse it with the place, but it designates the members not the location too many grounds folk.

grounds function is crucial. It is played between men and women, the men using their stickball clubs, and the women only their hands. The rules of the game are simple and with few restrictions, the goal being to strike the target which is at the top of a twenty foot pole made from a cedar tree. This target may be several things but most often is a carved wooded fish or a cow's skull affixed atop the pole. Striking below the target for several feet scores a point, a direct hit on the goal several more.

The initial throwing of the ball into the sky and the raucous calls of the players are said to signal to the Creator that the traditional people are carrying on for one more year the ancient and powerfully centering cycle dances and ballgames which were bestowed on the Indian people in the time of the Creation. That such a sacred and mysterious task could be accompanied with such laughter, frivolity, and precocious horseplay is a trait common to people of the ceremonial grounds way of life. Nothing is sacred and everything is sacred. The tempo of the game is relaxed and fun with no unduly rough horseplay or intentional efforts to hurt one another allowed to be a part of the struggle.

Wise elder men and watchful clan mothers watch the proceedings and quietly counsel those who may have a tendency to go too far or roughhouse too often. There is design in the fun. Its point is to teach the children, young people, and men and women of the grounds, persons of all ages how to enjoy time together, to learn fair play, and to be active and healthy. This concern for health is central to grounds life and tradition. Stickball games and a sacred feast of wild meat within the precincts of the men's arbors in the ring start out the year's ceremonial cycle. Once the opening ceremonies like ballgames and the Squirrel Soup Day are completed, the grounds will host visitors from other grounds at its several all-night stomp dances occurring monthly. During these stomp dances members will "touch medicine"[15] and remain awake all night as they dance intermittently until daybreak, after which they may visit with friends, play stick ball, clean up the grounds, then head home to sleep. There will be several of the all-night stomp dances leading up to the eight days of the Green Corn Dance, the highlight of the year.

This annual religious festival involves many daytime dances, naming ceremonies, scratching, and smaller ceremonies which mark and celebrate the cycle of natural destruction and renewal which is mirrored in the ceremonies of the grounds. After the corn dance week ends, several more all-night stomp dances will be held monthly until the ceremonial year ends in the fall, and the grounds will lie dormant for several months,

---

[15] "Touching medicine" is a grounds term for the practice of bathing in and consuming in small amounts several teas made from various plants used for the purposes of strengthening and preserving the participant's health by preventing sickness and disease. According to grounds tradition the practice of stomp dancing all night while using medicine came from the stipulation that while one is touching medicine it is imperative to remain awake. Dancing and singing fulfills this stipulation.

after which the cycle will begin again. With the next spring's gathering for ball play a few familiar old faces will be missing; a few new babies will sit in their hammocks in the shade next to grandma while mom and dad tussle in the grass for the buckskin ball. The cycle will repeat again as it has for countless generations.

What is the appeal of the ceremonial grounds and why does it persist among many tribal peoples to this day? Its persistence is attributed by the elders to its focus almost completely on the health of its members.[16] All activities are directed towards this ends from ball play, to dancing, to touching medicine. Health is the primary concern of the traditional Creek culture. Through the participation in the life of the community the life of the individual is strengthened; through the engagement of the individual the whole of the community is strengthened.

---

[16] Mental, physical, and emotional health is stated as the ONLY reason that grounds meet in the words of several elders, and the "gatekeepers" of the tradition seek to pass it along unencumbered in religiosity or political ideologies, despite the tradition still bearing the baggage in many aspects of its organizational structure of its political/religious/social past.

FIGURE 15 PHOTO: AUTHOR SCOTT AND DAUGHTER SEHOY

Roots of the Ceremonial Grounds

The ceremonial grounds are at the very heart of the traditional Creek life, and health is at the heart of the ceremonial grounds activities. The architecture, layout, and protocol of this tradition are millennia old, stretching back to the pre-Columbian mound builders. Located in what are today parts of Georgia and Alabama, the ancient Mound Builders are the origin of the culture of the Muscogee peoples as well as others tribes in the Eastern part of North America. Called the Mississippian culture, the remnant mound sites, some over fifty feet tall and covering many acres, as well as other archeological remains of this once wide spread and powerful collection of peoples, number in the thousands. Oral history speaks of an alliance of towns arising a thousand years ago including Coweta, Cussetah, Ahbika, and Tukabatchee. This alliance was to grow and count in its ranks dozens of towns when the Spanish arrived in the Southeast four hundred years ago.

These ancient Southeastern Indian towns sometimes were large and fortified, in some cases located atop large mounds, with a central plaza surrounded by four large cabins in which the men of the community would meet, where dances and ceremonies would take place and which was the political and social heart of the settlement. Smaller satellite communities would be tied to the larger towns and these would host large annual renewal ceremonies called the Green Corn Dance. Complex and interconnected networks of trade, marriage, and military alliances tied these many and widespread communities together.

Massive council houses and public buildings could be found around the central plaza, around which the various neighborhoods of the different clans would be scattered, as well as ball fields and other ceremonial spaces. In the central plaza would burn a sacred fire, a flame which was said to be entrusted to the people from the Sun itself, The Sun, viewed by some as the "face of the Creator", was an entity seen as the ancestor of the tribal leadership among some tribes. Elaborate ceremonies would take place in the confines of the ceremonial grounds surrounding this sacred fire, and sacred ball games would be played at the nearby stick ball court, games which when observed by the Spanish who arrived in the sixteenth century sometimes involved thousands of players and lasted for days at a time.

In the early 1500s, reports of strangers began to be known throughout the lands of the Muscogee peoples. With the arrival of the Europeans on the scene, the several large and powerful chiefdoms in which the Indian people had lived for centuries would collapse into smaller and fractured groups as disease, and then warfare and slavery increased exponentially. With the appearance of Desoto in 1539 in the land of the Muskogee speakers, a cascade of death and destruction would occur that would halve, then halve again the population as tens of thousands died in the wake of Spanish expeditions into the Southeastern interior, visits which introduced death and destruction to the ancient mound builder way of life for the few tribes like the Natchez and others who still lived in large mound communities. Having no genetic protections from the diseases introduced by the Europeans, the large and well established tribal Chiefdoms would collapse and only two generations later little would remain of the original ancient communities. In the aftermath of waves of epidemics the large palisaded towns, which were built atop mounds and which would had tens of thousands of citizens in some cases, would be completely abandoned. Then populations would crash across the eastern half of the continent and a full appreciation of the depopulation and its consequences are only now becoming known. Scholars writing at the end of the 19th century had estimated the pre-Columbian population of Native Americans at about 10 million, but due to research advances and newer data models used, by the end of the 20th century the consensus by the academic world had shifted to closer to 50 million (Taylor, 2002).

In its place evolved a less architecturally elaborate, though no less complex, cosmology and religious system. Still retaining many aspects of the ancient Mississippian worldview the surviving remnants of the ancient cities would reorganize into smaller social groups, called Etvlwv, or tribal towns. These communities would be organized much like the older and much larger mound cities of the past, though on a much reduced scale. In the center would still burn the sacred fire, which would be surrounded by several cabins or arbors in which the men would assemble, and where the business of the community's leadership would be handled and where public gatherings and religious ceremonies take place. Nearby would be a large and spacious building called a *Cukofv*, or council house. The ball field where the ancient "little brother of war" as southeastern stick ball was called would be nearby and the annual games would still be held. Much was like it had been but the massive earthworks and erection of public buildings was for the most part a thing of the past.

The Indian people of the Southeast spoke many different languages and were organized amongst themselves in differing social patterns. The ceremonial grounds, the Sacred Fire, and the ceremonial ball game were a commonly shared tradition in the Southeast, with a cosmology which was alike as well. As the European powers' arrival led to social disruption on a large scale, tribes jostled for position and the struggle for survival intensified, slavery and war became common, and hundreds of tribes were lost to history as they were broken and scattered.

Others would become more unified in this process and the larger tribes such as the Creek, Cherokee, Choctaw, Catawba, and Shawnee would steadily assimilate other groups seeking refuge. This being so, the tribal social structures would become more flexible and inclusive, and the presence of persons from multiple tribal origins and even of other races would accelerate as the colonial powers and tribal groups tussled for dominance.

With the Americans throwing off the yoke of colonial rule and becoming contenders for lands and resources, the Creek people would find themselves with a steady and growing stream of outsiders pressing in closer and closer to Creek lands. Eventually missionaries would establish contacts within the large tribes of the Southeast including the Creeks, and in the years leading up to the removal, preachers and American government officials would work together to push policies of "civilization" and "Christianization." Factions would evolve within Creek society based on the level of adherence to the age old Indian communal ways of life and those who were increasingly embracing ways of life that were introduced by non-Indians and adopted by Mixed elite who were becoming increasingly powerful in the affairs of state of the Creek people. With outsiders pressing in on all sides troubles increased.

The communal aboriginal way of life with its focus on community first would feel the effects of efforts by Mixed Blood leadership to change social choices. These elite families, many of whom who had become entangled in the lifestyle of the non-Native southern planters, practices which included slave labor, individual capitalistic endeavors, and the accumulating of private resources, challenged the "Indian way" which the vast majority of Indians still followed.

In the traditional way of life, individual gain was hardly known and even less respected. The piling up of personal riches and imbalance in social standing which would occur among community members would lead to a slow but steady weakening of the fabric of tribal life. An ancient maxim of the traditional people which stated that "No one should have more until everyone has enough" was tested to its limit during the period of the Creek peoples' struggle to remain on the ancient lands of the ancestors, a battle which would ultimately be lost for the largest part of the people in the 1830s and 40s as the removal of the large tribes to lands in the west by the United States government would lead to large-scale suffering from hunger, homelessness, alcoholism, and violence.

With heavy hearts and the few things which they could carry, most of the Creek people set off for the West prodded by the bayonetted rifles of the American military. In the aftermath of these events only a few hundred Muscogee Creek would be left in the Southeast within the boundaries of the lost nation by the 1850s. In the struggle against the forcible removal of the Indians, many bands associated with the Creek Nation had been steadily streaming into the lands to the South. Moving out of the collapsing and surrounded Creek Nation and into Florida, several groups would establish new communities in the panhandle and around the big bend area. With time some of these would move deeper into the peninsula and find refuge from any social interaction with outsiders in the inaccessible reaches of the Everglades. These were the ancestors of the Seminole and Miccosukee tribes.

Not all Muscogee would migrate south with the passing years, though. Some number of families of Creeks remained in the Tensaw area north of Pensacola on the edge of the formerly Creek lands, while others congregated in small hamlets scattered across the panhandle. In several of these settlements, the remaining Creeks who lived marginal existences on the edge of the White society would intermarry with families of Lumbee, Catawba, and other Carolina Indians who were migrating in to find work and refuge in the relatively sparsely populated recesses of the Escambia, Apalachicola, Choctawhatchee, and other river valleys.

The Creeks scattered across lower Alabama would congeal steadily into a tighter more insulated community, and by 1836, the Tensaw settlement was populated by these remnant Creeks. Nearby to these Creeks homesteads, the timber companies had purchased large tracts of timber land a situation detrimental to the Indians clustered there. The stranglehold on the land which timber interests had left little land available for land grants or acquisition. Those families receiving 1836 land grants moved inland and away from the river where they had been concentrated. They migrated into the Poarch area near the Head of Perdido and Huxford area. Here they were able to find sufficient tracts of grant land. A new community as well as identity was born. In this community the Indian families intermarried with each other for the most part. The interactions among the families evolved into a web if interrelated families, a distinct group emerged which became the Poarch Creek.

This group was small and self-reliant, insular and reclusive. It was distinguished from neighboring white people as well as the other descendants of Creeks still in the area. With the Civil war and other events leading to a rise in racism and Jim Crow persecutions of non-whites, in later years the Poarch Creeks would be discriminated against by them. These few southern Alabama Indian settlements over time became tightly clustered geographically, with many families on landholdings of individual Indians. The Poarch Creek Indian Communities at Hog Fork, Bell Creek, and Poarch became more strongly based on a network of close kinship and mutual support, avoiding interactions with outsiders and living simple lives farming and hunting. The several Catawba communities in Florida at Scott Town, Scotts Ferry, and Woods would have a very similar experience.

For the rest of the nineteenth century and into the mid twentieth these small and isolated hamlets would live for generations under the radar, outside of contact with the federal government and having little to do with outsiders. Subject to the racist and Euro-American-centric authorities' power in the rural counties of south Alabama and northern Florida where they dwelled, they would eke by forgotten and ignored in the lands in which they had once owned in the case of the Creeks. Avoiding involvement with outsiders where they could, these Indian people would only re-emerge into public view in the 1950s as Native Americans everywhere began to advocate for better lives and inclusion in the American ideal of self-determination and freedom for all.

With the Creek Indian Land Claims ruling finding in favor of the Creeks' claim that lands had been seized from ancestors in violation of agreements made, the Creek Indians in the Eastern United States would once again emerge from their isolation as small semi-autonomous settlements, and efforts would be initiated to establish political organizations which represented their interests, with several being in contention for state and federal acknowledgment by the 1970s.

In 1984 the Poarch Band of Creeks centered in Escambia County, Florida and Munroe, Baldwin, and Escambia Counties, Alabama would secure recognition by the B.I.A. as a federally acknowledged tribe. Other small groups such as the Principle Creek Nation, and the Lower Muscogee Creek Tribe in southern Georgia as well as several communities of Creek-Cheraw in the central panhandle of Florida and in the Pensacola area would continue as petitioners for federal status, as state recognized tribes or as Independents, in their battles for social and political survival.

From the years after the removal throughout the decades the Indians which known to outsiders as the "Seminoles' would survive in the harsh and demanding environs of the Florida peninsula. Unlike their kinsmen further north, who were reduced to marginal lives navigating a treacherous path in the Southern

Jim Crow society, the Seminole sought complete separation from the people they felt they were still at war with. Several flare-ups in the late 1800s with state authorities did little to improve the relationship between these staunch holdouts and the authorities.

After the Second World War, the population of the Seminole people's Florida homeland began an exponential increase, and within a few decades there was little room left for them to maintain their once isolated and independent existence. Unable to maintain their former independent way of life, some in the tribal leadership began to develop a relationship with the BIA and federal authorities. Soon plans were underway to become a part of the Bureau of Indian Affairs system and accept American citizenship and move onto reservations which were set up for them as part of this settlement. Change was coming to the Seminole people at an exponential rate and political strife became more pronounced.

Despite intense internal struggle over culture, social, religious and political identity, and other areas of dispute within the tribe, in the late nineteen fifties the Seminole Tribe of Florida (and soon after the Miccosukee Tribe of Indians) would achieve federal acknowledgement, with the Poarch Band of Creek Indians located on the northern end of the state of Florida in Escambia County receiving the same by the mid-1980s. Before the federal recognition of the Seminoles, they had been isolated and independent for the most part. Though not completely outside of interactions with the state of Florida which surrounded their swampland and Everglades settlements, the Indians of central and south Florida were mainly a people governed completely by the tribal Chiefs and the Medicine Men of their bands' decisions.

FIGURE 16 PHOTO: GREEN CORN FEED FIRE

The tribal membership, organized by clan, would meet annually at the Green Corn dances and from the proceedings there these half dozen bands of a few hundred Muscogee Creek and Miccosukee speakers would forge the decisions which bound them as a people respectively, each group making decisions regarding their welfare communally as it had been for thousands of years. These Corn Dance council meetings, along with clan based leadership, would operate as the government of the people, rooted in the traditional values and ancient customs of their communities. Even today the Seminole and Miccosukee are still very attached to the values which allowed them to survive on of the most challenging experiences of any tribe in North America.

Some of these customs and functions stretched back to the mound builders thousands of years ago, but with the world that they lived in by the 1960s; Seminole life would change swiftly and significantly. Within a few decades the Seminole and Miccosukee peoples would both find attendance at the Corn Dance falling, and the impact of modernity being felt, many would no longer adhere to the traditional culture of their ancestors. The allure of the modern American society was constant and readily available in nearby urban areas.

Much like their ancestors who lived to the north, who fled to Florida to resist assimilation, there were several families of traditional people would refuse to take part in the federal recognition and would establish communities of "Independent traditional" people. Unenrolled in either B.I.A. recognized tribe, they would plot a course of their own rooted in the values of the traditional Native American heritage, rather than American capitalism in which the Seminole and Miccosukee tribes both were deeply involved after federal acknowledgment. By the dawn of the twentieth century only a minority of the Seminole and Miccosukee would continue the age old cycle of the Corn Dance, or live lives infused with the traditions of a century before, though that small number who did were and are dedicated, strong, and in the early years of our new century, growing in number.

This spirit of renewed investment in the cultural identity of these communities is stirred by a younger generation interested in the traditions of the community, and walking in the footsteps of leaders like Abeka, a Seminole war chief whose memory still bespeaks courage and tenacity to survive. When the American Army captured the resistance leader Osceola, the defiant young chief Coacoochee and nearly all of the Seminoles leadership through a disgraceful ruse, things looked dim. This act of treachery by Americans didn't discourage Abeka though. He was a light in the darkness of war to his people and was the last of the major Seminole leaders to avoid capture.

Besides frustrating the efforts of the American army, Abeka infuriated U.S. Army General Jesup by joining with Osceola to free 700 Seminoles from a holding camp near Fort Brooke, close to Tampa. Here the general had steamer ships prepared and waiting to haul them to the Indian Territory in the west. "Grandma Mary Frances" Johns once told us at Corn dance about here grandmothers grandmother who leapt from a ships dock to avoid shipment west. Jesup soon realized he had been taken and issued orders that his officers seize Osceola and the others despite the white flag of truce. Osceola would die in custody of his captors, and Abeka drew a deep and lasting insight from this. He had found out of the underhanded taking of the captives from Coacoochee, a Seminole leader who had escaped from the old Spanish fort at St. Augustine where they had been held. When he related to Abeka the details of their capture, the Maker of Medicine never again risked capture, refusing to attend negotiations with the Army or American representatives, writes Michael Gannon in The New History of Florida. Abeka played a major role in the shaping of the Seminole identity through the more than century long life he lived in Florida. The Seminole leader Billy L. Cypress writes in Perspectives on Arbiaka (Sam Jones), ``There were a number of leaders like Osceola who were better known by the Europeans, but Arbiaka played just as great a role in keeping the Seminole people together and surviving through war times to peace times." The hand of Abeka is still on his people today. Patsy West, a historian for the Seminole Tribe of Florida, said that Abeka "was a powerful religious leader and his career ... far eclipsed Osceola," adding that" there would be no Seminoles and Miccosukees left in Florida were it not for the strength and determination of this one individual." His era was one of the hardest to be an Indian in Florida.

As an example of this an August 1850 edition of a St. Augustine newspaper set a $1,000 bounty for warriors brought in dead and a $500 reward for the capture and delivery of Seminole women and children. His life spanned 111 years according to oral history and he guided the Seminole people in the long journey from the days of being a part of the Creek Nation and having plenty in the land to the north to the life of the hunted Seminole of the early twentieth century trying to survive in a Florida fast filling up with other people.

For Indian people anywhere in Florida, the middle of the twentieth century was a time of change, a period marked by a loss of social isolation, growth of political involvement in the wider Indian and American world, and a diffusion of the population centers. Where the Corn Dance had been the focal point of the calendar and the ceremonial grounds the center of the world for generations, the decades of the second half of the century that followed saw change affecting all Native communities, though this would have differing outcomes on both ends of the peninsula. While in the Indian communities of south Florida, the involvement of the people with the outside world led to a lessening of the role of Corn Dance and ceremonial grounds among them, a role that had been absolute only a couple of generations earlier, the same forces of change would lead to a renewal of traditions in northern Florida and in south Alabama. Indians there would commence to recovering aspects of the traditions worn away by Jim Crow segregation and missionary inroads to community identity.

Across the mainly agricultural and still rural area of the Florida panhandle, lower Alabama and southwestern Georgia, the small remnant settlements of Indians had retained some of the traditions of their forebears to varying degrees. According to oral traditions in my own community of Blountstown, while not intact to nearly the degree of Native-based cultural survival found among the Indians in the Everglades, Creeks in the north had been sending representatives to the centrally located Corn Dances while they were still centered in the Ocala area according to oral history. While this large Corn dance held in central Florida would devolve into several smaller ones after the First World War, at least some members of the panhandle Creek Indian community would still gather for small and isolated dances, stickball games, and Green Corn Busks.

In some of these communities the work of the missionaries had been complete and the traditional Creek ways were lost for the most part. Indeed there was and still is hostility by many of the more rural and fuller blood Creeks around Atmore and Blountstown to the ways of the Square ground tradition, which rural preachers decry as "devil-worship" and "heathenism." In other settlements, however, there were individuals and families who not only worked to preserve the ceremonial grounds and traditional culture's values, but worked to establish new ties between the "grounds people" in south Florida, in the panhandle and southern Alabama and Georgia, and in Oklahoma, as well as to strengthen already existing relationships between these far flung descendants of the mound builders.

In the 1970s and 80s when I was growing up, there was only one Corn Dance being held anywhere north of the Big Cypress Swamp, and this was that of the Apalachicola grounds in Blountstown. This Corn Dance ground, which was moved from its old location in Wakulla County in the early 1980's with the securing of property for it by Chief Andrew Ramsey, has been at its present location for forty five years. From across the panhandle and beyond, representatives from several Indian settlements and dozens of families would gather to take part in the renewal and cleansing that is the Busk.

This ritual of fasting and ceremonial rebirth that today has nearly a half dozen groups practicing in the panhandle alone has found an exponential growth in interest in the hearts of many descendants of Creeks who remained behind after the removal scourged the South of most of the larger tribes. In southern Florida the traditions of the Corn dance and traditional Indian culture are being sought out by many young people among the Seminole and Miccosukee people even as the tribe enjoys economic success after generations of sheer survival.

The Ceremonial Grounds and the Tribal Town

Throughout the ups and downs of the history of Creek people, the ceremonial grounds and ceremonial calendar continue to be practiced by some, even as others adapted

Christianity to the Creek world view and established many "Indian churches". Today though not as proliferate as in times past the ceremonial square grounds of the Creek, like the Euchee, Seminole, Miccosukee, Shawnee, and Cherokee continue to play an important role in the tribal identity. Called the ceremonial grounds, as well as stomp ground, square ground, or Big House, the institution of this "public plaza" around which the Muscogee universe revolves is fundamental to the Creek identity and continues to define the very root of the Muscogee way of life for many. It is the home to a force which is known to represent the creator of all things and hosts a framework for the preservation of health and a balanced life for those who attend.

The Sacred Fire which is rekindled yearly at its heart, the many animal and stomp dances which take place in its ring, and the raucous and enthusiastic ball play which occurs on its ball field are all important focal points for the Creek people who continue to carry out a cycle of ceremonies and particular activities associated with them. Called the "tribal town," the people who are members of a ceremonial grounds community are often connected by blood as well as by affiliation. Though the network of ceremonial grounds which stretch from the Florida Everglades to the prairies of Oklahoma have a diverse set of protocols and varied social and organizational schema, they all share basic tenets and practices which emerge from a common pre-Columbian origin.

Ancestry and Identity

At once a social, political, and religious center, it is also the place where childhood memories with family members are made, tribal ties to other branches of your community are renewed, in which the very values that define Creek people are transmitted across the generations; some verbally, others more abstract. The values threaded throughout the activities are subtle, poised and natural.

The central point of the entire ceremonial grounds way of life is simply put: health. As some elders have been heard to say, "The (ceremonial) grounds are for the spirit, the church is for the soul." This gathering place is almost always difficult to locate and not easily disturbed by the outside world when the Creek people gather there. With a complex and subtle ceremonial calendar underlying all activities which take place there, a group of knowledgeable and committed elders guide the community in the annual cycle of stick ball games, sacred feasts, all night stomp dances, "touching medicine," and the countless other activities that denote the continuing function of the grounds as a socio-religious "government in exile."

Since the appearance of other governments the place of the tribal town as a binding authority has faded among almost all Muscogee peoples. The last tribal groups to lose the ceremonial grounds as a functionary of the governance of the people as well as a religious institution was the Seminole and Miccosukee tribes of Florida a half century ago. Today the ceremonial grounds in most tribes have a status as a respected religious institution but few view it as their government outside of a ceremonial setting. Tribes like the Muscogee (Creek) Nation as well as Seminole Nation of Oklahoma, the Seminole Tribe and Miccosukee Tribe of Florida, the Poarch Band of Creek Indians and other Bureau of Indians Affairs supported governments have all experienced this trend of the loss of traditional forms of governance to more modern ones. There are no longer of tribal governments set up by BIA through the years in Indian Country, not to mention the many layers of local, county, state, and federal authorities that have all led to the devolution of political powers once exercised by the Mekko of the tribal town in generations past. Today the Mekko of a ground acts as a spiritual leader more than a political one. He will guide his people in their annual journey through the seasons as they gather voluntarily to take part in the activities that he alone is responsible to orchestrate and sustain.

Across the Universe of the Muscogee world the passage of time has created a spectrum of practices and traditions which are unique to the many groups which share a common root in the Southeast. Today there are three distinct groupings of ceremonials grounds. Each area has a distinct social and religious context. These three regional groupings are Eastern Oklahoma; North Florida, South Alabama, and South Georgia; and South Florida.

FIGURE 17 PHOTO: JEWELL DEAN & ELAINE HILL

Eastern Oklahoma

In Oklahoma, there is a clustering of ceremonial grounds in several groupings among not only Creeks, but among the Euchee, Shawnee, Cherokee, and Seminole peoples. It is here among the tens of thousands of members of the Creek Nation that were removed that the ceremonial grounds traditions still have the most intact ceremonial infrastructure and affinities to the architectural and cosmological worldview of the ancient mound builders of a millennium ago. Depending on the year and circumstance there are from sixteen to eighteen Creek ceremonial grounds holding dances annually, often including the three Euchee grounds. There are also at times a few grounds being revived or atrophying due to lack of participation.

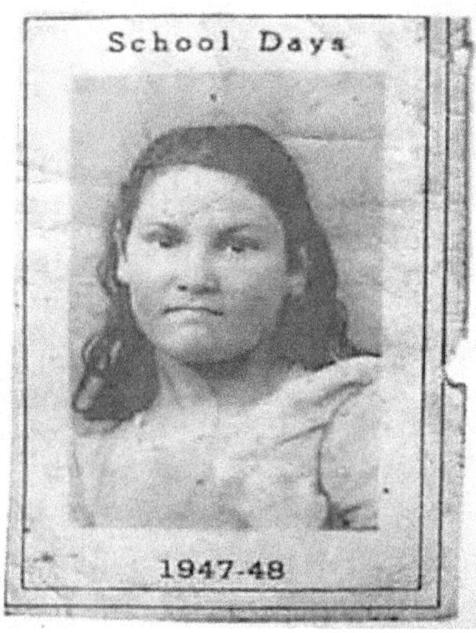

FIGURE 18 INEZ SISTER OF LOLLY

Many of the grounds in the Creek Nation belong to one of several established distinct sets of ceremonial protocols which vary slightly from each other but which are generally similar. Many grounds have been revived in the last fifty years and some have been revived only to fade away within a few years. The large main grounds which have been up throughout the years of the Creeks residing in Oklahoma have slowly dwindled in number to what remains today, with a slow process of consolidation going on as certain grounds slipped away and the members would migrate over to a "related" grounds. In this way the grounds are like a family with a genealogy where names recur and blood lines are shared.

Florida's Panhandle and lower Alabama and Georgia

In the "tristate" area of the Florida panhandle and lower Alabama and Georgia there are several ceremonial grounds today. Oldest is the Apalachicola Grounds which has been holding Busk in the panhandle for generations. My own grandmother as well as countless family members attended the Corn Dance in Blountstown in the central panhandle since it was moved there in 1983, and some attended at its old location seventy miles to the east at its former location, the Oak Hill Corn Dance Grounds in Wakulla, Florida.

The Apalachicola ground has four arbors, a ribbon dance, and a host of animal dances and other traditions similar to those kept in Oklahoma, with which many members maintain contact. In the last couple of decades there have been several grounds established in parts of the Florida panhandle separate from the three splinters of Apalachicola, Kunfuskee, (New) Pine Arbor, and White Earth. There are now during the years since the turn of the millennium newer ceremonial grounds which are located in areas near Perry, Chattahoochee, and other rural areas. From information gleaned from internet sites administered by members of these grounds, the cosmology and ceremonial protocols they use are nottransmitted directly through established ceremonial leadership lines in Oklahoma or North or South Florida.

The Hassossa Tallahassee Grounds, located on the Poarch Creek Indian Reservation in Atmore, Alabama, were established a decade and a half ago along the lines of protocol used by its benefactor tribal town and parent ground among the Oklahoma Creeks, the Tallahassee Grounds. With its ceremonial ashes restored by Dave Lewis, a Medicine Maker from Creek Nation in Oklahoma, and in the year 2000, it is identical in protocol and architecture to the Tallahassee grounds in Oklahoma. The hard work of Mekko Slick and ceremonial leaders like then Speaker Locv Haco and others over two decades of "practice grounds" work led to the restoration of the ceremonial grounds to the Poarch Creek Reservation. Despite a split within its lineage within a year of the ashes coming up, with Hassossa Tallahassee Grounds remaining on the reservation land and a faction led by Mekko Locv Haco crossing the line into nearby Florida and establishing the Kunfuskee (Tallahassee) Ground near Fountain Florida, both grounds continue to honor and maintain the traditions each worked so hard to reestablish in the Creeks original homeland.

Elders say that Hillis Haya Dave Lewis told those assembled in 2001 when he was restoring the ashes to Hassossa Tallahassee Ground at the Poarch Community to "reach back" and carry the tradition forward without being caught up in the building up or tearing down of grounds that sometimes happens, to keep the protocols passed on to them and to work together with other grounds. Nearing two decades since this event, the two grounds which were born from the restoration of the sacred ashes to Poarch have a minimum of interaction despite ties of kinship and heritage each share. Hassossa Tallahassee has many visitors from Oklahoma at Corn Dance while Kunfuskee (Tallahassee) sees more Seminole and Miccosukee participation as well as the Creek and Catawba from the panhandle.

South Florida

In the South Florida the several annual Corn Dance grounds still hosts the brightly garbed Seminole and Miccosukee traditional people. Though the Creek speakers and the Miccosukee speakers once were very separate and their Corn Dances held separately and with little cooperation, today the lines are less clear and a renewal of the traditions is growing yearly. The Corn Dance tradition here has lost most of the elaborate ceremonial in its appearances. The countless wars and intense struggle to survive shaped the religious traditions and practices of the Indians there to a point where they are well adapted to the watery environment to which the early migrants in this fierce region retreated. The Corn Dance is marked by a single arbor, by various songs and traditions, and by unique protocols very different from those followed by Corn Dances in Oklahoma.

The participation in the grounds traditions by Indian people throughout the Muscogee universe is alive and well today, with a vibrant and surging interest by young people during the last several decades and with a growing support, institutionally as well as financially by the "modern" BIA governments that displaced them in the past. The intrinsic value of the cultural traditions of the Indian people once dismissed as backwards and not of any practical value in a modern America, is now being understood as necessary for a balanced and strong social fabric. In Florida, Alabama and Georgia, and especially in Oklahoma, the leaders of tribal ceremonial grounds communities are networking, documenting, and strengthening the role that this most ancient of institutions plays in the lives of modern southeastern Indian people.

Among the humid evenings during the summer, sitting at Green Corn Dance with my grandmother in times past was dear to me and of the most cherished memories of my life. The rustle of stomp dance shakercans prepared in place of now rare and hard to obtain turtle shell shakers, the crackling of the new fire in the center of the square, and the quiet conversation among elders in their camps, all are among the cherished memories. The idea of clan is not as important among Creek speaking peoples in Oklahoma as it once was in generations past; though among some Creek-Seminole people in Florida it is still important in many ways, as it is among our kinsmen the

Miccosukee, with whom we share the Florida peninsula. Though the Miccosukee were the hardline resistors to the encroachment of the Americans while many "Lower Creeks" like my own family took measures to accommodate the newcomers, we both share the common root of the Southeastern Indian culture of the ceremonial grounds traditions.

"Family" Relationships in the Creek World

Many aspects of the world that the Doyle sisters lived in has changed immensely during the two centuries that separate their lives from our own today. Besides the apparent changes of the removal of the Creek Nation from its southern homeland of millennia to the West, and the adaptions to modernity that have led to fundamental changes in the lives of the Creek people and cultures, some things are still rooted in the perspectives, beliefs and practices of the pre-Columbian Muscogee Creek, and these we often call "traditional."

FIGURE 19 PHOTO: THE AUTHOR HODALEE SCOTT SEWELL FAR LEFT WITH FAMILY AND TRIBAL MEMBERS AT THE KUNFUSKEE CORN DANCE 2012 IN FLORIDA

FIGURE 20 PHOTO: THE AUTHOR AND SAM PROCTOR, MEDICINE MAKER IN DUSTIN OKLAHOMA 2000

The constant and unending process of adaption to changing social, economic and developmental conditions that all cultures face to survive has led to all tribes facing challenges to preserve what was most important, even as they would discard other things as no longer useful. Before the removal the Muscogee Creek were a very diverse collection of tribal towns, with a half dozen different languages in use among the dozens of distinct and fiercely independent tribal towns. The tribal town or *etvlwv* was the basic system of government, and each was sovereign in its own right. Many larger tribal towns would have several smaller "daughter" towns as well, there being dozens of clans scattered across these tribal towns.

The process of building the Creek Nation began millennia ago with an alliance between four founding towns, most often said to be Coweta, Cussetah, Tukabatchee, and Ahbeka. With the advent of the colonial struggle for domination by European powers in the South, dozens more tribal groups would join the Creeks' Confederation for protection and refuge from the warfare, land grabbing and slavery rife on the frontier of the time. Though by 1800 nearly half of the Indians who made up the Creek Nation were from non-Muskogee speaking groups, Muskogee proper would be the language of affairs and trade. Groups such as the Euchee, bands of Shawnee, Natchez, and other non-Muskogee speaking peoples would join the

Creeks' expanding nation, finding safety from the incessant slave raids, tribal war and colonial intrigues of the times.

The once disparate and barely functioning "Creek Confederacy" of the pre-colonial era would evolve into a much stronger integrated unit as pressures from the colonial powers and tribal adversaries demanded an increasingly complex political infrastructure. The Creeks had always been divided into an Upper and Lower factional society with the Muscogee proper dominating among the Upper Creek while the Lower Creeks would have substantial numbers of smaller non-Muskogee speaking peoples such as the Apalachicola, Alabama, Miccosukee, and others allied. For the next two centuries, decisions made in councils on the eve of the removal would lead to many peoples being a part of the Creek Nation who were originally independent tribal groups from then on. By contrast, after the removal a half dozen tribal groups who were originally integrated parts of the Creek body proper would be left to themselves into the twentieth century, such as the Miccosukee and Seminole of Florida, the Alabama-Coushatta of Texas, the Poarch Creeks of Florida and Alabama and others.

The inspiration for this work, the Doyle sisters I spoke of earlier, were destined to lose touch with one another as their lives moved on from that bright spring morning when the three took vows of marriage. Though I refer in this text to Amanda, Sarah, and Nancy as "sisters," the former had a different mother than the latter two, and they would be considered "half-sisters" today in the American mainstream understanding of "family." In the traditional culture of the Creek people, a person is considered to be "related" only to their clan, which is always inherited from the mother. If two persons were of the same clan they were thought of as being brother and sister, nephew and uncle, and the like, whether they actually knew how they were connected or not. The dozens of various clans were a network across the Creek Nation. Clan was at the root of Creek life. Children would be born into their mother's clan and belong to it throughout their lives. When a man married he would live with his wife's clan. Clan provided safety, identity, and social and political structure to Creek lives. Each clan had head women who were the authorities in the village, a sort of civil law which they dominated within the confines of the village, while men would have authority in war and external matters.

Clan was ever present and a Creek person travelling to other villages could count on assistance and help from anyone of their Clan family. Much as the nuclear family is the basic unit of Americans' concept of the meaning of family, so was the matriarchal clan identity a couple of centuries ago throughout the Native societies of much of the Southeast.

In the traditional Clan structure, your relationship is paramount in the identity of tribal ways. A person's primary identity and social responsibilities, obligations, and benefits come from their Clan. Most villages would have had representatives of each clan family and people in the town visiting would find lodging and food, information and networking of tribal affairs and news among these kinsmen and women. Nancy and Sarah's mother Susannah Islands was a member of the Bird Clan (*Fuswvlke);* therefore her descendants would be accepted as such among all the tribe. This line of descent as a member of the Fuswvlke would pass down through the daughters for many generations down to me and my descendants.

The monthly all night dances which are held at the ceremonial grounds are generally well attended by a few hundred Creeks and other tribal people. The various stomp grounds dance schedules are staggered so each weekend there is at least 2 or 3 grounds having stomp dances, and members from those which are not holding dances that weekend go to the ones who are. Through the night dancers, who are lined up in a spiral, male-female-male-female alternatingly, circles the sacred fire, singing ancient songs in praise of the creation which tell the stories of the Creek people's journey through time and space.

FIGURE 21 PHOTO: WILLIAM AND CARRIE HABBARD, GRANDSON OF INDIAN TISH

When one leader finishes his songs the dancers disperse to the sidelines of the dance grounds only to reassemble a few moments later behind the next leader. People from grounds which are not hosting dancing that particular weekend will go to neighboring grounds which are. Most stomp dancers know all the other stomp dancers and the annual cycle of reciprocal dancing allows the 16 or so Creek grounds to continue to dance. When I attend a stomp dance on Saturday night, or the Green Corn Dance during mid-summer at the ceremonial grounds , like every other Creek Clan Member, I will find the place in that square grounds arbor where the Bird Clan people sit and take a seat there. When I visit at other ceremonial grounds besides my own I will seek out a person who has a Bird Clan camp and visit and eat and fellowship among these "relatives," some of whom I may not have met before. Through the two centuries that separate my life from those of my third great grandmothers Nancy and Sarah, the traditions of clan identity and its place of importance to many Creeks continue for many even to this day.

It is especially dear to those still associated with the traditional world, and though no longer "law," it does play a part within the modern Creek communities, though it is diminished substantially from the older times. The vagaries of life on the frontier would separate these Clan women's lives. While Amanda would eventually find her place in the new Creek Nation west of the Mississippi, Nancy and Sarah would spend the rest of their lives in the sleepy, rural southern lifeways of South Georgia and Florida, their descendants intermarrying with other Mixed Blood families, and often into lines from the same set of ancestors.

Among many Eastern Creeks, and especially the Poarch Creeks who live mostly in Monroe, Baldwin, and Escambia counties in Alabama and in neighboring Escambia County, Florida, enrollment in the Poarch Band is important since there are easily ten thousand people throughout the region of documentable Creek or Lumbee Indian ancestry. . Requirements for enrollment were designed to capture those ancestors living in the Indian settlements there a century ago, not two centuries ago. The time from the removal in the 1830s to the formation of clearly intermarried insular Indian communities took several generations and by the late 1800s had occurred. By using the federal census of those few counties in lower Alabama where these mostly Indian settlements were concentrated, the Poarch band avoided having the countless thousands who descended from a single Creek ancestor after removal on their modern roll of tribal members.

At enrollment of the contemporary tribe in the mid 1980's half the tribe was at the one quarter blood threshold according to the Bureau of Indian Affairs response to Poarch bands petition for recognition. Today according to Poarch Bands bylaws, to enroll in the Poarch Band of Creeks, you must be descended from the American Indians listed on one of three "rolls": the 1870 U.S. Census of Escambia County, Alabama; 1900 U.S. Census of Escambia County, Alabama; or 1900 U.S. Special Indian Census of Monroe County, Alabama. These documents are not "Indian rolls" as usually referred to, such as the Lakota or Crow in the west. These are federal census for the most part, rife with the opinion of the census taker shaping the stroke of his pen, who is an Indian, who is white, who is Indian. Poarch Band goes on to require that besides being of Creek heritage, (leaving aside the fact several of the founding families listed as Indian on these census were of Catawba or Chickasaw lineage), they must have a minimum blood quantum of 1/4 American Indian blood (equivalent to one full-blooded Creek grandparent) and not be enrolled in any other tribe.

Each group that is accepted as a federally recognized tribe has the right to make its own rules of citizenship, so this extremely arbitrary framework was crafted to enroll the thousands who had formerly been working within the framework of the Creek nation east of the Mississippi for twenty years into the Poarch Band. The roll used by Poarch and based on federal census are riddled with opinion and racism of the era when you examine the identity of the persons who are listed as Indian on these specific documents over time and on other documents.

Many of the people listed are identified as white or as mulatto on other documents. The base roll put together by Poarch Band was crafted to bring the maximum people into the tribe with the most identification as in din on these documents from a century ago. So if you're not from those counties, or are listed as white or mulatto,-though kin- you don't qualify for the roll In the Poarch Band of Creek Indians today, almost all Indians share the same set of a few dozen ancestors to some degree; and it's the same to a lesser degree among the members of Creek Nation in Oklahoma. The ancestral ties of the Clan are the binds that tie the tribe together and is still an intimate and important part of tribal identity. These cultural practices are still present and functional among only the minority of Creeks today who are "tribally active" as it is known generally; involved in the life of the community as a familial people, socially, religiously, and still using the Creek language.

FIGURE 22 PHOTO: TOM, DAISY, ELMON, ALBERT, AND CARL SCOTT, JACKSON CO 1930

Ancestral Ties

All families have stories. How persons describe who and what is considered family does vary in many cultures and regions. The importance of family is also something that's varied and different across time and place. When we stop to think about whom our ancestors are, and who we today are, that gulf of time can seem vast and our fates hardly connected. Especially in the American mainstream, with its focus on material possession, social mobility, and entertainment and diversion, the impact of the lives of great-grandparents, or indeed their grandparents on anyone today is worthy hardly of a passing thought for most.

But for the people who continue to live in proximity to the language, culture, and values of the Muscogee Creek world, this is not the case. From "full blood" members of the surviving ceremonial grounds in the Muscogee (Creek) Nation in eastern Oklahoma to the weekend Powwow enthusiast at a tiny gathering in Tama, Georgia, the descendants of the historic Creek Nation everywhere are all drawn to this honored and storied heritage. It is one of struggle, fortitude, heartbreak, accomplishment, and a singular "love for the land" that's undimmed since the founding of the *Mvskvlke* a millennium ago.

Creek culture has not in the past been in the written form and is passed down through means of oral and cultural traditions and ceremony. The need to preserve tribal language, history, and values has in recent years led to the written recording of many stories, experiences, knowledge, and wisdoms, which in times past would have been kept only oral and private within family and Clan. Indeed many areas of knowledge regarding ceremonial affairs, medicine, and other forms of *Mvskvlke* patrimony[17] are still regarded as best kept and unrecorded by the gatekeepers of traditional practice. Tales of ancestral exploits include the legends of family ancestors as well as the many traditional characters such as Cufe[18] and the Deer Woman.[19]

---

[17] Patrimony is an inheritance or legacy, and often refers to the aboriginal aspects of an Indian tribal culture today such as clothing, language, sports, and other long time markers of specific tribal identity, i.e. Seminole tribal patchwork, Iroquois lacrosse etc.

[18] Cufe is the ancient "trickster" of the Southeast and plays a role in southern Indian cultures like that of the coyote among western tribes, teaching through his own folly those willing to learn lessons from another's foolishness.

[19] The Deer Woman is reputed to seduce the unwary men who aren't watchful of their virtue, and symbolizes for many the dangers of unbridled passion and lack of decorum.

Ancestry and Identity

My daughter Sehoy has a piece of such a puzzle of our past in her name. To my knowledge, there are several girls today named Sehoy among Creeks as well as one among the Coushatta in Kinder Louisiana, according to my friend Ernest Sickey. Many of the names that women were traditionally given would relate back to the exploits of male relatives from their clan. Sehoy is such a name, though there have been several Sehoy of note in the past; the name is one which is rooted in lives long ago. The story I was told by an elder in the 1980's was that once a party of Choctaw attacked out town while many of the men were away on a hunt, leaving only enough men, mostly the elders and young boys behind to take care of things.

The Choctaw happened to attack and though the Creek men put up a good fight they were unable to stop them making away with several girls and many of the towns supplies. The hunters returned and soon were on the trail of the Choctaws fleeing westward back towards their territory. The head start they had was too great and the Creek men agreed the large group would never catch up before they were too deep into their stronghold, so they came up with a plan, though one felt unlikely to succeed. Two of the men whose nieces were among the captives would journey alone to catch them faster, this being viewed a little as a suicide mission some said.

None the less the two headed out after the enemy war party, after the other hunters had given them the little ammunition they had left after hunting for weeks far way. The two had the medicine person tie them up a small war bundle and with their weapons, the extra ammunition, and the small war bundle they left quickly. After their departure the rest of the party returned to their town with heavy hearts, not only having lost several girls, but these two brave but foolish uncles as well. A few days later, the two uncles returned to town not only with their nieces but all the people taken as well as with other captives the Choctaw had with them. The Creeks celebrated and soon one of the girls was given a name commemorating her clan's courage; Sehoy, two who bear something go on. The old traditions of each family, clan, and tribal town are full of such stories.

Deer Woman is one of dozens of entities who are the primary characters in the "old time stories" we learn at home and the grounds. She is a witch who though a deer takes human form to lure away young men who aren't discriminating in their judgment of partners for "after the dance" activities. The moral of the stories about her is that she appears at a dance, an unknown woman who is ready and willing to sneak away with the young man and that when one's behavior is rooted in the community and knowing people that there is safety and those fast and loose relationships aren't a good idea, even are dangerous. And the ball playing bat of the old times would've been shared around winter fires and passed along in the home.

When my son Harjo was a boy I would tell him these old stories of the Creek past before bed reminding him of the lessons which they hold for us today.

When my daughter Sehoy was a little one I did the same. For a growing number of Creek people the opportunities to learn through this time honored and disappearing way are no longer possible and many seek to know more about what it means to be Creek, to be Indian, to understand our tribal heritage and ancestors, by reading and study of the growing body of work from Creek and other southeastern Indian writers, researchers and descendants.

In a 2001 book called *"A Sacred Path: The Way of the Muscogee Creeks"*, another descendent of the Hill family, Jean Hill Chaudhuri, gives a riveting and knowledgeable account of the struggle of full blood (traditional) Creek people to maintain the ties to the ancient ways from the pre-Columbian past, unaltered by the centuries of efforts to dismantle the institutions of Creek life which missionaries, government officials, and even fellow Creek people undertook. [20]In Florida the ties between the Hill family and the Scott family, like that of Jean Hill Chaudhuri in Oklahoma, were strong. Growing up I viewed men like Tom and Jim Scott as heroes, community leaders of Scott Town during the segregation era. I am a descendent of Sarah Scott Etheridge, who in the darkest of days in the 1870's lived in

---

[20] (Chaudhuri, 2001)

Scotts Ferry. She and her family was a next door neighbor to Ruben Blanchard, a veteran of the American's Civil War who, though serving honorably in the confederate army as well as Navy and who was held as a prisoner of war in a Yankee internment camp, would later would be denied his confederate pension in his old age by vindictive racist local authorities in Calhoun County.

They repeatedly denied his request saying he was a mulatto, a Negro, and that Negro's were not allowed to serve in the confederate forces. Though he eventually won his struggle against them it illustrates how much the world had changed for the Scotts Ferry Indians in the fifty years from the Civil War to the time of his application in 1900. My ancestor Sarah Scott and the other families of Scotts ferry settlement faced tremendous challenges to their assertions of their rights as Americans, as many court cases from the times document. The will of the racist local authorities to push their community across the color line and into a "mulatto" identity was met by a greater will asserting their native heritage and refusal to be bullied by Jim Crow customs of the time.

These men of Scott Town and Scotts Ferry courageously asserted the Native identity of their family and community even as county officials dismissed them as "mulatto" and colored. Across the South dozens of remnant Native American communities, especially with no contact with federal officials, would confront the same difficult reality of Jim Crow segregation. The struggle was especially difficult for those Catawba and Lumbee descendants in the central panhandle like those of the Scott, Copeland, Porter, Oxendine, Jacobs and other family's whose members appeared phenotypically Indian. With no legal status as Indians in Florida, many fell into the mulatto category as far as officials were concerned despite most being consistently identified as Indian on records in the Carolinas. Like some families in Oklahoma and many at Poarch, the Indians of Scotts Ferry and Scott Town settlements met the challenges to their identity as natives with a determined embrace of who and what was their own despite the social costs. Many would intermarry with Creeks through the last hundred years and the resulting Creek-Cheraw tribal group that is todays Apalachicola River Community of Indians would carry on that struggle in the twenty-first century.

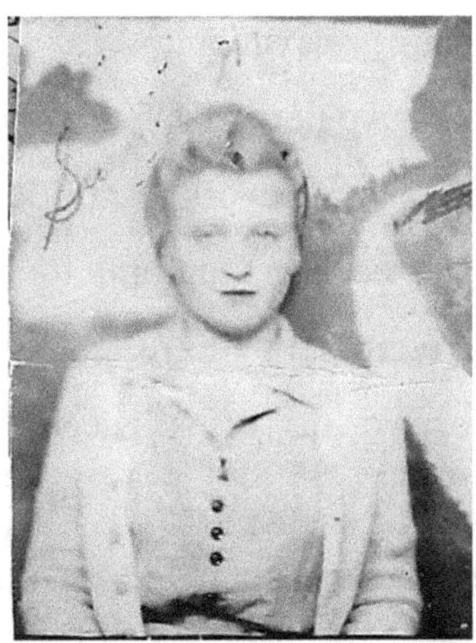

FIGURE 23 PHOTO: SALLIE KEVER

Everywhere people who have ties to the Creek Nation want to know more about the people, events, and motivations that were responsible for bringing us to the place we stand now. Unlike some of the Indian tribes from the western part of the continent, the four hundred years of sustained contact and interaction between the Creek people and the Europeans and Africans whom they came to know has led to a uniqueness that is the Muscogee people and our universe. It's a realm where race, identity, and belonging are not defined as in many other communities by skin color, and the mark of all three peoples can be seen in the faces of countless Creek and Seminole today. One can find woven into the fabric of beliefs and practices of modern Creek ceremonial ground and Indian church people threads from the Europeans and Africans who came to call the Creek Nation home. Our cosmology is a tapestry of medicine, magic, and a timeless spiral turning again and again back to itself, rather than in a straight line. Time is cyclical.

The Creeks have never been a homogenous people. Historically there was patchwork of polities, with over a hundred tribal towns each maintaining their own full sovereignty and right to self-government still reflected in what remains of this pre-Columbian world. It is still seen in how the Creek Nation and the other tribes who were spun from the common root are organized and "go about" to use an old Creek concept. The Seminoles both in Florida and Oklahoma, the Poarch Band of Creek Indians in Atmore, Alabama, the Alabama-Coushatta tribe of Texas, the Coushatta Tribe of Louisiana, the Thlopthlocco, Kialegee, and Alabama-Quasartte tribal towns of Oklahoma, the people of the Tama tribal town of Lower Muskogee Creek in Georgia, and several groups of Creek descendants in the Florida panhandle in Blountstown, Pensacola and points in between, as well as dozens of other groups I could mention, all share roots in the common heritage of a thousand years of Creek lives in the Southeast. This isn't even mentioning the millions of people worldwide, including Americans, Mexicans, and peoples throughout the Caribbean and others who have some small genetic tie to a Creek ancestor during the last five centuries of struggle, of whom they are unaware.

FIGURE 24 PHOTO: OXENDINE SISTERS ON BACK PORCH
BRISTOL FLORIDA 1920

Even within the 11 eastern Oklahoma counties which
also overlap the Muscogee (Creek) Nation of today there are
many identities and ways of life which are still ongoing, some of
which tie to the deepest and most ancient foundations of Creek
tradition. Some are of course uniquely American, while some
remain Creek in the traditional sense. As an example of how
differing identities have grown from a common root, consider
the impact of the course of American history on the family, or
possibly the impact of a family on history, depending how you

might look at it. I reflect on the lives of individuals from particular lines of descent over several generations and in differing parts of the United States, to illustrate the persistence of the American Indian identity, even those far from the mainstream of the contemporary Native American world.

The genesis of this story of some of my families' journey is with Nimrod Doyle, a man who lived out a full and long life in a time of transition unparalleled in American history. Called an "Indian Countryman", as the white men who came and lived in the Creek Nation among the Muscogee came to be known, he was one among many who would play a significant role in this crossroad of American history.[21] (Frank A. , Creeks & Southerners, 2005, pp. 27-31).

Like a few Indian Countryman he married two Creek women, and fathered many children with his wives as well as others, including his "negro children" who petitioned for full citizenship in the Republic of Texas as did his Indian children did, a petition which was denied. The Indian Countrymen were a unique breed on the frontier of the young America and the ancient Indian nations it met as it expanded.

The Indian Countrymen

The history and identity of the "Mountain Man" of the American West is well known to many people today from

---

[21] (Frank A. , Creeks & Southerners, 2005)

television documentaries and western movies. Countless have been the depictions of the rugged buckskin-clad trapper and his long-suffering Indian wife traveling through frigid landscapes and trading among the tribes for furs. Like the fur trapper Pasquinal of the "Centennial" television series, the iconic symbol of strength and endurance in the face of nature and hostile Indians that is well known to most Americans was precipitated a full century before by another such rugged individualist, though one less well known to the public; the Indian Countryman of the old Southeast. These individuals known as Indian Countrymen were found throughout the towns of the large tribes of the Southeast previous to their removal to the West. Unlike the roving French fur traders of the Rockies much later, the Indian Countrymen found residence among the Indian people in their communities, many times as town members and trusted associates. Today their surnames live in among the families in leadership among many of the tribes who have roots in the south before removal.

The Indian Countrymen were a fixture as part of the societies of many of the Southeastern tribes in the eighteenth and early nineteenth century. Because of the matrilineal nature of the Southern tribe's social organization, men of European ancestry could be found cohabitating with as well as married to Native women among the Creek, Cherokee, Choctaw and other tribes. During that era thousands of children were born to the unions of Native women and Euro-American men, and many of them would themselves marry into fellow Mixed Blood families, in a network of intermarried related families that stretched across the tribes of the old Southeast and was found in all the major tribal groups such as the Creek, Cherokee, Choctaw, Chickasaw, Catawba, and others. Though racial identity was a strong factor in the Native American community for the last century, it wasn't so pronounced formerly.

Tribal identities were based on a multiplicity of factors, and the actual racial ancestry of an individual within a community mattered little in comparison to their contribution and standing, as the large numbers of primarily Euro-American ancestry among the Cherokee, and numbers of persons of African ancestry among the Creek and especially the Seminole today illustrate.

The Indian Countrymen would play a significant role in the unfolding of the fate of many of the large tribes of the South, a relationship which would eventually culminate in the removal. The role of Indian Countrymen, such as Andrew Brissert, an Englishman who had come to live among the Creeks and was married to a Tallapoosa Fus-hatchee Creek woman with whom he had several Creek children, is illustrative of the "bridge" that many were between the frontiers of the many nations in play at the time. Arrested in 1783 by Spanish authorities while buying supplies in Pensacola, he was charged with being "dressed and painted like an Indian." Apparently his appearance in the clothing of his community violated a local ordinance which didn't allow for the wearing of disguises while in the city (out of concern for spies).

As an assistant to the powerful Mixed Blood Chief Alexander McGillivray, his arrest was met with determined protest and threats of diplomatic repercussions if he wasn't released, threats which McGillivray as well as Brissert's tribal town compatriots were sure to keep. Needless to say he was eventually released, but confusion and consternation regarding the unique and oft perilous niche that such people occupied was constant.

During the colonial era many hundreds of Euro-Americans would come to live among the Creek for varying lengths of time, some for short periods, others for their whole lives. Even to this day the names of many of these Indian Countrymen are found throughout the Muscogee (Creek) Nation as well as the half dozen tribes which were once a part of the Creeks' empire. Many of the Indian Countrymen would have positions in the several European trading firms operating in the Creek Nation, as well the Cherokee, Choctaw, and Chickasaw nations. Despite this many were important go-between for the families, clans and tribal towns of their Creek wives. Many Indian Countrymen had several wives, not uncommon in Indian societies of the time.

Ancestry and Identity

The marriage of Nimrod Doyle to both a Coweta wife and a Cussetah wife is an example. Both tribal towns played important roles in the Creek nation and especially among the Lower Creek, who often had a closer relationship with the Americans. Leadership of Coweta from the Islands and McIntosh families was slanted towards maintaining good relations with the nearby white settlements, and the members of the leading families often had blood ties to them as well. The Indian Countrymen would in their marriages to females from leading families create bridges across the racial and cultural divide. Frequently among those the who had much to gain from the conflicts and jockeying for position between tribal and international interests, they often were at ease in the Indian communities in which they settled, taking part in ceremonies, translating for the leadership, and at times holding position of power themselves. An episode documented in which Doyle rides at the head of a hundred Coweta warriors is an example of this type of involvement. His role as an important figure in the life of the Lower Towns is found on a dozen documents from eye witness observers from the time. The Indian Countrymen were drawn from many backgrounds, with French, English, Spanish, Scottish, and Irish being most prominent, though several Jews and Arabs are documented as well. Most were fluent in one or more of the dozen or so Indian languages used in the Creek Nation in those days, including Hitchiti, Alabama, and Euchee.

FIGURE 25 PHOTO: JOHN FRANKLIN SCOTT JACKSON COUNTY 1933

Though Indian Countrymen who lived for years in the towns of their Creek wives would be viewed as much a part of the tribal town community as any other man who married into the female-based social system, outsiders would see them as troublesome factors which didn't fit into the race oriented social structure which was prevalent to westerners. Where authorities would see an Indian Countrymen as a wildcard and possibly dangerous to the attempts by some of the powers competing for tribal alliances, many tribal leaders came to depend on the insights and skills of these unique men. The dynamic and inclusive nature of some Native American tribal social structures couldn't be fathomed in the minds of those from the non-Native world.

Ancestry and Identity

They often viewed Indians as a monolithic, unchanging people and uncontrolled by the social forces which were known and reliable, namely those of the common European social norms. Though outsiders would view the Indian Countrymen and their Mixed Blood families as "others" within the tribal mass, the Native American communities themselves viewed them as members and participants in the established system of kinship. When any Indian woman married her husband he would then move to her community and into her clan's compound in the town. He would be under the authority of her family until such time they were no longer married, and marriages as well as divorce were simple affairs then.

Any children born to her would belong to her clan and remain with them and her when the father, whatever his racial makeup, left as some did to return to white families back east or to the British isles where many of them were from, as in the case of the father of Chief William McIntosh, a leader of Coweta after my own ancestor Joseph Islands. Indeed, a non-Native man's lack of a clan of his own to "have his back" made him an even more valuable husband too many Creek women, whose families and clans were often engaged in fierce battles with rivals to maintain leadership in a changing time. The protection and stability provided by her clan would be the most important factor in the survival of many Indian Countrymen's fortunes as well as lives. When the terrible day of removal came many chose the life of their tribal town in a new land rather than staying in the now enlarged states of Alabama and Georgia; being white many could have severed ties with their Creek families and communities, though many did not.

During the struggles of the colonial era for hegemony by the many tribal and European powers, a great upheaval swept through the Native American Southeast and dozens of tribes were dislodged from their original territories, with many being forced to flee to larger stronger tribes for refuge. Cherokee, Euchee, Catawba, Shawnee and dozens of other tribal groups as well as intermarried individuals could be found scattered among the Creek Confederacy's towns during the 1700s, with many hundreds of Euro-Americans and Europeans from a dozen nations making their homes there as well. As Andrew Frank stated in *his Creeks and Southerners,* "the Creek Confederacy was in a constant state of re-creation."

The effort by the Shawnee in the 1770s to recover a "Peoria woman who was a prisoner among the Creeks" to bring her again to her tribe is an example of the distance which some individuals and communities could travel. Neither Creek nor Peoria could have foreseen that in two century in the future both tribes would wind up sharing the same fate as exiles in eastern Oklahoma. While touring the Creek Nation in 1790, a U.S. Army lieutenant stated there to be at least three hundred Euro-American men residing in the Creek Nation, many with large

Creek families. These men could be found in almost every village, some communities with several. Though many of the Whites who came to live among the Creek were interested primarily in trading, some were not. The same military official said that "There is in almost every town one family of Whites, and in some two, who do not trade, these last are people who have fled from some part of the frontier to this asylum of liberty." [22] The light skin and occasional blue eyes that unexplainably emerge in an individual from a family known locally as full blood around Okmulgee or Henryetta in the Creek Nation is usually from such a forgotten ancestor.

Records reveal that there were even at least two dozen Euro-American women married to Creek husbands, a situation that though uncommon is interesting. One would wonder how these women fit into the Creek clan system. One story passed down among the people of my ceremonial ground speaks of the founding of one of the clans by a Creek man who married a White woman found in the woods and unable to remember her previous life. The members of the White Potato clan are said to descend from this woman. . The Big Town Clan was established among Florida Seminole with the inclusion into the tribe of two white girls lost in the woods and taken in by the tribe long ago. n Florida as well, there were members of a small clan known as the Little Blacksnake clan who are said to originate from an

---

[22] (Chaudhuri, 2001)

African woman who found a home among the Indians generations ago. Indian Countrymen such as Thomas Marshall, who had two Creek wives much like Nimrod Doyle, during the dozen years he lived and traded among the Creeks, would establish families which would shape the future of the Creek people for centuries to come. Benjamin Hawkins was the Indian agent for the U.S. government to the Creeks and documents which he left behind mention over eighty-eight such Indian Countrymen by name and other commentators of the time such as Stiggins and Woodward name at least fifty-five.

FIGURE 26 PHOTO: UNCLE BUCK

Such Indian Countrymen mentioned in these records were only those who were involved in politics and the deerskin trade, so it is safe to assume there are hundreds of others whose names most likely will never be known. According to some records, at least eight hundred Euro-Americans found spouses and homes within the Creek society between 1700 and the removal. The great number of mixed blood Indian people among the 80,000 citizens in Creek Nation today attests to the openness of the Creek culture then and now.

Many times the Mixed Blood children of the Indian Countrymen would marry Euro-Americans themselves, and some of them descendants are the tens of thousands of Creek Indian descendants who remained in the east. Others established large networks of intermarriage among mixed blood families across the Creek nation and even into neighboring tribes such as the Cherokee, Chickasaw, Choctaw and Shawnee. Intermarriage with whites by Creek women was common before removal especially in the Lower Creek towns which bordered the American settlements in Georgia.

Such was the case with the descendants of Nicholas White, an English trader who was married to a Creek woman and had four children with her, at least one of whom married a Euro-American. In some cases the marriages among the many Mixed Blood families were arranged ahead of time, and in others it was a natural fit as all involved were "between nations," with a common experience as Mixed Bloods. Laughlin Durant was the son of an Indian Countryman and married a girl from the Hall family, while George Cornell's daughter would marry fellow half-blood Billy McGirth. Hundreds of such marriages are recorded before and after removal among the mixed blood class that we know of.

Many of the Mixed Blood children would come of age assisting in the business ventures of their Indian Countrymen fathers. Sam Moniac and Adam Hollinger, both ancestors of many in the Poarch Band of Creek Indians, as well as William McIntosh, Joseph Islands, and Jesse Wall were such examples of half-blood children who came to inherit their father's ability for business. George Galphin would establish business ventures that would be continued by his children. The above mentioned McIntosh would marry the half-blood Creek daughter of Benjamin Hawkins, Eliza, and just one such Mixed Blood among his many wives. It was said that the appearance of their children was that of someone "completely White," according to one observer at the time. [23] Marriage amongst the fellow Mixed Blood elite families was a path to security and success for some.

An example of Mixed Blood intermarriage continuing over generations in some families is the marriages of (Euchee) Billy Barnard to (Creek) Peggy Sullivan, and (Euchee) Polly Barnard to (Creek) Joseph Marshall. The Grayson family, whose members would hold positions of leadership a century later in Indian Territory, was founded by Scotsman Robert Grierson, whose children would be residents of Hillabee town. Mixed

---

[23] (Frank A. , Creeks & Southerners, 2005)

Blood Joseph Wright was the son of Indian Countryman William Wright and was one of many Creek Mixed Blood that tried to live in American society and would find his genuineness as an American questioned due to his mixed parentage.

Sometimes the Indian slave trade would be the route which would bring Whites to their lives in Creek communities, unfortunately. John O'Reilly was a Euro-American trader who was married to a woman of the Tuskegee tribal town. He is documented as having tried to buy back Whites held captive, which he failed to do. Though he wouldn't be successful in his efforts, dozens of such ransoms are documented as having occurred with success. On occasion there were whites who were captured as children that would grow to adulthood in the Indian settlements, like John Hague. He would eventually intermarry with his "captors" and have many children. There are dozens of documented cases of such situations, most often the captives feeling more at home with the Indians and refusing to return to live with the Americans.

Hannah Hale, a White girl who was taken as a captive by the Creeks when only ten years old, is an example of the successful integration of such persons into Creek society. Adopted into a Creek tribal town after her capture, she would eventually wed the Mekko (Town Chief) of Fish Pond Tribal Town and bear five children for him. Even though her parents attempted to have her brought back to Georgia in 1799, she refused to leave her home among the Creek people. This was a common occurrence among such captives once they had adjusted to the tribal life.

The most common ethnic background of the best-known Indian Countrymen is that of the Scots. Some scholars believe that the similarity of the tribal and clan structures of both peoples made the transition to Creek society by such Scotsmen easier. The persecution of Scotsmen in their Highlands Scottish homeland as well as in the colonies made the freedom and opportunities of the Creek lands appealing. On balance those with Scots backgrounds are the majority of the Indian Countrymen who are found among the Creek and Cherokee peoples. As a colonized people the Scots much like the Irish could in some degree identify with their adopted Indian kin.

Kept on the fringe in the English society of the colonies, many would journey into the Indian nations to find opportunities offered there which couldn't be had elsewhere. Despite attempts by the Spanish, American, and British authorities to regulate the flow of "Buckskin Scots" and their trading endeavors within the tribal communities across the Southeast, most such efforts were ineffective at best. The deerskin trade was indeed a lucrative one for any man with the gusto to accept the risks involved and many of the Indian Countrymen did well for themselves in time.

Not all the Indian Countrymen were of the caliber of individual that Native American leaders would hope to find residing in their towns. Leaders of several Creek towns issued orders for Indian Countrymen Richard Bailey, John Shirley, William Lyons, Francis Lessly and Robert Kilgore to leave the nation, which they did, with their Creek wives and children remaining behind. This was the fate of such relationships on many occasions. Albert J. Pickett would recount that "hundreds of unprincipled men of vagrant dispositions…were to be found at this period, in all parts of the Creek Confederacy…" [24]Probably the best known Indian Countrymen after William McIntosh is Charles Weatherford. Having been wed to a sister of Alexander McGillivray of the prestigious Wind clan, he would have been exiled himself for his questionable dealings, had it not been for an Ochiapofa tribal town Mekko vouching for his behavior henceforth.

The Wind clan was rooted in tribal leadership for generations and intermarried with Whites more frequently than others, gaining important economic and social advantages through such unions. The access to markets and power that these relationships represented was sought after among the chiefs, and the ties that were created from them would play an important role in the ultimate loss of Creek lands in the South. In the 1750s, the acclaimed naturalist William Bartram commented concerning the wives of the Indian Countrymen that "White traders are fully sensible how greatly it is to their advantage to

---

[24] (Frank A. , 2010)

gain their affections and friendships," as these wives would "labor and watch constantly their interests and direct and prevent plots or evil designs which may threaten their persons, or operate against their trade or business."[25]

Though there were indeed many relationships between Indian women and Euro-American men which were short term and would be viewed as marriages of convenience, others were long lasting and close. Kendall Lewis was one such Indian Countryman who would live with his Creek wife for three decades, finding refuge among the Indians after being charged with murder in Georgia. In time he would become a well-respected interpreter for Creek Chief Big Warrior as well as the United States Indian agent Benjamin Hawkins. Lewis's attachment to his wife and adopted people was so strong that he would remove west with them when the Indian removal happened.

For over half a century Abram Mordecai, an Indian Countryman of British Jewish ancestry would reside with his Afro-Creek wife until his death in the 1830s. Several hundred British men would find refuge among the Creeks when loyalists were expelled from the newly declared United States of America. John Chisholm commented in 1797 that there were at least fifteen hundred Tories residing among the Five Tribes. [26]

---

[25] (White, 1930)
[26] (Galloway, 2008)

Ancestry and Identity

Such refugees would include Indian Countrymen like James Walsh, George Wellbank, James Russell, Timothy Barnard, William Augustus Bowles, Abram Mordecai, and Sam Mims. Tories such as William Simory, James McQueen, and others would abandon their lives among the Whites for a refuge among Creek people, where many were welcomed as allies. The Red String affair, an incident in which fifty Irish indentured servants attempted to overthrow the local colonial order after seizing weapons and then escaped to the Creek lands, is an example of the refuge which Indian nations offered to those who would be free, even if that liberty must by necessity be found in another culture than their own. When this rebellion was put down, many of the rebels found safety among the Creeks, and they wouldn't be the last to do so. Creek Nation was truly an asylum of liberty in that time of turmoil and uncertainty for many.

The oral traditions of the Creek people are full of accounts of communities, clans, and identities founded by such groups seeking asylum. The "Big Town" clan among the Florida Indians today is said to have been founded by such a group, and another story speaks of both the Thlekatchka and Mikasuki tribal town communities being initially composed of refugees. Such stories of the origins of the Thlekatchka people may account for the ease of intermarriage with Whites that would accelerate into the early 1800's among them and neighboring towns of Lower

Creeks on the Chattahoochee and Flint. Despite this, the comments of Hector St. John Crevecoeur are telling in his *Letters from an American Farmer* (Crevecoeur, 1957), "There must be in their social bond something singularly captivating, and far superior to anything to be boasted of among us, for thousands of Europeans are Indians, and we have no examples of even one of those aborigines from choice becoming Europeans."[27] The capacity of the Indian communities to assimilate outsiders is common and found throughout the history of the Southeastern tribes, and is a part of the values of the Creek culture. The survival of the Apalachicola ceremonial grounds lineage now located in Blountstown Florida is one based on the identity of the Apalachicola Tribal Town as a community of refugees.

The education of their Mixed Blood children was often of some concern to their Indian Countrymen fathers. John Pierce established the first American school on the border between the American state of Alabama and the lands of the Creeks in 1799, with dozens of Creek students enrolled there. The noted Mixed Blood David Moniac attended school at West Point and was a courageous individual in his military service. The interpreter David Tate, another ancestor of many Eastern Creek families today in Alabama and Florida, was educated in Philadelphia and Scotland. David Cornels, another common ancestor of many

---

[27] (White, 1930, p. 75)

today in the Pensacola, Florida and Atmore, Alabama area, was educated in the language and customs of his Euro-American father.

The presence of Nancy, Sarah, and Amanda Doyle for education at the Asbury Missionary Institute in the late 1820s was a typical experience of some Mixed Bloods from families of Indian Countrymen. The "civilization plan" devised by American federal authorities included facilitating Christian missionaries in setting up and operating schools among the Indians. The Methodists and Baptists both did so until the removal from the Southeast.

The above mentioned Asbury Institute as well as the Withington School served to provide educational opportunities in a region with few options otherwise. The Choctaw Academy was another such school, and was founded in 1825. Chief John Blount, the leader of the Apalachicola Band of Creeks of the reservation located in today's Blountstown, Florida, used his son's absence at this school as a reason to delay his people's removal until 1839. The children of Indian Countrymen and tribal leaders were frequently enrolled at these schools, though not all would remain long, as poor health would afflict many.

Mixed Blood children such as Indian trader's daughter Sarah Waters, siblings Peggy, Polly, Elizabeth, James, Daniel, Richard and Dixon Bailey, and Poarch Creek ancestress Sophia Durant, all faced social minefields in their choices of marriage partners and way of life. The three Bailey sisters would marry other assimilated Mixed Bloods, a common occurrence by many such children for Indian Countrymen families. In such relationships they were more comfortable and found a familiar way of life.

The understandings which the Mixed Bloods before the removal had of their "unique" status among both Indians and Whites can be discerned in the statement of Slafecha Barnett in the *Niles Weekly Register* in 1817. "When the White people first came amongst us the Great Spirit had forbid our mixture-we did mix- and to avoid the pain of separating the husband from his wife, and the father from his children, and brother from sister, he has continued the course of the Mixed Blood in our veins. We must remain in this situation because God is upon the top of us and directs that it be so." [28] The difficult space that the children of the Indian Countrymen occupied socially was one that demanded them to be doubly cognizant of the intricacies and pitfalls therein.

One of the best-known is Mary Griffin Musgrove, the daughter of Indian Countrymen Edward Griffin and his Creek wife, a relative of Emperor Brim. Known as Coosaponakeesa among the Creeks, she is an example of the treacherous path Mixed Bloods trod in the mid-1700s in politics and social circles of the times. Though reared and educated in colonial South

---

[28] (Gazette, 1500-1926)

Carolina, she found that her life's path was rife with political intrigue and social entanglements at every turn. Married at least three times (her first husband Johnny Musgrove was himself a Mixed Blood and interpreter) she would move between the Creek and colonial worlds countless times on behalf of many interests in both.

Being able to adapt to changed social circumstances; being "White" when need be and "Indian" as custom dictated, was a hallmark of many of the children of the Indian Countrymen. Interpreters like Alexander Cornells would use their abilities and ties to the Indian Community to assume roles as intermediaries for negotiation, activities which would facilitate a growing place of importance for them in Creek society. Dealings with the growing American power would lead to their role becoming increasingly central to political affairs.

Lynn McGhee, another ancestor of many Creeks in the East today, is an example of the child of an Indian Countryman "making good" in those perilous times. U.S. Indian Agent Hawkins stated that he was "a prudent, honest, sober, and industrious half breed..." in a 1797 letter. [29] Many of these men like McGhee would found among the Tensaw settlement on the border of Creek and American domains, north of Pensacola, an area which would ultimately be home to many of the Creeks who would choose to remain as was stipulated they could in the

---

[29] (Frank A. , Creeks & Southerners, 2005)

Treaty of Fort Jackson. This treaty, known in the oral history of the Eastern Creeks as the "Red Jacket" treaty, was the avenue used by dozens of Creeks and Mixed Blood families to remain in the East while most of the Creek Nation was removed to the Indian Territory in the West.

John Davis was another half blood and son of an Indian Countryman who, though of partial Afro-Creek ancestry, would be of value to the American authorities who were growing in power and presence on the social and political stage leading up to the removal. He worked as an interpreter for the Reverend Compere who was laboring to establish the Withington School among the Creeks and would himself become a missionary of the gospel to his fellow Creeks. Davis assisted the reverend in penning a few hymns, the Lord's Prayer, and excerpts from the Bible in Muskogee. Indeed, one of the hallmarks of many of the Indian Countrymen is their acceptance of the Christian faith.

Missionaries had become increasingly central to the United States government strategies to assert control of a restless Creek population which was quickly being subsumed on all sides by landless White squatters, with the inevitable conflicts that arose. Religion was thought by some in power to be one avenue for "civilizing" the Indians, and getting them off of their lands as well. Many full blood Creeks rejected any infringement on their ancient traditions. "The efforts at civilization seem only to reach the Mixed Bloods and then only in proportion to the

White blood in their veins" said William Sparks in his *Memories of Fifty Years: Containing Brief Biographical Notices of Distinguished Americans and Anecdotes of Remarkable Men* in 1872. (Sparks, 1870)

Assuming that all the children of Indian Countrymen were "pro-American" and at the service of Christian missionaries and government officials would be erroneous though. The examples of several such people are Red Stick Prophet Josiah Francis, also known as Hillis Harjo, William Weatherford, and the red Stick war Leader, and the noted Creek-Seminole War Leader Osceola, as well as others. All these men had small amounts of Native American racial ancestry yet played important roles in the activities of militant traditionalists resisting American encroachment.

The place of Mixed Bloods on the spectrum of political ideologies that the Creeks were struggling over would come to a head often. The attack on Fort Mims and the dozens of Indian Countrymen's families killed in the ensuing massacre is one example. The range of reactions to unfolding changes confronting Creek society would be seen in the activities of many with ties to the Mixed Blood elite, both pro and anti-American. Leaders such as this little fit the mold of the War Chief fighting for tribal preservation against the invading White man so common in history books and the media.

The Mixed Blood children of the Indian Countrymen were as confusing to the authorities of the American government as were their fathers, especially as efforts to remove the Indians west ramped up. Though Colonel Gilbert Russell, an American military official charged with allocating lands to be allotted to Creeks remaining, was confounded by several of the Indian Countrymen's status as members of Indian communities and was reticent to allot to them therefore, his struggle is obvious in a statement he made.

He said "There are about ten White men who have long resided within the limits of the Creek Confederacy and have been viewed as adopted citizens thereof- they not only took the part of the United States throughout the war, but they and their families suffered greatly in the loss of lives and property. In what light ought the Indian-Countrymen to be viewed-whether as Indians or citizens of the United States?" (Clarence Edward Carter, 1938) He decided to not allot land to the Indian Countrymen, an action which unsurprisingly made more land available to White Alabamians.

Despite this we do still see a few Indian Countrymen able to find their way onto the Parsons and Abbott Roll of 1932, including Nimrod Doyle. This type of identifying with the Creeks on a very fundamental level was, surprisingly enough, even acknowledged in some limited instances by White authorities. George Stinson, another Indian Countryman, who was charged in 1824 with "trading without a license" with the Indians by the Georgia state authorities, illustrates this. Despite attempts to prosecute him in the case as a non-Indian and so under the authority of the state, the jury found him not guilty as he was a "Creek man." even if not an Indian. The ties between the Indian Countrymen and the Indian people they resided among were strong for many, and would link their fates together throughout their lives.

Even in the years after the removal, it was possible for some few children of the Indian Countrymen to reconcile their lives and their heritage with the circumstances in which they found themselves. Living into old age in an Alabama which had expelled the Creek Nation of his mother's family many decades earlier, part-Creek Thomas Woodward came to be viewed by many Alabamians as one of the "state's patriarchs."[30] George Stiggins, another son of an Indian Countrymen who chose to live his life after the tumult of the removal years in Alabama as a southern gentleman, wrote his *Narrative of the Creek Nation as Written by a Member of the Tribe.* (Frank A. , Creeks & Southerners, 1970, p. 124) Despite having chosen to remain behind he was still tied to his Creek heritage even decades after the Creek people had been banished west.

According to historic sources, some of the descendants of Indian Countrymen who remained behind after the Creeks'

---

[30] Woodward to Hooper, Dec 20th 1858, in Woodward's, *Reminiscences*, 153-62, esp. 160

removal were able to find success in the Alabama society, the best example of this being Alabama politician Robert Jemison Jr. His mother was a direct descendent of Samuel Mims who was killed at Fort Mims during the massacre there in 1814. Robert Jemison served in the Alabama State House of representatives, the Secession Convention of Alabama, and, during the Civil War, the Confederate State Senate. Eventually one of the newly created divisions of Alabama was named after him, now known as Jemison City, Chilton County.

Unlike those remaining Creeks who chose to cluster around the several smaller Indian hamlets in southern Alabama and live tribal lives in the Atmore region and nearby areas, Creek descendants who embraced southern values and lifeways could move up the social ladder, and away from their Indian roots.

The role of Indian countrymen in the life of the Creek Nation, and indeed the old Southeast in general, is an important one. To this very day the names of dozens of these men from centuries ago is found among the Creeks and other Indians who were removed from the South.

While their roles in the affairs of the Creek Nation varied and their personalities differed from loyal and brave to scandalous and full of treachery, the importance of the impact that they made on the history of the Creek Nation, and thereby in American history, cannot be denied. As their descendants continue to plot a course for the future as Native American communities in an increasingly diverse American landscape, their wherewithal and lust for life is still found in the lives of many of those who walk in their footsteps among new peoples and circumstances.

Nimrod Doyle's colorful life would exemplify the time of great transition in which he lived out his days. His life would span from birth and youth in the Northeast and participation in the French and Indian War and presence at General St. Clair's Defeat, to the struggle of the Creek Nation to keep its homelands in the Southeast and would eventually find its conclusion on the lonesome prairies of the Republic of Texas. His many descendants would be found among several races and in various regions of the America he helped to build. His progeny today are scattered from the isolated pine barrens of north Florida's panhandle and the rolling hills of Oklahoma, to the coast of California and most states in between.

As interesting as Nimrod Doyle's life was, some of his children's lives were almost as colorful and in some cases would span the entire length of the nineteenth century. Some of his children, such as Nancy, Sarah, Amanda, Muscogee, Jackson, and Winchester, we have been able to locate in records and can follow over the decades without too many gaps. We know little of others, such as his "mulatto" children who unsuccessfully sued for freedom in Texas in the 1800ss. Though not an Indian himself, being of Irish extraction most likely, he was part of a wave of immigration into the Creek Nation and other tribes by fortune seekers, traders and rascals, missionaries and patriots, loyal friends and traitors.

For several generations Creek women from leading families had formed alliances with White men who could bring something to the table to help their families and factions in the political intrigues which abounded. Large families of Mixed Bloods were already established and involved in the leadership of some Creek Communities, particularly the key Lower Creek towns of Coweta and Cussetah. The physical proximity of the colonial Georgia American settlement led to a growing familiarity and at times alliance between the Lower Creeks and the early American settlers. The large numbers of Mixed Bloods and intermarriage between them, as well as, to frontier Whites would continue to impact the fortunes of the Lower Creeks for generations.

As anti-American sentiment grew among many of the Upper Creeks located in what is today central Alabama, to the Lower Creeks of today's Georgia river valleys like the Chattahoochee and Flint, the Americans were neighbors and in some cases trading partners. Ultimately this difference in affinity for the Americans would lead to a Creek internal struggle, a civil war which would end in the removal of all Creek Nation people to the West and the stranding of several small bands of Creeks afterward in Southern states unfriendly to Native Americans in their midst. The McIntosh and Islands families, both of whom I descend from, were leaders among these towns.

Families of Mixed Bloods were established that would continue to impact the Creek social structure and leadership for centuries to come, such as McIntosh, McQueen, Carr, Marshall, Kinard, and others. Dozens of these families would have members who remained behind after the removal to found the many eastern Creek families scattered throughout south Alabama, southern Georgia, and north Florida today.

Even with all that had transpired with the treaty making, negotiations and fighting, eventually the steamroller of American manifest destiny would roll through Creek life and the Creek Nation itself would be removed to the Indian Territory west of the Mississippi. With the imminent occurrence of the Indian removal becoming a reality, all Creeks and many Indian countrymen faced a choice between resistance which could well mean death, acceptance of the Americans' policy for eastern Indians which could mean removal to an unknown and frightening far-off land, or accommodation, which would mean "social death" as acceptance of remaining behind meant loss of Creek Nation citizenship and possible enslavement. Despite substantial efforts to remove them, by the Treaty of Fort Jackson, some Creeks would remain in the Southeast and their descendants are still there today. The time of the removal was full of bloodshed and social struggle on a widespread scale. Countless thousands died in the matter of only a few years.

The genocidal policy of the forced removal from their eastern homeland of the majority of the Muscogee Creek and other large native nations in the 1830s to the Indian Territory would greatly impact the lives and future destiny of all Creek Indians. The travails of the tens of thousands who made the journey west on the infamous "Trail of Tears" to the Indian Territory, and the less well known struggles of those Creeks who remained behind and became "strangers in their own land," both deserve closer inspection and appreciation by our present generation.

In the decades before the birth of the Doyle sisters, the Creek Nation had become more divided and its position more precarious as the great game of colonial expansion and American manifest destiny rolled across the frontier. By the time of the opening decade of the nineteenth century hostilities between upper and lower Creek factions was intensifying. Leaders such as Brim and Alexander McGillivray had welded a "Nation" out of dozens of tribal towns who all jealously guarded their sovereignty and territory and who often fought among themselves as much with those outside the tenuous coalition.

The Creeks had navigated a course between the British, Spanish and French, dealing with ambitions to expand their colonial presence, and with the American Revolution this process intensified. The role which European powers would play would steadily decline and the might and involvement of the American government would increase along with divisions within the Creek country about how best to accommodate or resist the growing strength of their American neighbors. Nimrod Doyle and his families would be caught in this struggle and the family would be splintered by the force of the events they would face. For generations to come these events would continue to affect the descendants of those who faced the removal, and each passing generation sought ways to adapt to the social realities they faced.

Chapter 2 Removal

Nimrod Doyle

A pivotal figure in this story is Nimrod Doyle, an Indian Countryman. Though a white man who chose to live among, marry into, and have children with Muscogee Creek people, Doyle, like more than eighty other Indian Countrymen that records identify in the historic Creek Nation, is something of a mystery in many areas (Frank A. , Creeks & Southerners, 1970). As with any research concerning the past hundreds of years ago, we have to build the story we tell from available archival information. We have to construct what we think persons then were really experiencing from precious few scraps and information fragments that have come down to us from the records that have survived, and from the oral histories of individuals and communities in the present.

We know some of the facts of the life of Nimrod Doyle from the archival records that do exist. They are truly dwarfed by the amount of information about him we don't know, and like the majority of lives lived in that era, we will likely never know. The further in the past an ancestor lived, the less likely we are to be able to pin down certainties of their life's journey. In this narrative I have tried to reconstruct episodes of his and his descendants' lives from the archival records. From the little bit we have been able to learn about Doyle he was a remarkable man. We know of his living in Boston, Massachusetts as a young man, his exploits during the conflicts that followed the American Revolution, his involvement as a soldier wounded in combat at the time of General St. Clair's defeat, and his participation in the affairs of Indian Agent Benjamin Hawkins during the Indian Removal which wrested the Five Civilized Tribes from their southern homelands.

We know some of his exploits as a Texas Ranger in the Republic of Texas late in life; indeed he was the oldest Texas Ranger on record at his passing. We know he had one wife named Susannah Islands of Coweta and another named Mary of Cussetah and had children with other women as well according to records from courts in Texas. We know he lived to an advanced age and during his long life knew some of the great figures of his day intimately, such as Shawnee War Leader Tecumseh, US Agent to the Creek Nation Benjamin Hawkins, noted Indian fighter and mixed-blood General Thomas Woodward, and the famous senator Henry Clay. Clay was a lawyer, politician and noted orator who represented the state of Kentucky in the House of Representatives as well as the Senate. As young men he and Doyle would travel west to Kentucky, and be reunited in Washington D.C. as elderly friends a half century later.

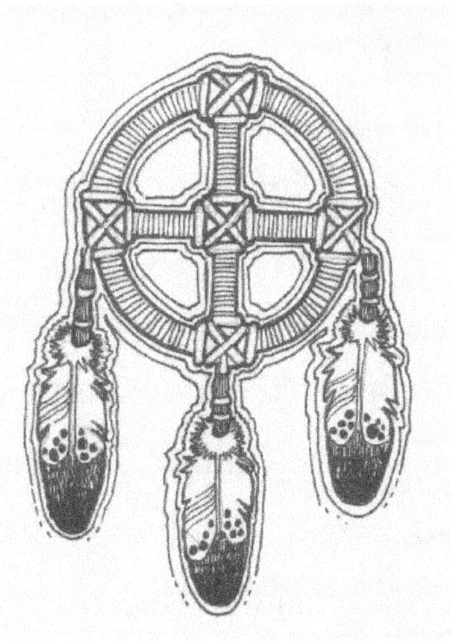

FIGURE 27 ARTWORK: TITLED: MEDICINE WHEEL

FIGURE 28 ARTWORK: TITLED: INDIAN SITTING BULL

Nimrod Doyle is but one minor character in a sweeping drama that played out across the frontier of the young America in the late eighteenth and early nineteenth century, but he did play a key role as did several other Indian Countrymen in the events leading to the eventual movement of the Creek Nation to the West. From the earliest days of contact between Native Americans and Europeans, there were some men who for their own reasons found their place among their own race less to their liking than one among the tribal peoples. Sometimes derisively known as "squaw men," they were also called Indian Countrymen, and many played key roles in fate of the Indian people they came to live among, some for better, others for worse. Indian countrymen such as John Hague, Benjamin Hawkins, George Galphin, and George Mims, would find a place amongst the Creeks. In the matriarchal societies of the Southeastern Indian people, these men would often marry into families of tribal leaders of the communities, bringing prestige and influence to the Indians, and economic gain and in some cases safety and refuge to the Indian Countryman.

The further we go back in American history, the harder it becomes to pin down solid details of the lives of our ancestors from the documentary archives which survive. Because of the time and places in which Doyle was involved during his lifetime, there are some records to give us a least an inkling of his experiences. Judging from his name and early residence in Boston, Nimrod Doyle was most likely of Irish ancestry, though he is quoted as being 'an American' which most likely means his parents or grandparents were immigrants.

Doyle was born around 1770 in the Northeast, probably in Massachusetts, as we find him resident there on the 1810 federal census. He first comes to prominence in the historic record during his participation in the Great Lakes War. In 1791 Nimrod served in this war with General St. Clair, and was wounded during this conflict, along with Bob Walton, (who will also show up in later conflicts in Creek Nation) at St. Clair's defeat. The Northwest Indian War (1785–1795), which was also known as, Little Turtle's War and by other names as well, was fought between the United States military forces and several tribes in that region for control of the Northwest Territory. This conflict was centuries in the making, with fighting over this rich territory, first among Indian nations, and then later with constantly shifting alliances among the tribes and various European powers, such as France and Great Britain, and their colonists.

In 1793, after the American Revolutionary War had ended and the Treaty of Paris gave the U.S. control of the Northwest Territory, troubles would occur. Despite the terms negotiated for the treaty, Britain kept its forts and policies there, many of which helped to support the political independence of Indians living in the Northwest Territory. With the encroaching American civilization drawing closer, this was important to the tribes.

FIGURE 29 PHOTO: AUTHOR SCOTT AND SON HARJO 2010
ROGER STATE UNIVERSITY GRADUATION POWWOW

Then President George Washington gave orders to the U.S. Army to put an end to the hostilities between the Indians and American settlers, and enforce American sovereignty over the territory the tribes held. The American Army, fighting with mostly under supplied and poorly trained troops, suffered several major defeats, including the defeat of Harmar in 1790 and General St. Clair's defeat in 1791, in which Nimrod Doyle was wounded. Both of these battles, which were Indian victories over the American invading forces, resulted in about a thousand soldiers killed and many casualties.

After the Native American forces' resounding defeat of General St. Clair, President George Washington ordered General "Mad" Anthony Wayne to form a force that could hold their own against the native warriors. He did so, and began to train a well-supplied force. General Wayne took command of the force, which was named the "Legion of the United States," in the fall of 1793. General Wayne took the American forces into battle, and accomplished a decisive victory against the Natives. He swung the tide of the struggle at the Battle of Fallen Timbers in 1794, a conflict which finally brought the war to an end. Due to their defeat at Fallen Timbers, the Native Nations were forced to cede extensive land, some of which included much of the present-day state of Ohio, to the United States as part of the Treaty of Greenville.

This treaty was finalized in 1795, and Native American forces would lose even more territory in the decades to come, with some of the defeated tribes being removed to Kansas and Indian Territory subsequently. Ironically, Nimrod Doyle and some of his children would find themselves "removed' to the West eventually, though at their own hand and fleeing from investigation by the government for fraudulent representation of the then children Jackson Doyle and Muscogee Doyle as eligible adults on the Parsons and Abbott Roll.

This roll was ordered to be taken as part of the treaty of March 24, 1832. It dictated a cession of lands from the Creek people to the United States inclusive of all lands to the East of the Mississippi river. Each head of household was allowed two tracts of land which included improvements. In 1833 Thomas

Abbott and Benjamin Parsons compiles a roll of Creek Indian heads of household and enumerated their names as well as the number of males, females, and slaves each family had. These were all listed by tribal town and numbered, which were then used for identification of those persons in later documents. While few and far between, there are some free blacks listed within this census.

Many slaves gained their freedom from their Creek masters and once their freedom was obtained, they in most cases received citizenship within the tribe and several are listed by name on the roll. Information we find on this roll is very telling. The fact that Nimrod Doyle (a white Indian countryman), his daughter Amanda (listed as "wife of James Callahan" who doesn't appear on the roll), and his daughter Muscogee and son Jackson (children at the time) all appear on this roll, yet Doyle's daughters Nancy and Sarah Doyle do not. This indicates that the two daughters by Doyle's wife Susannah Islands had already crossed into a life with their husbands George and Alexander Hill, outside of the Creek lands.

The fact that Doyle, who is White, appears on the roll along with two of his children is an indicator of the difficult choices confronting people in those times. His willingness to be involved in such fraudulent activity wasn't unknown and many Indian Countrymen were documented as involved in such schemes. In *Woodward Reminiscences*[31] a series of letters in which Thomas Woodward, a Mixed-Blood and Indian Countryman, 'friend of Nimrod Doyle,' Woodward reflects back on his life and times, and events leading up to the removal of the Southern tribes and the subsequent American settlement of an enlarged Alabama.

This valuable document has many mentions of Doyle, including a story from one letter that states that Nimrod Doyle was wounded in battle under General St. Clair in the Northwest Indian wars for what would become the present day state of Ohio. Though barely twenty years old at the time, Doyle enlisted with the American forces and was wounded in battle in 1791. After recovering from his wounds, he was released from service. He then re-entered in the military in 1793 and fought at the Battle of Fallen Timbers under General "Mad" Anthony Wayne. He is listed as a private in Russell's Regiment Cavalry, Kentucky Volunteers in 1793.

This is at the same time that he and Henry Clay, the future senator and distinguished statesman, would have journeyed there together. We find the next documentation to mention him in the book *The Mississippi Territory and the Southwestern Frontier 1795-1817* [32] where Robert Haynes mentions Nimrod Doyle in a series of letters and other

---

[31] Woodward, T. S. (1939). Woodward's reminiscences of the Creek, or Muscogee Indians, contained in letters to friends in Georgia and Alabama. Tuscaloosa, Ala: Alabama Book store.
[32] Haynes, Robert Vaughn. The Mississippi Territory and the Southwest Frontier, 1795–1817 (University Press of Kentucky; 2010)

documents of the time. Soon after this Nimrod Doyle appears on the 1810 federal census with his family (consisting of himself and two females between the ages of 26 through 44), at his home in Boston, Ward 6, Massachusetts.

After this appearance on the federal census though, he begins to appear in the records relating to the events unfolding in the interior South, in the Creek Nation. We find that after the struggles in the Ohio valley, Doyle shows up involved in the unfolding struggle for the Southeast, as the Creek Nation became more and more embroiled in the battle for supremacy between the United States and Britain, and eventually for its own survival. The Creek Nation, always a patchwork of various peoples and political ideologies, had become divided into hostile parties, known as Red Sticks and White Sticks. When Tecumseh the Shawnee war leader visited the Creeks in 1811, Nimrod Doyle was there, as an agent of the United States and assistant to Benjamin Hawkins.

In 1813 in multiple sources he is listed as a "subagent" and 'assistant" to Benjamin Hawkins, the US Indian Agent to the Creek Nation, and is recorded in Woodward's Reminiscences as running a "trading post" in the Polecat Springs settlement this same year. He was at the cutting edge of manifest destiny as American strength grew and Indian resistance increased.

A letter to Benjamin Hawkins dated 3 May 1813 records:

"With him were a number of his colleagues; John Halstead, the Indian trade factor at Fort Hawkins on the Ocmulgee, Christian Limbo and Nimrod Doyle, the agent's assistants, and Alex Cornell, a mestizo who serves Hawkins as an interpreter." (Hawkins, 1980)

From the same chapter in Nimrod Doyle's life we find this passage in "The Second Creek War: Interethnic Conflict and Collusion on a Collapsing Frontier"[33]

"Undoubtedly this party had numerous members but existing documentation mentions only a portion of them; John Crowell the Creek Agent and his brother Thomas, William Walker the son in law of the late Big Warrior of Tukabatchee, the colorful Thomas S. Woodward and his friend Nimrod Doyle..." (Ellisor, 2010)
On page 215 it continues:

"...and finally Captain Nimrod Doyle, an elderly Indian Countrymen also involved in land deals, offered his assistance riding at the head of nearly one hundred Coweta and Cussetah warriors..."[34]

The information in this passage isn't surprising since one of his wives, Mary (possibly Barnett), was listed as a Cussetah, and another wife named Susannah Islands was a Coweta (Coweta), and he was reputed to have great influence among

---

[33] John T. Ellisor. The Second Creek War: Interethnic Conflict and Collusion on a Collapsing Frontier. Lincoln: University of Nebraska Press, 2010.
[34] (Ibid p.; 215)

some portions of the Lower Creeks. In another reference to Doyle found in Woodward's Reminiscences, he is said to have been the only white man that Tecumseh would speak with when he visited the Creek Nation seeking allies, having known him during the wars in the North.*Woodward's Reminiscences of the Creek, or Muscogee Indians* by Thomas Woodward of Louisiana, formerly of Alabama. 1859"[35] includes the following passage:

> *I (Thomas J. Woodward) became acquainted with an Indian countryman by the name of John Ward; and the first time I ever visited the Creek agency, which was then on Flint river, was in company with Ward, an old uncle of mine and one Andrew McDougald. Col. was then holding a council with some chiefs from various parts of the nation. I met with Ward occasionally from that time until the war commenced. When Gen. Floyd moved his troops to Flint River, Ward was the interpreter for the officer that was in command at Fort Manning. He then came into Gen. Floyd's camp and remained with the army until it reached the Chattahoochee, and commenced building Fort Mitchell. He was often sent out with Nimrod Doyle as a spy. Christian Limbo, John Ward, Bob Walton and Nimrod Doyle saw Tecumseh at the Tallassee Square, opposite Tuckabatchy, and the*

---

[35] (Woodward, 1859)

reason why they were permitted to see him, was, that Walton and Doyle had known him in his younger days..."

In recent years, the impact that Doyle and his children made on the state of Alabama was publicly celebrated on August 25th 1985 when a historic marker was erected at Ward's Mill in Chambers County, Alabama. This marker read:

Side 1 "Where Oakfuskee Trail crosses Oseligee creek: Nimrod Doyle, first White settler in present day Chambers County built a trading post and grist mill here in 1816-1818. Doyle was in the Great Lakes Indian Wars under General St. Clair. He knew Indian leader Tecumseh at Detroit and was the only white man Tecumseh would talk with at Tukabachi. Doyle was subagent under Indian agent Benjamin Hawkins. Nimrod Doyle married daughter of Coweta Indian Joseph Islands and fathered two sons and two daughters.

Side 2 "Children of Nimrod Doyle, first white settler of present day Chambers County: daughter Muscogee Doyle's land from the 1832 treaty became site of Fredonia. Amanda Doyle married James Callahan at Asbury Mission near Fort Mitchell in 1829. Callahan was the last survivor of the confederate congress. Son Jackson married a Creek Woman and owned Ward's Mill site in 1832. Son Winchester Doyle married a White woman. Doyle's family went with Creek Indians to Oklahoma. Since then many whites have owned this place, including revolutionary veteran Stephen Nolan, and later Solomon Ward. Erected by the historic Chattahoochee Commission, the Chambers County Commission, the Leonard B. Blanton family 1985"[36]

While researching in the early 1990s, a great find in the search for documentation and records relating to the story of Doyle and the ancestors of the Apalachicola River Indian people was unearthed at the Florida State Archives (R A Gray Building, Capital Complex) in Tallahassee, Florida. It was a reference in a South Carolina Marriages Index book to the marriages of Nancy, Sarah, and Amanda Doyle, all called "Belles of the Creek Nation" in the reference to them and the 1829 marriage event that inspired this work.

In that year, Amanda Doyle married James Hill, and this event was recorded in the *Cherokee Phoenix* in an article. It was also picked up by a half dozen other local newspapers from the area. Nancy and Sarah Doyle, Amanda's half-sisters, also married James brothers, George and Alexander Hill on this same place and day, which was covered in some of the newspapers as well, though only Amanda's marriage to James received treatment as a full article in the *Cherokee Phoenix.*

---

[36] (Commission)

The *Cherokee Phoenix* was the national newspaper of the Cherokee Nation, as well as the first published by an Indian nation in a native language. The first issue was in English and Cherokee and was published on February 21, 1828 in New Echota, the capital of Cherokee Nation. It continued until it was shut down in 1834 as the Indian removal played out. It was edited by Elias Boudinot. As the issue of removal of the Southern tribes loomed, he expanded the paper's scope and had subscribers from all over the US and even Europe. This historic newspaper is available in searchable digitized form through the University of Georgia Libraries and the Digital Library of Georgia, and transcriptions of the English-language portions of the newspaper can be found at Western Carolina University's Hunter Library's Web site. (Cherokee Phoenix)

As recorded in index book records[37] found in the stacks of the Florida State Archives, (as well five other periodic sources from the times, including an April 29, 1829 edition {Volume 2 number 7} of the *Cherokee Phoenix*,) on March 3, 1829 the brothers Alexander, George, and James Hill, all brothers from Darlington District in South Carolina and stationed at Fort Mitchell, Creek Nation, were married by the Reverend Mr. Hill, to Sarah, Nancy, and Amanda Doyle, Creek Indian girls attending the Asbury Missionary Institute. The

---

[37] Evans, Tad. "Milledgeville, Georgia Newspaper Clippings (Southern Recorder), Volume II 1828-1832"

details of this marriage were captured in the *Cherokee Phoenix* article from 1829:

> Married on the 3rd of March, at the Asbury Missionary Institute, near Fort Mitchell Creek Nation, by the reverend Mr. Hill, the Mr. James Hill of the US Army, to Miss Amanda Doyle, a Creek Pupil of the Institution. This establishment is under the charge of Mr. and Mrs. Hill, who were desirous of showing the natives how this ceremony is performed in a refined state of society, and the highest encomiums are due them for their entire success. Great exertion and ingenuity were necessary to accomplish it. The company consisted of about twenty white persons and one hundred and fifty natives. The bride and her two maids were dressed with great taste and propriety, according to the fashion of the age. The groom and his two associated were in full military costume; and those persons present accustomed to wedding scenes, pronounced this bridal party one of the handsomest they had ever witnessed. After the marriage ceremony, the happy pair were congratulated with all good wishes; cake and wine were passed around, and in due time a bountiful supper was partaken of by the whole company, and the evening passed on in the most agreeable manner possible. All parties seemed delighted with the occasion. A number of strangers present will

never forget the kind and hospitable reception given
them by Mr. and Mrs. Hill.-Georgia Courier

-transcribed from the Cherokee Phoenix 1929 [38]

We also found in the marriage index records the
following information, the indexed reference in *Milledgeville,
Georgia Newspaper Clippings (Southern Recorder), Volume II
1828-1832* which states:

> HILL, Mr. James of the US Army m. DOYLE, Miss
> Amanda, a Creek pupil of the Asbury Missionary
> Institution near Fort Mitchell Creek Nation, m. there 3-3-
> 1829 by Rev. Mr. Hill. AC 3-18-1829; CP 4-29-1829; A
> th 4-7-1929; SP 3-21-1829; SR 4-21-1829. DG 4-19-
> 1829 gives wedding date as 4-3-1829 HILL, Alexander
> of the US Army m. DOYLE, Miss Sarah, a belle of the
> Creek Nation, m. there 3-3-1829 State of Georgia CP 4-
> 29-1829 HILL, George W. of the US Army m. DOYLE,
> Miss Nancy, a belle of the Creek Nation, m. there 3-3-
> 1829 State of Georgia CP 4-29-1829

Three Marriages at Ft Mitchell 1829

As described earlier in the narrative, in March of 1829
three Creek Indian girls of the Creek Nation married three
brothers from the Hill family of Union County in South

---

[38] (Frizzell)

Carolina. Nancy, Sarah, and Amanda Doyle, all described as "Belles of the Creek Nation" by the South Carolina Marriage Index listings records from the Florida State Archives, married George, Alexander, and James Hill. Such marriages were not uncommon in these times, but to find such documentation is. These three brothers were stationed at the federal military post at Fort Mitchell, in the Creek Nation.

The three young soldiers joined the American Army in 1828. Near the Hill boys' duty station of Fort Mitchell, Creek Nation was a school for Indian Girls called the Asbury Missionary Institute, with which the Hill family was already involved. According to several sources, this school was the first Indian educational endeavor in Alabama, and was authorized by the South Carolina Conference of the Methodist Episcopal Church, that was held at Augusta, Georgia, Saturday, February 23, 1822.

The mission or school was built, as near as can be determined on the section line between the Southeast quarter and southwest quarter of section 22, township 16 north, range 30 east. It was near to and a few hundred yards west of the Central of Georgia, 1 ¼ miles north northeast, of Fort Mitchell, and less than ½ mile southwest of the present Tickfaw. This point is less than ½ mile from the site of Coweta, and was therefore apparently just outside the limits of this town. The source goes on to state that Coweta, it will be remembered was the capital of the Creek Nation and the establishment of the school in the proximity of the town, indicates the desire to exert that much more influence.

Reverend William Capers, afterwards Bishop, was the first Methodist missionary to the Indians, and in 1822, when the appointments were made by the conference, he as superintendent, with Isaac Smith, and Andrew Hammill were assigned to this work.

Rev. Mr. Smith was given charge of Asbury Mission, while the Rev. Mr. Hammill was given charge of McKendree Mission, which was to have been established at Tukabatchi, in the Upper Creek Nation, but which never materialized. Mr. Smith was sixty-three years old, when appointed, Mr. Hammill, was twenty-four, and Superintendent Capers, was thirty-one.[39]

Fort Mitchell was built by the Georgia militia in 1813 during the Creek War on the main Indian trade route to the Tombigbee River. It was the trading post for the Southeast from 1817 to 1820, and a military post until 1840.

In September 1821, the South Carolina Annual Conference sent the Rev. William Capers to Fort Mitchell as "missionary in South Carolina and to the Indians. After

---

[39] Excerpted from ASBURY MISSION
http://alabamapioneers.com/index.php/Early-Alabama-Stories/early-history-of-alabama-part-a.html

negotiations with the chiefs of the Creek Nations, he opened the Asbury Manual Labor School and Mission in 1822 to teach Creek children reading, writing, and other "civilized" skills.

The mission was one mile north of Fort Mitchell near the Indian village of Coweta and may have been the first formal educational effort in the Chattahoochee Valley. The school opened with twelve pupils under the direction of Rev. Isaac Smith. Throughout its history, the school had, on average, 35 to 50 students. There were soon three teachers, several buildings, and a farm of about 25 acres. The school closed in 1830 with the forced removal to Oklahoma of much of the Creek tribe.

William Capers (1790-1855) was a native of South Carolina. He was the Superintendent of the Asbury Mission from 1821 to 1824, and during most of this time was also pastor of the Milledgeville, Georgia station. In 1829 he began a mission to slaves in the Charleston district, and later was Superintendent of slave missions on islands off the Georgia coast. Capers was elected Bishop of the Methodist Episcopal Church, South at its first General Conference in 1846. He died at Anderson, South Carolina on January 29, 1855.

Isaac Smith (1758-1834) was a Revolutionary War veteran who crossed the Delaware with Washington. He was General Lafayette's aide near the end of the Revolution. He was converted by Francis Asbury, and is considered one of the founders of Methodism in South Carolina. In 1796 he left the ministry and became a businessman in Camden, South Carolina.

In 1820, at the age of 62, Smith re-entered the ministry, and the following year was named a presiding elder in Athens, Georgia. He was dubbed the "St. John of the South Georgia Conference." Smith served the Asbury Manual Labor School until his retirement from the ministry in 1827, at the age of 69. He died seven years later at his daughter's home in Marion County, Georgia. [40]

HILL, Henry, murdered 11-1824 by Joseph S. Loring; Loring escaped. Hill was a ferryman at Macon, Ga. GJM 12-1-1824 GSL
HILL, Mr. James of the U.S. Army m. DOYLE, Miss Amanda, a Creek pupil of Asbury Missonary Institution near Ft. Mitchell, Creek Nation, m. there 3-3-1829 by Rev. Mr. Hill. AC 3-18-1829; CP 4-29-1829; Ath 4-7-1829; SP 3-21-1829; SR 4-21-1829. DG 4-19-1829 gives wedding date as 4-3-1829
HILL, Jeremiah m. SIKES, Mrs. Margaret in Tattnall Co. by

FIGURE 30 DOCUMENT: EXCERPTED FROM SOUTH CAROLINA MARRIAGE INDEX BOOKS AT THE FLORIDA STATE ARCHIVES IN TALLAHASSEE WHICH DOCUMENTS THE MARRIAGE ON MARCH 3RD 1829 OF AMANDA DOYLE TO JAMES HILL AT FORT MITCHELL CREEK NATION

---

[40] (Hill, 1829)

Married on the 3d of March, at the Asbury Missionary Institution, near Fort Mitchell, Creek Nation, by the Rev. Mr. Hill, Mr. James Hill of the U. S. Army, to Miss Amanda Doyle, a Creek pupil of the Institution.— This establishment is under the charge of Mr. and Mrs. Hill, who were desirous of showing the natives how this ceremony is performed in a refined state of society, and the highest encomiums are due them for their entire success. Great exertion and ingenuity were necessary to accomplish it.— The company consisted of about twenty white persons and one hundred and fifty natives. The bride and her two maids were dressed with great taste and propriety, according to the fashion of the age. The groom and his two associates were in full military costume; and those persons present, accustomed to wedding scenes, pronounced this bridal party one of the handsomest they had ever witnessed. After the marriage ceremony, the happy pair were congratulated with all good wishes; cake and wine were passed round, and in due time a bountiful supper was partaken of by the whole company, and the evening passed off in the most agreeable manner possible. All parties seemed delighted with the occasion. A number of strangers present, will never forget the kind and hospitable reception given them by Mr. and Mrs. Hill.— *Georgia Courier.*

FIGURE 31 DOCUMENT: A COPY OF THE 1829 ARTICLE FROM THE CHEROKEE PHOENIX ABOUT THE MARRIAGE AT FORT MITCHELL CREEK NATION OF AMANDA DOYLE (THE DAUGHTER OF NIMROD DOYLE) AND JAMES HILL

Returning to the impending removal, in 1832 the U.S. government mandated that a roll be taken of the Creek tribal towns and their members before the removal, the Parsons and Abbott Roll mentioned earlier. It stated:

> "…By a treaty of March 24, 1832, the Creek Indians ceded to the United States all of their land east of the Mississippi River. Heads of families were entitled to tracts of land, which, if possible, were to include their improvements. In 1833 Benjamin S. Parsons and Thomas J. Abbott prepared a census of Creek Indian heads of families, which gave their names and the number of males, females, and slaves in each family. The entries were arranged by town and numbered; these numbers were used for identification in later records. [41]"

The first part (upper Creek towns) was taken by Benjamin S. Parsons and the second part (lower Creek towns) was taken by Thomas J. Abbott. They were certified on May 1st and May 13th, 1833.

---

[41] http://www.usgwarchives.net/special/native_american/

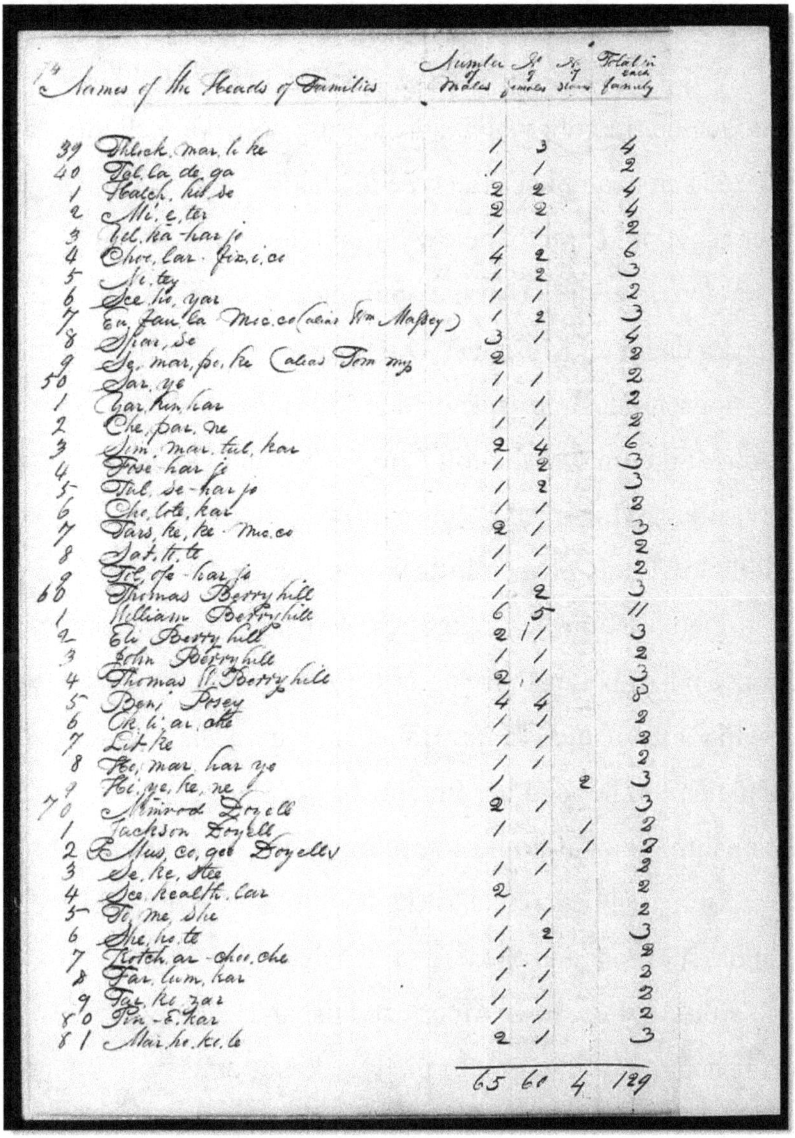

Names of the Heads of Families	Number of males	No. of females	No. of slaves	Total in each family
39 Thlock.mar.li.ke	1	3		4
40 Tel.la.de.ga	1	1		2
1 Hatch.hil.se	2	2		4
2 Mi.e.ter	2	2		4
3 Tel.ka-har.jo	1	1		2
4 Chee.lar.fix.i.co	4	2		6
5 Ne.tey	1	2		3
6 See.lie.yar	1	1		2
7 Eu.fau.la Mic.co (alias Wm Massey)	1	2		3
8 Spar.se	3	1		4
9 Se.mar.pe.ke (alias Tom my	2			2
50 Sar.ye	1	1		2
1 Yar.hin.har	1	1		2
2 Che.par.ne	1	1		2
3 Sim.mar.tul.kar	2	4		6
4 Fose har jo	1	2		3
5 Tul.se-har.jo	1	2		3
6 Che.lote.kar	1	1		2
7 Tars.ke.ke Mic.co	2	1		3
8 Sat.ti.te	1	1		2
9 Tel.ofe-har.jo	1	1		2
60 Thomas Berryhill	1	2		3
1 William Berryhill	6	5		11
2 Eli Berryhill	2	1		3
3 John Berryhill	1	1		2
4 Thomas W. Berryhill	2	1		3
5 Ben. Posey	4	4		8
6 Ok.li.ar.oke	1	1		2
7 Lit-ke	1	1		2
8 Hee.mar.har.ye	1	1		2
9 Hi.ye.ke.ne	1		2	3
70 Nimrod Doyell	2	1		3
1 Jackson Doyell	1		1	2
2 Mus.co.gee Doyell		1	1	2
3 Se.ke.hee	1	1		2
4 See.kealth.lar	2			2
5 Te.me.she	1	1		2
6 She.he.te	1	2		3
7 Kotch.ar-chee.che	1	1		2
8 Far.lum.kar	1	1		2
9 Tar.ke.zar	1	1		2
80 Pin-E.kar	1	1		2
81 Mar.he.ke.le	2	1		3
	65	60	4	129

FIGURE 32 DOCUMENT: PARSONS AND ABBOTT ROLL SHOWING NIMROD, JACKSON, AND MUSKOGEE DOYLE IN BROKEN ARROW TRIBAL TOWN (HORSE PATH)

This roll shows the heads of households in the Creek tribal towns. He appears with his son Jackson and daughter Muscogee on the roll, which considering both were children at the time is an example of the type of shady dealings that Doyle was engaged in. Directly below him on the roll is his son Jackson Doyle with two in the household, and below him is Nimrod's daughter Muscogee Doyle, also showing two people in her household. Both Jackson and Muscogee were actually children at the time of the roll being taken and Doyle would later be investigated for fraud because of this, but as he was in the Republic of Texas by then little would come of it!

One of Nimrod's daughters, Amanda, also appears on the Parsons and Abbott roll, living in Cussetah and listed as the wife of a white man named James Callahan, whom she had married after the end of her and her first husband James Hill's relationship. Soon after the compiling of the Parsons and Abbott roll, the removal began in earnest, and unlike Doyle's children Amanda, Jackson, and Muscogee, his daughters Nancy and Sarah would follow their American husbands southward to Florida and out of the orbit of the Creek Nation.

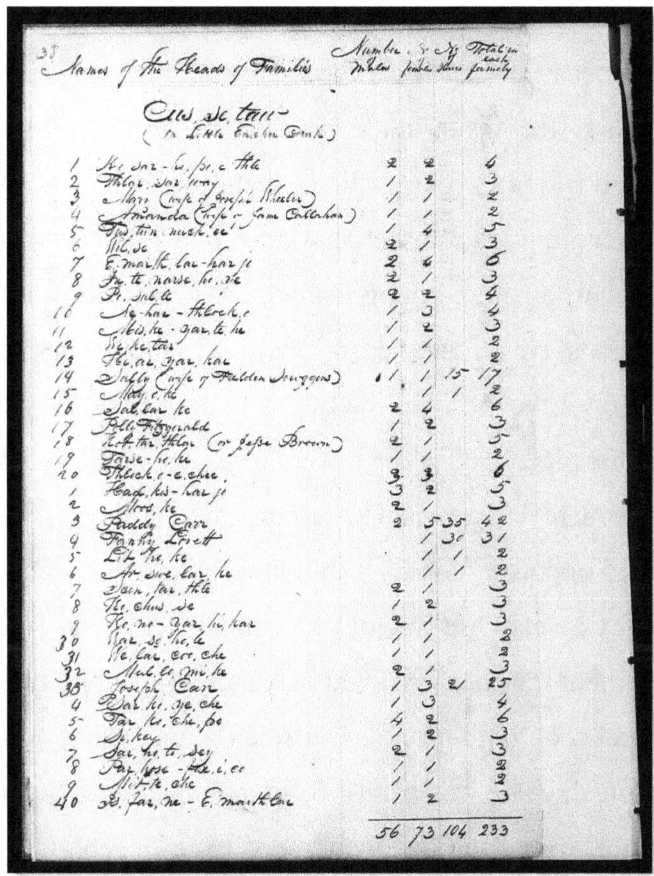

FIGURE 33 DOCUMENT: 1832 PARSONS AND ABBOTT ROLL OF CUSSETAH (CUSSETAH) TOWN SHOWING AMANDA DOYLE

The Wives of Nimrod Doyle

Though Nimrod Doyle had many children by several different women according to the documentary historic evidence, I have focused for the most part on his three daughters; Amanda, the daughter of his Cussetah tribal town wife Mary Barnett, and Nancy and Sarah, his daughters by his

Coweta tribal town wife Susannah Islands. I have focused on these three because their lives as well as the lives of their descendants reflect the struggles for survival and identity that many Mixed Blood Creek people of that time in history faced. Forces of accommodation and resistance played out in their lives on many levels as these young women charted a course during one of the most chaotic and costly periods in the history of the Creek Nation. Like many of the Indian countrymen, Doyle cemented his place within the lower Creek society through his marriages to Creek women. This arrangement also provided him security and opportunities for exploitation of his position.

His Coweta wife was of the Bird Clan and was from two very prominent families involved in leadership among the Lower Creeks, on both her father's side (Islands) and mother's side (McIntosh). She was named Susannah Islands, a member of Coweta tribal town, and the daughter of Chief Joseph Islands and his wife Bissey McIntosh. Susannah's father Chief Joseph Islands is documented as having signed a treaty for Coweta in 1802, the Treaty of Fort Wilkinson. This Chief Joseph Islands the senior died around 1836 in hostilities. Susannah had a brother also named Joseph like their father.

He went on to be a preacher in North Fork Town, Creek Nation West after the removal. He was converted to Christianity in 1842 by a slave named Billy, and went on to pastor the North Fork Indian Church there for many years. He died on the 8th of

March in 1848, which was reported in the *Indian Advocate* in April of that year. His Creek name was Cho-so-gee. Other significant Creek leaders from the lower Creek town of Coweta were William McIntosh, Paddy Carr, the aforementioned James Islands, and Benjamin Marshall, among others. Coweta and Cussetah were physically very close, just across the river from one another. They were near modern day Fort Benning, near the Alabama-Georgia line. Nimrod's other wife was Mary Barnett, and she was a member of Cussetah Tribal Town, according to her daughter Amanda's 1886 Roll of Self-Emigrants application a half century after the removal.

Doyle's ties to both Cussetah and Coweta were strong because of his strategic marriages. Both were leading towns of the Lower Creeks. The Cussetah were a respected town. Creek history says that after the Yamasee War, the people of Cussetta moved from the Chattahoochee River area and rebuilt their tribal town on Ocmulgee River, where it was until the 1830s when the forced removal of the Creek Nations lands and their seizure by Georgia and Alabama. Most agree that Cusseta was one of the oldest and most significant Creek towns, and was populous as the census of 1832–33 recorded 1,918 residents living there. It is significant as well that at this town on 24 March 1832, tribal representatives of the Creek Nation signed the Treaty of Cusseta. This treaty ceding all the Creek Nations lands east of the Mississippi River, which would be divided into individual allotments, was the beginning of the end in many ways. That Doyle would be married to a girl of Cussetah makes sense in context of the aspirations he displayed for leadership and adventure.

The Treaty of Cusseta mandated that the Creeks would relinquish all claims to land east of the Mississippi River, including the territory that they held in Alabama. The treaty stated that individual Creeks be granted land claims in the former Creek territory, as many eastern Creeks ancestor did. Altogether, each of the ninety Creek chiefs was to receive one section of land and each Indian family was allotted one half-section of land of their own choosing, a stipulation which in many cases did not occur. This treaty made clear the Americans aims. The intention of the Americans to remove as many Creek as possible to the lands in the west in the least amount of time was the motivation for the treaty requirements. Though the United States agreed to pay expenses for Creek who would remove for the first year after relocation, this in many cases didn't happen or if so was inadequate, leading to privation and suffering by many. The Cusseta treaty also called for the American government to make payments to the Creeks, an amount totaling approximately $350,000 and provide for 20 square miles of land to be sold to support the many Creek orphans left homeless by the disease outbreaks sweeping the

Indian towns at times. The treaty would not benefit the Indians, as many didn't.

Once the treaty went into effect, its effects began to be felt by the Indian towns. As would be expected, many of the new Creek landowners found their supposedly good fortune to be a detriment. Being for the most part simple tribal people and not being aware of the value of land, many of them were quickly taken advantage of by unscrupulous businessmen and land hungry settlers, many of whom often purchased land for a pittance from the Creeks. Those few Creeks who managed to keep legal title to their lands were soon overwhelmed by squatters and fortune seekers.

Compounding the difficulties for the Indians, the state and federal officials generally refused to evict these squatters and troublemakers, who in time were one of the severe banes to the already afflicted Indians. The tribal leaders seemed powerless against the tide of squatters and when individual Creek men attempted to enforce their treaty stipulated property rights against the illegal squatters, many were retaliated against by the local militia, with some being killed. By 1835, the situation became even worse as violence broke out between Creeks and squatting settlers. The treaty had dome its work and one more finger slipped from the tenuous grasp Creeks were maintaining on their homeland. Doyle

Doyles other ties were to the tribal town of Coweta, through his marriage to a women from a leading family of this town, the Islands family. The Coweta's had supplied many influential peoples through the years including Malatchi (1720-1756), Emperor Brim (died 1733), William McIntosh (1775–1825), and Mary Musgrove (ca. 1700–1767) among some.

The first place that the Coweta would settle in colonial times was the Chattahoochee river area. It was probably at a place which there afterwards was called Coweta Tallahassee. In colonial times American records speak of it being occupied by people from Likatcka, which was itself a branch of Coweta Town. Voices from the time give us some insights to the old Coweta, as D. I. Bushnell, Jr., has published parts of a journal kept by a member of General Oglethorpe's expedition to the Creek towns in 1740. The records give some account of the people of Coweta Town in those long ago days.

A chronological examination of the records which mention Coweta include one that states that in 1761 they had 130 hunters and their trader was George Galpin. Another says that in 1797 Hawkins gives the names of five traders, Thomas Marshall, John Tarvin, James Darouzeaux, Hardy Read, and Christian Russel. There were of course many more but some of these names recur with time, among those leading the tribe at times.

William Adair counted Coweta as one of the six principal towns of the Creek Confederacy but does not mention Cussetah strangely. The census Parsons and Abbot in 1832 lists five bands of Coweta Indians, as follows: "Koochkalecha town, 276 besides 12 slaves; on Toosilkstorkoo Hatchee, 85 and 15 slaves; on Warkooche Hatchee, 30; on Halle-wokke Yoaxarhatchee, 191; at Cho-lose-parp Kar, or Kotchar, Tus-tun-nuckee's town, 275 and 24 slaves; total 857 Indians and 51 slaves."

The smallness of Coweta Town in numbers to the larger Kasihta was probably due to it had given off another settlement in the past. This community which afterwards under Creek tradition constituted an independent tribal town with its own ceremonial ground was Thlikatcka, or "Broken Arrow". Founded by families who went off by themselves to a place where they could break reeds with which to make arrows according to tradition by some and as a site where arrows were broken as a symbol of peace with the Choctaw by others, it became in time large.

In ancient times the Lower Creek were closer to the Atlantic Oceon, and they moved in land later. After the Yamasee war, the Coweta re-settled on the west bank of the Chattahoochee River between the Yuchi on the south and a town known as Chattahoochee. The Coweta were settled on the Chattahoochee River for many years and was said to have been established at the location it was there to facilitate open trade with the nearby Spaniards. Bartram in his writings states that the people of the town spoke the true Muskogee language. The older location of Coweta was in Troup or Heard Counties, in today's Georgia, and was abandoned before Hawkins's time, 1798-99.

Creek tradition describes the Coweta, Cussetah, Tuckabatchee, and Arbeka as the four "founding towns" of the Creek Nation, and Coweta and Cussetah were closely related and exercised great influence among the Lower Creeks of the Chattahoochee River, as the historic records show. Families like the Islands and McIntosh of Coweta had strong sway over the other Lower Towns such as Upper Chehaw (Chiaha), Hitchiti, Oconee, Okmulgee, Okawaigi, Apalachee, Yamasee (Altamaha), Ocfuskee, Sawokli, and Tamali, to name some.

Tribal town leaders of settlements among the Tuckabatchee, Okchai, Okfuskee, Talassee, and Abeika tended to dominate political affairs among the Upper Creeks, and were less dominated by individual families like some Lower Creek towns.

Doyle's Coweta wife Susannah Islands was the daughter of Joseph Islands who, like Doyle, was involved in the politics and the unfolding situations which led to conflict within the Creek Nation. Joseph Islands's wife Bissey McIntosh was herself a Mixed Blood and from a leading family among the Lower Creeks, and a kinsmen of William McIntosh. Of all the dozens of Mixed Blood elite families among the Creeks, the McIntosh family was the most influential and powerful. It would remain so for generations to come. It all began with a Scotsman named William McIntosh, a white man much like Nimrod Doyle, who established a place for himself among the Creeks and a family line that is among the leadership of the Creek Nation to this day.

The McIntosh Family in Creek Nation

The McIntosh family is one of the best known of the Mixed Blood families who came to power in the Creek Nation in the late eighteenth and early nineteenth centuries. Chief William McIntosh is most certainly one of the most colorful and well known characters of Creek history. His death, like much of his life, was a statement of his split identity, and of the precarious position in which many of the Mixed Bloods found themselves with the removal.

As dawn broke over the lands of the lower Creeks in what is today the state of Georgia, the early morning stillness would be shattered by war whoops and gunfire. On April 30th of 1825, four hundred Creek warriors gathered before daylight near the home of Chief William McIntosh to conduct a grisly and yet sacred duty. They were there to execute him as demanded by Creek tribal law for signing the Treaty of Indian Springs penned the past February, an action which transferred a substantial amount of the lands in the eastern part of the Creek Nation to the

United States and exacerbated the growing divisions among factions of the Creeks.

The National Council had passed a law regarding the leadership and growing loss of lands, with some of the leaders using their tribal connections to grow wealthy and powerful at the expense of the Creek people. The Creek warriors who surrounded the house were bound by law to execute any chief who signed such a controversial treaty as the Treaty of Indian Springs. McIntosh and his family members were not the only ones who were held accountable for their actions; others included a tribal leader who was visiting McIntosh, Etomme Tustunnuggee.

The assembled warriors set aflame the large sumptuous plantation house that McIntosh had constructed on his vast private landholdings. In a manner much like the wealthy White planters of the South it was palatial and its surrounding fields were worked by his many slaves. With that long ago dawn, his time of leadership and controversy, politics and business, would come to an end. In the growing light warriors gathered round the large house and prepared to bring to justice an outlaw, their firearms doctored for the sacred task they would be used for, the men fasted and prepared by the medicine people for the serious business of taking human life. When the doomed McIntosh emerged from the flaming structure he was brought down in a volley of gunfire, his years of leadership and bravery in battle finally silenced at the hands of his tribal brethren.

Two American witnesses who survived the attack would later recount to others that the "banditi were busily engaged, from the commencement of the horrid scene until a late hour of the morning, in plundering and destroying everything of value, as well the property of the white men who were present.[42]

Though it would seem that this killing was one of chaos and banditry on a frontier rife with murder and struggle, it was actually a part of the internal balance of the Creek world, which was reflected in the traditional laws of the Nation, and the cost in blood for violating what was and still is viewed as the laws which represent the universal and eternal order as granted in the creation time by the Creator and sustainer of all things. The hundreds of Creek men, the law-menders, who had gathered to take action that spring morning, were acting under the laws of the Creek people to bring to justice one who had violated this law, knowingly and without reservation.

These men bent on justice, known as the "Law Menders", were acting in the defense of the Creek people's overall welfare, after years of land losses and incursions by outsiders. The loss of any lands, which were held in common by the tribe, was not allowed and "chiefs" who did sign on to such

---

[42] From the affidavit of Harris Allen and Francis Flournoy, May 16th, 1825, in Mrs. J. E. Hays, "The Murder of General William McIntosh, Treaties of Indian Springs 1821-1825

agreements were to be held responsible under the law with their lives forfeit if they were found to be party to agreements which transferred lands. As the *Niles Weekly Register* reported in May 1825, "McIntosh was not murdered; rather that he has been duly executed, according to the known laws and usages of the nation to which he belonged."[43]

Interestingly, McIntosh had enthusiastically supported this law when it was passed by the Creek Nation National Council, an edict which "called for the execution of any Creek leader who ceded land to the United States." (Frank A. K., 2002). When the Nation's leaders had met to pen this into law at the square at Broken Arrow, he spoke as an advocate for it and signed as did almost all the Creek leaders present, much unlike the Treaty of Indian Springs, which was controversial and not in any way representative of the will of the Creek people.

As Frank stated "Although fifty-two Creeks signed the document, only six were headmen, and only McIntosh was a member of the Creek National Council." This treaty, which ceded 6, 700 square miles of Creek tribal land in exchange for payment of $10,000 immediately with $190,000 being paid over the subsequent fourteen years to McIntosh and his faction, involved most of the Creek lands remaining in what is today Georgia. This land transfer was not to include lands held by

---

[43] Niles Weekly Register (Baltimore Md.), May 28, 1825; "treaty with the Creeks at Indian Springs," February 28, 1825, in American State Papers, Indian Affairs, 2 volumes (Washington D.C., 1934), 2:767-68

McIntosh and a few of his supporters. As historian Michael Green said, this treaty was clearly "fraudulent by the standards of any society, [was] concluded in violation of the clearly expressed orders of both interested governments, [was] riddled with bribery, chicanery, and deceit." (Green, 1982)

Though McIntosh was executed for his crimes, this historically significant incident was not an indication of his "whiteness," but was rather more an indication of his identity and inclusion as a tribal town chief and as a Muskogee Creek. As historian Theda Perdue has posited, children of Native women in matrilineal societies should be viewed as fully native, their clan and tribal town ties demanding such. Terminologies used today which indicate a mixed racial identity or status as "part-Indian" do not represent the realities of the Indian world and its complexity of identity and kinship either during the pre-removal era, or for several generations afterwards. (Ellisor, 2010)

James Carson, a scholar of the Native American Southeast states that being a part of a Southeastern American Indian community did not have a racial component.[44] The children of White fathers and Native American women would play a crucial role in the unfolding of authority and political intrigues, using their clan ties and tribal connections, as well as

---

[44] James Taylor Carson, Searching for the Bright Path: The Mississippi Choctaws from Prehistory to Removal (Lincoln, Neb. 1999) (PUBLISHER?)

knowledge of English and connections to Euro-American enterprises to rise to positions of leadership.

Although a Mixed Blood who lived a life rife with privilege and power, wealth and prestige, McIntosh's journey across the stage of history reflected the difficult position he was in personally, constantly having to navigate the treacherous waters of political intrigue and societal expectation. Born in 1778, he lived during a time of fantastic transition among the Creeks, a time when the Creek Nation was reaching the height of its power and would begin a slow downward spiral of land loss, military defeats, and increased violence and death from all sides, a situation which would ultimately end in a complete loss of the lands held dear for hundreds of years and a journey westwards to an unknown fate a thousand miles away.

As a member of the prominent Wind Clan and a leader of Coweta tribal town of the lower Creeks, he was fully invested in his community as a tribal member, which scholars Theda Perdue and James Taylor Carson have both shown through their works; although controversial as a leader, he was indeed fully Creek in his identity. Although he was a Creek leader and a warrior of unquestioned courage as the son of a Tory Euro-American father, he was involved in depth in the capitalist economy emerging among the Creeks, and especially prominent among the Mixed Blood elites.

McIntosh's life and death reflected the realities of the clash of civilizations unfolding with increased Creek-American interactions, which with the passage of years and increasing pressures from a restless American population became more violent and distrustful with each passing year. Each day of his life McIntosh had to balance the two opposing sides of his identity. As a successful and prominent chief, Creek expectations that McIntosh would share the benefits of his wealth were not disappointed, as several of his kinsmen and tribal town people were benefited.

His redistribution of cattle, money, food, and trade goods to others was the responsibility of a man and a warrior, as well as a leading chief, in the Creek society of McIntosh's day, a responsibility which until near the end of his life, he fulfilled. What was not beneficial or normative was the concentration of wealth and unbridled political power that went along with it, influence and means which were not norms in traditional Creek society, and almost never concentrated in the hands of a single individual as they became with McIntosh in the fairly communal lifestyle of the Creeks.

Being the son of a Wind Clan Creek woman and a White father, McIntosh grew up with two conflicting standards of identity and culture constantly pulling on him. In the traditional ways of the Muscogee Creek, an Indian youth's father played only a small role in his upbringing and teaching, with the mother's brothers (who were of the same clan) being the primary shapers of a youth's identity. With McIntosh and his brother, this was not the case, as his British father played a significant role in influencing his son's life. McIntosh's father taught him English, exposed him to interactions with other Whites and instructed him in the capitalist economic values which were a large part of the elder McIntosh's business among the Creeks. The elder McIntosh was very involved in the lives of his young sons and sought to help them "rise above" the life that traditional Creeks sought as in balance with others and nature.

The Wind clan uncles of McIntosh were men who took their clan responsibilities seriously, and the elder McIntosh went too far when he tried to have his young sons sent away to be educated in Scotland, an action which was protested, and ultimately foiled by, the Wind Clan uncles. His mother's brothers were determined that their charge would not be taken away from them or from their people.

Indeed their views on the matter would have carried much weight with fellow Creeks, though the elder McIntosh indeed tried to take his sons with him upon leaving for Scotland, with the promise that he would return them after schooling was complete, something not unknown among the Mixed Blood sons of other elite families. The story says that McIntosh's father went against the wishes of his wife and her clan and left with his sons to await transit aboard ship to Scotland. While they were waiting to board the ship, the boys' maternal uncles came and took them while their father was otherwise engaged.

The tale states that the men of the Wind Clan had acted swiftly to reclaim their charge when the elder McIntosh had "joined the other passengers in the lounge area. Later in the evening when the Captain had returned to the stateroom, the boys were missing…Nothing could be done now for the ship was at sea and the Captain was taking the trip alone."[45] Though the actions of the Wind Clan men are seemingly underhanded and selfish from a modern perspective, they were doing what would be expected from them under Creek law. This close scrape for the young Creek McIntosh and his brother with a differing future than that of most other Creeks would not be his last. Despite this, he and his brother would remain upon the lands of their people for the rest of their lives.[46]

Twice in his life, the Creek law clearly reached out to firmly grasp McIntosh and shape his fate; on the day that his Wind Clan uncles returned their charge to the Creek Nation and his responsibilities as a Wind Clan member, and on the day of his death when the Law Menders' bullets, some fired by men of

---

[45] Harriet Turner Corbin "A History and genealogy of Chief William McIntosh, Jr. and His Known Descendants," 23-24, typescript in Mississippi Department of Archives and History, Jackson, Mississippi.
[46] Benjamin Griffith, Jr., McIntosh and Weatherford, Creek Indian Leaders (Tuscaloosa, Alabama 1988), 3, 36; Bonner, William McIntosh, 114-43; Jones, "A Lettered Portrait of William McIntosh, " 77

his own clan, would fulfill the requirements of the law and hold him accountable for his actions.

Much like another Creek of a similar background, the war chief William Weatherford, McIntosh would participate fully in his tribal town and clan responsibilities and would ultimately pay the greatest of prices for his beliefs regarding them. As an advocate of policies which would lead the Creeks into a closer relationship with the United States and assimilation to its values, McIntosh and other chiefs found themselves between the steadily increasing presence of Americans on their lands and the calls by more conservative leaders for military actions against the newcomers.

Though both McIntosh and Weatherford were sons of White fathers and Creek mothers, their allegiances could not have been more different. McIntosh was called "a steady friend of the United States and of civilization" by the U.S. Secretary of War James Barbour. (Frank A. , Creeks & Southerners, 2005, p. 101) Though this movement for acquiring the trappings of "civilization" among the Creeks never caught on with the majority of Creeks, leaders such as McIntosh are known to have influenced ; factions whose descendants are still recognizable among the politics of the Creeks today, east and west of the Mississippi.

The notions of capitalism, individual land holdings, Christianity, slave based agriculture, and other ideas and practices new to the Creeks were spread among and by the Mixed Blood elites and found footing particularly among the Lower Creeks, whose progressive outlook would continue down to our own time in some ways.[47] In his time, many American officials viewed McIntosh as like them, and he used this to expand his business interests and ties politically.

He took a similar tack among the Indians, as strategically he cultivated the clan ties among the Wind people, one of the leadership clans among the Muskogee speaking Creeks, to his personal advantage. The United States government's choice of singling "cooperative" leaders out for monetary rewards and positions of authority during treaty negotiations, with him as a "lead" Chief in many cases, would work for McIntosh for much of his political career. In the end, however, it would be his undoing, and his ultimate choices to act beyond his capacity as sanctioned by the laws of the Creek people would be a pattern repeated among many other tribes over the next century.

The United States policy of "setting up" chiefs would be repeated multiple times across the continent as the wave of American expansion moved westward. Countless times leaders chosen by the American authorities for their pliability would be

---

[47] In the Creek Nation today the sixteen ceremonial grounds are primarily descended from the Upper Creek faction whom settled in the lower part of the new lands asset aside for the Creeks in Indian Territory, whereas none of the lower Creeks' ceremonial Grounds survive. In many cases, the numerous "Indian Churches" bear the names of the lower Creek towns, and indeed the Mixed blood elites surnames can still is heard throughout the office holders of the modern Muscogee (Creek) Nation in Oklahoma during the last century.

led to sign agreements not sanctioned by their people. Few however would be held ultimately responsible for their decisions as fully as McIntosh was. It was not solely the Americans who were at the root of the situation, as their understanding of McIntosh as "one of their own" facilitated their interactions with him in many ways, an identity which he did little to refute. Indeed, he himself cultivated this representation in his dealings with the white authorities, state and federal. His participation on the American side during the War of 1812, engaging in political opposition and eventually armed conflict with Creek traditionalists known as "Red Sticks" was not the first of his actions which clearly communicated to all his American values and allegiances. During the Treaty of Washington in 1805[48] McIntosh would facilitate transfer of the lands between the Ocmulgee and Oconee rivers to the Americans.

---

[48] This was a treaty which was also signed by Joseph Islands of Coweta and the father of Susannah Islands who married Nimrod Doyle.

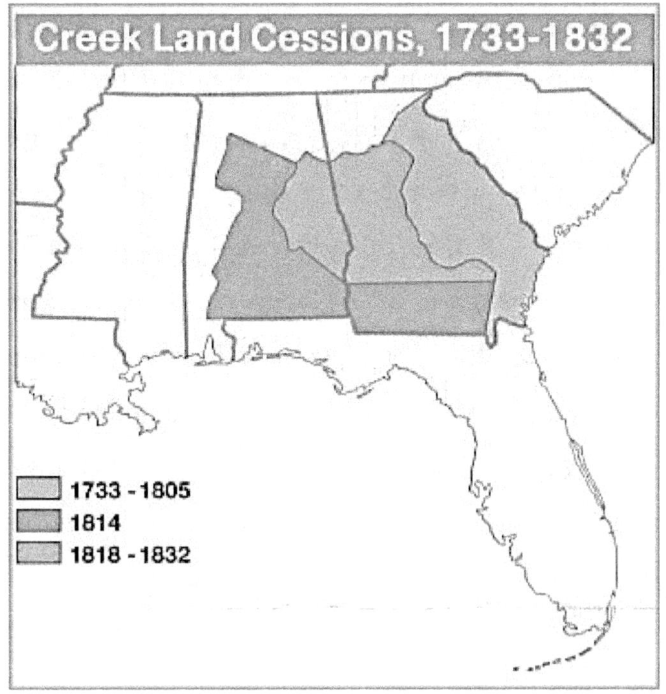

FIGURE 34 MAP: CREEK LAND SESSIONS 1733-1832

He would also make access for a road from Mobile, Alabama to the Ocmulgee valley possible, a route which he would use to expand his growing fortune and power. During the War of 1812 General Jackson would comment on McIntosh's valor in battle, stating "Major McIntosh the Cowetan who joined my army with part of his tribe, greatly distinguished himself.[49]" McIntosh's choice to ally himself with the Americans would cause much resentment among the majority of the Creek people, who did not live the Southern planter lifestyle and materialistic,

---

[49] Andrew Jackson to General Pinckney, March 28, 1814, in the Niles Weekly Register, April 23 1814.

capitalist, non-traditional values which McIntosh and other Mixed Blood elites throughout the Southern tribes did.

On many occasions afterwards McIntosh would barely fend off attempts by his adversaries to unseat him, and his alienation from chiefs from other towns, especially outside of his alliance of a few lower towns who were pro-American and supplied by United States interests, would grow with time. McIntosh's friendship with United States Indian Agent Benjamin Hawkins would lead to much personal benefit for him and until Hawkins died in 1816, they would work together on many projects to implement American policies slated to assimilate the Indians, with McIntosh a primary beneficiary of these activities.

His role as a distributor of goods and monies relating to negotiations and annuities would increase his power among his faction, and his personal wealth as well as tribal power base would grow steadily. When his in-law David Mitchell became the Indian agent to the Creek Nation after Hawkins's death, McIntosh's control over the flow of goods and funds became even more pronounced. McIntosh and members of his "party" received over $80,000 in goods in 1817 and 1818.[50]

Decision after decision and choice after choice, McIntosh showed his orientation away from the communal values, non-materialistic lifeways, and harmony and balance of

---

[50] Creek Agency Records, Accounts 1817-1818, David B. Mitchell Papers, Newberry Library, Chicago Illinois.

the *Nene Hvtke*, the "White Road of Peace" of the Creek world which was foundational to the law codes that governed Creek society. Throughout McIntosh's life he continue to live his dual identity; his American values exemplified through his ambitious and expansive business interests, even as he continued in his clan and village responsibilities and distributed some of his wealth among his Coweta people as was expected of a warrior and town chief.

Materially his wealth grew through the years, exemplified by his establishing two plantations, a toll road and ferry, and large business ventures on several fronts. A visitor to McIntosh's home in 1797 commented that his habitation was a *"poor sorry place, little better than an Indian hut,"* but by 1820 McIntosh would host countless visitors in his two story plantation house, estimated to be worth $1,500 dollars. Upon his death, the United States government estimated his properties to be valued at over $10,000.[51] The lifestyle and accomplishments of Mixed Blood such as McIntosh strengthened the views of many Americans that Indians could and eventually would be subsumed and absorbed into the American population.

President Thomas Jefferson said "The ultimate point of rest and happiness…is to let our settlements and theirs meet and blend together, to intermix, and become one people."[52]In

---

[51] Thomas McKenney to James Barbour, January 5, 1826, OIA, M-21, 2:345-349

[52] Thomas Jefferson to Benjamin Hawkins, February 18, 1803, in Paul Liecester Ford, ed., The Works of Thomas Jefferson, 12 volumes (New York

individuals such as McIntosh and others of the Mixed Blood elite this was a reality already in full swing years before the removal, though the vast majority of the Creek people still lived the communal village life of their ancestors.

Like many Mixed Bloods mentioned in the historic record, McIntosh's perplexing identity would be the object of interest and comment for the many Europeans and Americans that would cross his path during his years of operating business in several ventures along the "government road." A visitor to the Creek Nation in 1819, Ebenezer H. Cummins commented on the uniqueness of McIntosh, as well as revealing attitudes of the time which reveal the ideas of the "disappearing Redman," a view which would linger into our own time:"In the very neighborhood of the country of which we have been treating, is a rising family of the name of McIntosh, commonly called half breeds, possessed of many of the higher virtues, and particularly distinguished of military achievements." [53] Cummins goes on to inform us of the genealogical ties established among the white Southerners and the Creek (and Cherokee) Mixed Bloods elites, "A son of the late governor of Georgia, General David B. Mitchell, recently married Miss McIntosh, an accomplished girl…though descended of an Indian mother."

The assumed ultimate fate of the Creek people to assimilation and eventual extinction is stated in his next

---

1892-1899), 7:214.

[53] (Frank A. , 2010)

comment of his travels observation. "The truth is, after the missionary system, and the system of taming by the arts, shall have failed in the benevolent purpose of rescuing the savage from heathenism and extinction, amalgamation will have preserved the precious streams of Indian blood, coursing through the veins of many generous loyal citizens."[54] His statements hint at the view of many Americans who viewed the way of life and beliefs of the Native people as inferior to the "civilized" ways, and with the proper changes in culture they could be accepted by Whites as equals.

The best efforts by the many among the Creek, Cherokee, Choctaw, and other tribes who tried to adapt to White cultural life ways were not rewarded as they thought. This would be a harsh reality revealed by the long walk to Indian Territory west of the Mississippi in years to come. The policies which the American authorities were advocating and sought to implement in any way possible were at the forefront of the Indian agent Hawkins's agenda, and the policies administered by his successor Mitchell. The Americans' support of the activities of Indian countrymen and the Mixed Blood elite families they established would accelerate already existing differences among various Creek factions.

These differences would lead to conflict and bloodshed before and after the removal, grudges and resentments that

---

[54] Ebenezer H. Cummins, A Summary Geography of Alabama, One of the United States (Philadelphia, 1819), 23-24

would last for generations to come, resurfacing a generation later in the clash between Creek factions which occurred in the American Civil War, and indeed even can be found in the Crazy Snake "Rebellion" of a century ago. The legacy of McIntosh and his party would be so strong that it would resound in the politics of the Creeks for the next two centuries. McIntosh did not establish his vast network of business and political connections overnight or easily.

He used strategic marriages to several wives to cement ties which would be important to his endeavors. The tradition of polygamy was not new among the Creeks but it was uncommon for any one man to have the number of wives that McIntosh did. Like Doyle, the McIntosh Scotsman who sired Chief McIntosh had married at least two Creek women and had children with both, as well as marrying a Scottish-American woman with whom he sired a family, with whom the Creek McIntosh was acquainted. He was cousin to Georgia Governor George M. Troup and half-brother to Georgia legislator William R. McIntosh as well as the collector for the Treasury Department at Savannah, John McIntosh. Chief McIntosh also created for himself through his marriages and relationships many ties within the Indian Country, a custom which he also arranged for the benefit of his children. Chief McIntosh's descendants removed with the Creek people to Indian Territory for the most part, with only his daughter Catherine remaining in the south after removal. His two sons served as Confederate officers during the American Civil War. Some of his known daughters including Rebecca and Delilah moved to Texas with their husbands, owning plantations there. Rebecca McIntosh Hawkins Hagerty married again after her first husband died young. By 1860 she was among the wealthiest people in Texas, owning three plantations with a total of 12,800 acres, and 120 slaves.

With the death of the elder McIntosh, his daughter Catherine, along with her husband William Cousins fled the Creek Nation for safer lives, eventually ending up in Florida. Their Creek Nation of 20,000 would be forcibly removed from its ancestral lands within the decade and forced to lands in the Indian Territory beyond the Mississippi. Dozens of families of Creeks would remain behind after the removal, for various reasons, like their own. The family of William and Catherine McIntosh Cousins was one such family. The Cousins family as well as several other related Creek families settled initially in south Alabama after fleeing the Creek Nation.

William Cousins was himself a half blood like Catherine, the grandson of a Creek Nation chief named George Cousins, a leader of Eufaula tribal town. It is said that Catherine McIntosh was present when her father and brothers were killed at the family's plantation. The descendants of the McIntosh-Cousins union would settle throughout the Shoal River area of Santa Rosa and adjoining Escambia counties Florida and would eventually intermarry with other refugee families who were dislocated by removal, and form one of several eastern Creek communities.

Chief McIntosh married Susannah Coe (Creek), Peggy (Cherokee), and Elizabeth Hawkins (herself the Mixed Blood daughter of a Creek woman and an Indian Countrymen) as well as having children with other women. Through the ties he established across tribal town lines and among other tribes, McIntosh more than any other Creek leader, exemplified the concentration of resources and political power which were a hallmark of the Mixed Blood elites, and contrary to the traditional communal values of the Nene Hvtke, the traditional Creek values of harmony and reciprocity.

Many Americans viewed the "Indian" marriages as lacking the same legitimacy as the "Christian'" marriages by assimilated Mixed Bloods among one another or even to Whites. Native women, such as Susannah Coe and Peggy, who were a part of these "convenience" or "casual" marriages in the eyes of some of the White visitors to McIntosh's residence, were hardly regarded by many of them as worthy even of comment. Though these relationships were fully accepted by Native law, they were often dismissed in "proper society." McIntosh's marriage to Elizabeth was held in higher regard due to her father's prominence on the political landscape of the time; the American

Stephen Hawkins was commented upon by many of those who stayed at McIntosh's Inn.

The ambition McIntosh showed throughout his life was not only restricted to his life and marriages, but was present in the marital arrangement he facilitated for some of his children.[55] Like him, they married well-connected individuals. One of his daughters married Thomas Spalding, a trader among the Indians.

Another of his daughters married the federal interpreter to the Creeks Samuel Hawkins, while a third married the son of Georgia's Governor David B. Mitchell.[56] The extensive ties created by the McIntosh family would continue to expand for generations to come, with the McIntosh family name becoming well established amongst leadership circles until this very day. A son named Chilly McIntosh would himself become a well-known and influential leader as well.

Though Mixed Blood Indian leaders such as McIntosh, Weatherford, Josiah Francis, Osceola, or McQueen would loom large over the narrative of the history of the experience of Indians of the Southeast, the forces which motivated their choices and actions were complex and often misunderstood by the Americans of the time. Thomas Woodward, himself of

---

[55] The total number and identity of McIntosh's descendants is still debated today.

[56] Absalom H. Chappell, Miscellanies of Georgia: Historical, Biographical, Descriptive, &c., 3 pts. (Columbus, Georgia 1928), 3:24 Jones, "A Lettered Portrait of William McIntosh," 77; Green, Politics of Indian Removal, 63-66

Mixed Blood origins, commented "General Jackson said to Weatherford that he was astonished at a man of his good sense, and almost a white man, to take sides with an ignorant set of savages, and being led astray by men who professed to be prophets and gifted with a supernatural influence."[57] Many Americans failed to grasp the expansive embrace of the Creek culture in its complexity, or the strength and breadth that the clan based culture of Creek Nation afforded to even the Mixed Bloods among them.

This lack of insight to the motivating influences among the Mixed Bloods among the Indians is easily displayed in the observations of Thomas Hart Benton, Senator and Chairman of the Committee on Indian Affairs. He said that "some of the Southern tribes…though still called Indians," were no longer meeting his expectations of such, because, "their primitive and equal government had lost its form, and had become an oligarchy, governed chiefly by a few white men, called half-breeds, because there was a tincture of Indian blood in their veins."[58] The patronizing attitude towards the Mixed Blood Creek leaders in this statement can still be found in the sometime adversarial relationship between Oklahoma political leaders and tribal leaders today.

---

[57] Thomas Simpson Woodward to Albert J. Pickett, April 25, 1858, in Woodward's Reminiscences, 43

[58] Thomas Hart Benton, Thirty Years View or A History of the Workings of the American Government for Thirty Years, from 1820 to 1850, 2 volumes (New York, 1852-1854), 1:163

The choices made at the crossroads of history by many Mixed Blood were driven by many complex influences. With the paucity of records regarding the lesser known lives of the majority of Mixed Bloods not of such celebrated stock as McIntosh, Weatherford, many stories of family struggles and challenges overcome are lost to time, represented only by the remembrances of the tenacity and courage of their ancestors in the wake of the removal holocaust... In the South as well as in Oklahoma today, many families have rich oral history stories of the measures taken by their ancestors to bridge the widening gap that resulted from the intensifying pressures on all the tribes to remove west, or be assimilated, or into White or "colored" identity.

With the explosion of violence that swept the Indian lands in the years before removal, incidents increased of the Mixed Bloods and their families, who were on friendly terms with neighbors in many cases fleeing to American homes and settlements for refuge from the hostilities between Creek traditional people and Americans. One observer penned that "The whites who have been resident among them and who are acquainted with their habits and character, are sending their families from the Nation."[59] Unlike some of the Mixed Blood

---

[59] Charles McDonald to George M. Troup, May 6, 1825, Records of the Office of Indian Affairs, Creek Agency, 1824-1876, letters received, M-234: 1686-1689

families of lesser power and investment, McIntosh and his relatives would stay in their villages during the hostilities.

Others, mainly the hundreds of Creek women, who were married to, or more often cohabitating with, what we will delicately term "frontier whites"[60] and living among the Americans would sever ties to their home villages for good. These women would make their way into the tales of family folklore across the South, attesting to an "Indian great-great grandma" that seemingly every family claims but few can prove.[61] In fact, recent advances in genetics have made it affordable and simple to find out one's degree of European, Native American, and African ancestries through direct to consumer DNA tests.

---

[60] Some derisively called them "squaw men"

[61] In the area of south Georgia, lower Alabama, and the Florida panhandle this isn't far from the truth as hundreds of thousands of people in this region are descendants of the Creeks who remained behind when the main body of Creeks were removed west in the 1830s, either as parties to the stipulations of the Treaty of Fort Jackson, or through slipping between the cracks of the round ups and retreating into isolated rural hamlets in inaccessible areas. The tens of thousands of persons in these states who received the Creek Indian Land Claim Docket settlements from the Indian Claims Commission paid out in the 1970's and 1980's are a testament to the many Creek ancestors who for one reason or another avoided removal. This population was augmented to some degree in the decades following the removal by the arrival of hundreds of Catawba and other Eastern Siouan Indians fleeing the Carolinas. Families such as the Hathcock, Dees, Gibson, Sizemore, Hansford, Perkins, Porter, Hill, Scott, Oxendine, Lowery, Jacobs, and dozens of other surnames common among today's Eastern Creeks such as those at the Poarch Band of Creek Indians reservation (near Atmore, Alabama) and across the small Indian settlements of the panhandle of Florida originate from this migration and the subsequent synthesis of identity.

During the last decade, hundreds of thousands of Americans have taken such tests, which have revealed that for Whites and African Americans, Native American ancestry is among the LEAST likely findings.

In most cases, the data coming to light is showing that a quarter of so-called "White" Southerners have "recent African ancestry" (within the last 5 generations), and the average Black Southerner has one quarter European ancestry. Genetics has revealed a hitherto unknown truth of the history of the South. More than any other region, a great amount of inter-racial mixture went on, for centuries (Sykes, 2012). The journey of McIntosh, like that of several prominent Mixed Bloods over time such as Weatherford, Osceola, and others would end in violence as civilizations clashed in warfare and struggle.

The exclusive land cessions he orchestrated for himself, including over a thousand acres at his residence at Indian Springs and six hundred and forty acres around his plantation on the Ocmulgee were extensive. Along with these cessions he also arranged to receive, and presumably distribute to his supporters, half of the four hundred thousand dollars the Creek Nation was to receive for its lands being relinquished. Additionally the Americans agreed to pay McIntosh forty thousand dollars for his participation and facilitation of earlier land cessions.[62] The tide turned for McIntosh when his in-law Benjamin Mitchell was

---

[62] Kappler, Indian Affairs, 2:215; Jones, "Lettered Portraits", 79

replaced by John Crowell, who was unsympathetic to McIntosh's and Mitchell's arrangements.

Samuel Hawkins, who was executed two days after McIntosh, would state that Crowell was using his position to line his own pockets and develop his own power within the politics of the American-Creek arrangement, an accusation which doubtlessly could be said of most and was likely true for many. With the appointment of Crowell, a new system was afoot, and the winds of fortune were changing. After decades of unbridled ambition and influence among the Creeks on behalf of the Americans, McIntosh would find that he was between a rock and a hard place with few options available to supply his need for goods and cash, important to maintain his position and ensure support for his policies.

Animosity between Crowell and McIntosh would continue and grow with time. McIntosh would find himself cut off from the flow of cash and goods which had been his for years and which he had built his network of tribal allies and political connections. This desperate situation would be a major influence on his decision to sign the Treaty of Indian Springs in 1825, and would be the opening sought by his many enemies among the conservative Creek factions to lawfully bring his power and his life to a violent yet lawful end. The historic record shows the limited extent of the power that McIntosh, as active and political as he was, wielded in the Creek Nation.

Members of only eight of the fifty-six Creek tribal towns signed the Treaty of Indian Springs, almost none of whom were leaders, and all of who had received goods and cash from McIntosh in the years directly preceding the treaty. The blow to his faction among the Creeks that this treaty exacerbated would reduce its sway in the council for years to come. The power wielded after McIntosh's death by his son Chilly would include only the close alliance of Coweta, Broken Arrow, Talladega, and Hillabee.[63] The illegitimacy of the Treaty of Indian Springs of 1825 was apparent to many. Even McIntosh's adversary John Crowell, the United States Indian Agent who had opposed him on many things, said "With the exception of McIntosh, and perhaps two others, the signatures to this treaty are either chiefs of low grade or not chiefs at all.[64]"

This situation was corroborated in the statements of the Little Prince, who had worked with, as well as against, McIntosh through the years. "We are Creeks. We have a great many Chiefs and headmen, but are they ever so great they must abide by the laws. We have guns and ropes and if and if any of our people break these laws those guns and ropes are to be their end. The laws are not made for any particular person but for all."[65]

---

[63] Interview between the Secretary & the McIntosh Party, December 10 1825, Office of Indian Affairs, M-21, 2:288-292

[64] Thomas Crowell to James Barbour, February 13, 1825 in Hays "Murder of General William McIntosh."

[65] Little Prince and others, August 24, 1826, Creek Indian Manuscripts, Hargrett Rare Books and Manuscripts Library, University of Georgia, Athens Georgia.

Though McIntosh met his end at the barrel of the guns of the Law Menders, he did so as an outlaw and violator of the values that the Creek people, his own nation, held as sacred. As controversial as McIntosh and his decisions were, they were both rooted in the Creek culture. Though he was racially a Mixed Blood and viewed by many Americans who knew him as "one of their own," the identity of William McIntosh as a Creek should not be doubted any more than that of Josiah Francis, William Weatherford, or other actors on the scene of the Creek Nation in those days.

In many cases they were men who "lived by the feud," individuals whose motivations and actions flowed from the decisions and loyalties they made in their lives to a swiftly changing social reality. All Mixed Bloods would find themselves having to make difficult choices during the years leading up to the removal. On the frontier of the Creek and American worlds, survival and security would be negotiated on an individual, family, and tribal town basis. Military strategies, marriages, and political alliances would determine the fate of several dozen large Mixed Blood families.

In the case of William McIntosh, many of his children including his son Chilly would venture to Indian Territory and start a new life, much as Doyle's children Amanda, Muscogee, and Jackson would. Others such as McIntosh's daughter Kate, would remain behind, much like Doyle's daughters Nancy and

Sarah, and like them her descendants would settle in southern Georgia, eastern Alabama, and the Florida panhandle.[66]

In the mid twentieth century, descendants of the McIntosh family living near Cairo, Georgia, Florala, Alabama, and other small communities would organize into a series of organizations along with other Creeks across the area, to petition for acknowledgment by the BIA as tribal groups. From the late 1950s throughout the mid-1970s various groups of descendants worked together in a large umbrella organization to seek acknowledgement as Indian people from the government. By the late 1970s this intertribal cooperative effort would dissolve into competing tribal governments seeking recognition on their own.

A half dozen would petition, but only one, the Poarch Band of Creek Indians, would accomplish the endeavor to become federally recognized, a task which they would finally accomplish in 1986. Other groups such as the Lower Muskogee Creeks of Georgia, the Principal Creek Nation, and several others would get negative findings as BIA searched records for documentation of the group's ancestry, and be denied acknowledgment as recognized tribal groups with a relationship with the United States government. Most would claim the McIntosh family among their ancestors, one of the few families to which many COULD prove ties.

---

[66] Some of McIntosh's descendants in the area of Cairo, Georgia would form the "Lower Muskogee Creek" Tribe a century and a half after his death, others would petition the Bureau of Indian Affairs as the "Principal Creek Nation."

FIGURE 35 ARTWORK: ORIGINAL BY THE AUTHOR, TITLED: EARTH

FIGURE 36 PHOTO: AMANDA HILL

Chapter 3 Southbound

Nancy and Sarah in Florida

Though all were wed in March of 1829 at Fort Mitchell, unlike their half-sister Amanda, Nancy and Sarah would remain with their husbands for the extent of their lives and have many children. Like many of our ancestors who lived a century and a half ago, these two sisters would have dozens and eventually hundreds of lines of descent, with the majority marrying into non-Indian families as the girls had done. But several lines of the descendants of the sisters would intermarry with one another and into families of Eastern Siouan Indians who like the sisters had migrated down from the Carolinas during the nineteenth century, some of which did maintain Indian identity. I am from such a family. Being Indian was present in many ways in our lives. This was no easy task in the tumult of the Southern society that was firmly rooted in a view that there were only two races, White and Black, and that Indians were something from the past which no longer existed, at least at the local level.

As stated elsewhere, George and Alexander Hill first moved first to Decatur County, Georgia and then on to Jackson County, Florida, along with their Indian wives, Nancy and Sarah Doyle. They were both born in South Carolina, around 1810. Upon researching the oral histories passed through the various Hill family branches in Florida, as well as those in the Creek

Nation in Oklahoma, we found indicators of where to search for historical records and documentation relating to the many oral histories. During our research, we found a South Carolina Marriage Index Book at the Florida State Archives in Tallahassee Florida (the R. A. Gray Building) which listed an indexed reference to the marriages of these three couples.

It seems from the documentary evidence that the *Cherokee Phoenix*, the national newspaper of the Cherokee Nation, covered the weddings as well as four other local Milledgeville, Georgia area newspapers. They were said to be very extravagant for the times. Using the Index reference as a guide, we began to inquire about the possibility of finding one of the original newspapers which carried the article possibly being in existence. We were eventually able to secure a copy of it with the (much appreciated) assistance of the research staff at the Cherokee Nation of Oklahoma's Tribal Headquarters in Tahlequah.. Included in this chapter is the letter sent with the document. We also were able to gather several documents compiled by the Decatur County Georgia Historical Society that listed all the many descendants of the George Hill- Nancy Doyle and Alexander Hill-Sarah Doyle marriages.

As recorded in *Milledgeville, Georgia Newspaper Clippings (Southern Recorder), Volume II 1828-1832* by Tad Evans, found in the stacks of the Florida State Archives, (as well 5 other periodic sources from the times, including an April 29

1829 edition (Volume 2 number 7) of the *Cherokee Phoenix*,) move to note on March 3, 1829 the brothers Alexander, George, and James Hill, all brothers from Darlington District in South Carolina and stationed at Fort Mitchell, Creek Nation were married by the Reverend Mr. Hill to Sarah, Nancy, and Amanda Doyle, Creek Indian girls attending the Asbury Missionary Institute. The details of this marriage were captured in the *Cherokee Phoenix* article from 1829:

> "Married on the 3rd of March, at the Asbury Missionary Institute, near Fort Mitchell Creek Nation, by the reverend Mr. Hill, the Mr. James Hill of the US Army, to Miss Amanda Doyle, a Creek Pupil of the Institution. This establishment is under the charge of Mr. and Mrs. Hill, who were desirous of showing the natives how this ceremony is performed in a refined state of society, and the highest encomiums are due them for their entire success. Great exertion and ingenuity were necessary to accomplish it. The company consisted of about twenty white persons and one hundred and fifty natives. The bride and her two maids were dressed with great taste and propriety, according to the fashion of the age. The groom and his two associates were in full military costume; and those persons present accustomed to wedding scenes, pronounced this bridal party one of the handsomest they had ever witnessed. After the marriage

ceremony, the happy pair were congratulated with all good wishes; cake and wine were passed around, and in due time a bountiful supper was partaken of by the whole company, and the evening passed on in the most agreeable manner possible. All parties seemed delighted with the occasion. A number of strangers present will never forget the kind and hospitable reception given them by Mr. and Mrs. Hill. -<u>Georgia Courier</u>" [67] - transcribed from the *Cherokee Phoenix* 1829

The indexed reference in the Milledgeville, Georgia Newspaper Clippings (Southern Recorder), *Volume II 1828-1832* states:

HILL, Mr. James of the US Army m. DOYLE, Miss Amanda, a Creek pupil of the Asbury Missionary Institution near Fort Mitchell Creek Nation, m. there 3-3-1829 by Rev. Mr. Hill. AC 3-18-1829; CP 4-29-1829; A th 4-7-1929; SP 3-21-1829; SR 4-21-1829. DG 4-19-1829 gives wedding date as 4-3-1829

HILL, Alexander of the US Army m. DOYLE, Miss Sarah, a belle of the Creek Nation, m. there 3-3-1829 State of Georgia CP 4-29-1829

HILL, George W. of the US Army m. DOYLE, Miss Nancy, a belle of the Creek Nation, m. there 3-3-1829 State of Georgia CP 4-29-1829 [68]

---

[67] (Cherokee Phoenix, p. 104)
[68] (Hill, 1829)

Below is a transcription of the "Alexander Hill" narrative, by Robert Earl Woodham, from the *Decatur County, Ga. Past and Present 1823-1991* a genealogy index compiled by the Decatur County Historical Society.

"The Hill Family has been in Seminole County since the 1830's. Several related Hill families moved to Spring Creek and nearby areas across the river in Jackson County (Florida). They came here from Darlington District, South Carolina.

The first to settle here was Alexander Hill Sr., who was born in 1812 and died in 1880. His wife's name is Unknown. She was the sister of the wife of his brother, George W Hill. Alexander had 7 children, all born at Spring Creek.

Alex's son Ferdinand Hill was born in 1839 and died 6 May 1864 as a confederate soldier at the Battle of the Wilderness near Richmond VA.

Alex's daughters Lovie and Mahalia Caroline never married. Nothing is known of sons William and Richmond.

Alex's son Harmon Hill (1849) married Julia R. Minton 15 February 1877. Their children include Ella, Noah Alonzo, Emma, Luther D, Zenie, Jewel, and Meck (married to Cleveland Conyers)"

FIGURE 37 PHOTO: CLEVE CONYERS, SON OF SUSAN
HILL

Alexander Hill Jr. was born 1852 and died 1923. He and his
wife Mary Ann (1852-1921) are both buried at   Spring Creek.
They had at least nine children: Marcus M. (1875-1904) married
Mary Hall; Sophia Ann (1881), married Tully Murkison;
Mathew D.; Rufus A. who married first Rhoda M.J. Thursby,
and later to Annie Wilson; Mary; Preston Ulysses (1889-1964)
who married first Corene Holt, then later Kate Shores; Alto E,
who married James K Braswell; Alma S. (1893-1952) married to
Joe Barber; and John C.

Alexander's brother, George Wesley Hill Sr. was born in 1804
in Darlington District South Carolina. His wife Nancy was the

sister of Alexander's wife, making the two couples (descendants) double first cousins.

George moved from South Carolina to Spring Creek (Georgia) about 1856. He lived for several years at the intersection of Desser Road and Spring Creek Road. Nancy (born 1815) died about 1856 and is buried in a family plot at the intersection. They had at least 13 children.

George's son John A Hill was born in 1835; He married Mary Ann Dowell on 22 June 1852. He was a confederate soldier.

George's son Rueben Ezekiel Hill was born in 1836, he married Martha Frances Minton on 7 September 1865, and they had one daughter Rebecca.

George's son Thomas Hill was born in 1838 and died on 12 November 1864 as a confederate soldier in a Yankee POW camp.

George's daughter Emma Elizabeth (1840) married Daniel Minton.

George's son Allen Hill (1842) married Amelia Conyers on 27 February 1868. They had one son, Asberry.

George's daughter Julia Hill (1844) married Waydon Hewitt.

A son, Dempsey Hill (1845) married Catherine McMillan on 18 August 1870. He lived in Jackson County (Florida)

A son, Johnathan H. Hill was born 2 February 1848 and died 18 October 1918. He married Nancy Melvina Summers; they had at least 14 children and lived at Grand Ridge (Jackson County, Florida)

William Cato ("Cate") Hill (1853) married Caroline Bennett in 1872. Cate and Carrie had seven children and lived at Grand Ridge.

Susan Catherine Hill was born 24 December 1853 and died 29 August 1931. She was married to Moses F.J. Conyers. George W Hill (1856) married first Caroline Conyers 2 February 1872. They had 2 children, James Wesley and Martha.

Large families were common in those times. The children of Nancy and Sarah lived in an era when the population of Native American people in the South was small and many of the children would marry Whites and assimilate into that culture. A few, such as my own great grandparents, would cling to one another and remain within their own small community of Mixed Bloods, eking out a living and avoiding the constantly changing social environment regarding race and identity that was characteristic of the late 1800s and early 1900s in the Deep South.

Post Removal

In the same year that the Doyle sisters married their American husbands, Andrew Jackson became President of the United States. The Treaty of Fort Jackson twenty years earlier had set in motion a chain of events that would culminate in the eventual removal of the Creeks,[69] as well as ceding 23 million acres of Creek lands to the United States. This would be followed by the Treaty of Washington in 1826, which ceded additional land in Georgia to American authorities. Within one lifetime the Creek lands had shrunk exponentially and sights were set on the complete eradication of Native Americans from the South.

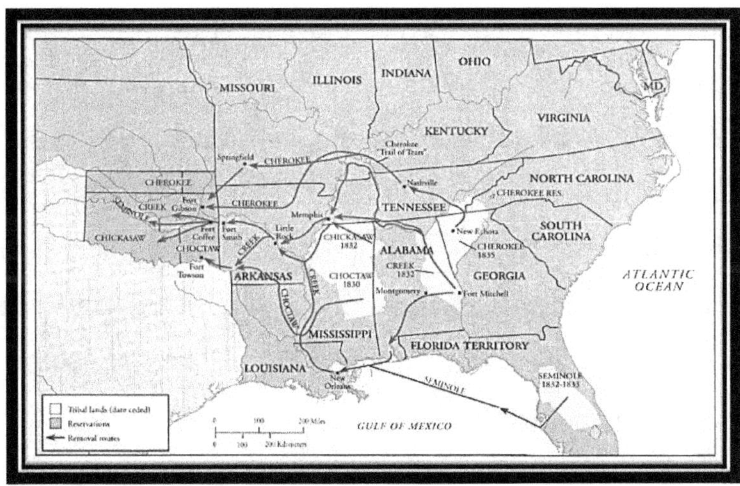

FIGURE 38 MAP: FORCED REMOVAL TRAILS

On May 26 1830, President Andrew Jackson signed into law the Indian Removal Act. With the removal of the majority of the Indians from the South those who remained faced difficult choices. In 1832 the final land cession took place with the

---

[69] Kohn, George Childs. "Treaty of Fort Jackson." *Dictionary of Historic Documents, Revised Edition.* New York: Facts On File, Inc., 2003. *Modern World History Online.* Facts On File, Inc. http://www.fofweb.com/activelink2.asp? ItemID=WE53&iPin=hisdc00930&SingleRecord=True (accessed September 25, 2014).

Treaty of Cusseta, which relinquished the last of the Creeks' lands in the East and accepted lands in the Indian Territory; 25,000 Creek people[70] would make their way there. The number of Creeks who remained behind in the old Creek lands is only an estimate but several hundred are likely, as well as thousands who fled to Florida to continue resistance as a part of the Seminole people. Several hundred people of mixed Indian and African ancestry were carried into slavery as well. Thanks to the archival records available to us we can follow the lives of Nancy and Sarah's families after the removal. A decade after the marriage of Alexander Hill to Sarah Doyle in 1829 at Fort Mitchell, Creek Nation, they appear in Decatur County, Georgia on the 1840 federal census, with one child, their son Ferdinand,[71] who was born in 1838. The area where Alexander and his family were living on the Florida-Georgia line was known as 'Spring Creek' and the brothers as well as a number of their descendants lived there for many years. Quite a few of their children would be buried there. On the 1850 census of Decatur County, Georgia both George and Alexander with their wives Nancy and Sarah and their children appear living as neighbors. Alex's family has

---

[70] Foreman, p. 47 n.10 (1830 census)

[71] Ferdinand Hill would die during the Battle of the Wilderness near Richmond, Virginia on May 6, 1864 in service of the Confederate Army. This engagement was the first battle in Grants Virginia Overland Campaign against General Lee, and both armies suffered heavy casualties of which Ferdinand was one.

four children age's four to twelve, and George and Nancy have six children ranging in ages from six to sixteen.

Decatur County bordered the Florida state line, and was dominated by farming like much of the Southland. The Spring Creek settlement where they lived was near Bainbridge, Georgia. By 1860 neither Nancy nor Sarah appears in the household of their husbands and children. Nancy is said to have died in 1856, the year her youngest son George was born. Alex aged 48 appears in the 1860 census still in Decatur County Georgia with five of his children, including the oldest Ferdinand, who would soon meet his end on the battlefield.

Sarah and Nancy both eventually disappear from the historic record, having lived through one of the most challenging times in the history of the Creek people. Nancy would pass during the civil war, her husband George remarrying in his elder years shortly before his own passing. Sarah would live longer but would soon leave behind many descendants like her sister Nancy had. They made choices about their lives that few of us today can understand, and were able to rear their families in a time and place that was extremely difficult. Among the many children of the two families, several of the children would intermarry with neighboring families. George and Nancy's son Reuben Ezekiel Hill would marry Martha Francis Minton in 1865, and Rueben's sister Emma Hill, my third great grandmother, would marry Daniel Minton in 1858.

Like many of the Indian hamlets that survived removal, the families that remained had a high rate of endogamy, with several intertwining lines of descend from the same small group being the norm among families like the Hill, Turner, Ward, Scott, Porter, Copeland, and many others. The Poarch Creeks would have dozens of such heavily intermarried families. Some of the descendants of Nancy and Sarah would marry among themselves, with George and Nancy's daughter Susan Catherine Hill (my second great grandmother) marrying Moses F. J. Conyers in 1868. Their son Cleveland Conyers would marry his cousin Meck Hill (the great granddaughter of George and Nancy Hill) in 1914. Their daughter Voncille, my grandmother would marry James Manning who was a great grandson of Sarah Scott of Scotts Ferry. Many people in rural areas have always married neighbors who to some degree or another are related. Even today there is a certain amount of endogamy among most small Native communities.

In fact this type of intermarriage among cousins has been extremely common throughout much of human history. Professor Robin Fox of Rutgers University states that it is probable that 80% of marriages throughout history have occurred between second cousins or closer.[72]) Cousin to cousin

---

[72] (Affairs, 1980)In the Bureau of Indian Affairs response to the petition for federal acknowledgement by the Poarch Band of Creek Indians during the early 1980's the degree to which some Eastern Creeks intermarried among related families was shown to be extremely high. Isolated Indian communities across the panhandle of Florida and south Alabama and Georgia often times

marriages, though common throughout the nineteenth century, declined in most communities during the twentieth century[73]

Once Nancy passed during the Civil War, George would live to old age. In 1869, in his late sixties, George Robert Wesley Hill (the senior) would remarry to Elizabeth Mercer, and would appear with her as well as with his youngest children, including Dempsey age 25 and George W Hill age 17, in the 1870 census residing in Jackson County, Florida, south of Decatur County, Georgia. His brother Alexander would appear alone with his children including his spinster daughters "Lovie" and Caroline, as well as sons Harmon and Alex Jr. living in nearby Holmes County, Florida. By the 1880 census Alexander and several of his children including Harmon Hill are back in Decatur County, Georgia, while George, now age 75, is still in Jackson County in Florida. During the decade to come both Alexander and George would pass away, having lived long and eventful lives. Their names would live on among many of their descendants with Alexander and George appearing in almost every generation in future years.

My great great-grandfather Harmon Hill, the second youngest son of Alex Hill, would marry his cousin and granddaughter of George Hill, Julie Minton in 1877. They spent

---

were especially apt to do so due to the racial pressures exerted on them by the surrounding white populations.

[73] . Richard Conniff, "Go Ahead, Kiss Your Cousin," August 2003 *Discover Magazine*

most of their lives in the Spring Creek settlement, moving to Liberty County, Florida and the Woods settlement in their elder hood, and being key persons in this community. The family ran a small store in this small settlement, with Harmon being a community leader in Woods in his late 60s where the 1920 census would find him. In 1922 he passed away. The Woods settlement in Liberty County would have several Indian families such as Hill, Oxendine, Jacobs, and Scott present there in the late 1800s and early 1900's. By the 1970's many of the core communities of Indian population such as Scott Town, Scotts ferry, and in this case Woods would lose much of their people to jobs and opportunities in other areas.

FIGURE 39 PHOTO: EMMA HILL AND FAMILY IN SPRING CREEK, GEORGIA CIRCA 1890

The Twentieth Century and the 'Woods' Settlement

Several other Indian families who had migrated south from the Carolinas about the same time as the Doyle sisters' families would come to settle in the Woods community. It would grow through the middle of the twentieth century. This tiny hamlet on the Apalachicola River was home to Hill, Oxendine, Jacobs, Brown and Scott families, who would find a refuge from the difficult racial climate of the time in this forgotten corner of Florida. In the Woods community, the men worked independent jobs in the logging and turpentine industries, work which allowed them some degree of independence from town and self-determination as to their communities' customs. The nearest town of Bristol was ten miles away and the people of Woods found their rural life one of family, quietude, and what the "big river" and its adjoining swamp offered in food and resources.

With the turn of the twentieth century, lumber companies in Georgia were dealing with dwindling availability of the hardwoods they were steadily cutting. Soon, they turned their attention to northwest Florida to find more. In the panhandle, there were huge supplies of timber standing, available and easily accessible for harvesting on both banks of the Apalachicola River. During the first few decades of the 1900's such companies as Graves Brothers, Cypress Lumber, Chipola Turpentine, Neal Timber, and Southern Hardwoods were installing large timber mills in both Liberty and Calhoun Counties.

Many Lumbee Indians of Robeson County, North Carolina had left their homeland in the mid and late 1800s for timber employment in Georgia, followed the industry down to Florida. The largest number of Lumbee's , including the Oxendine, Revels, and Jacobs families, settled into Liberty County on the Eastern side of the Apalachicola, where they came into close continuous contact with long-established Indian families like the Hill family who ran the community store at Woods, who had settled in the area in the late 1800's led by Harmon Hill. The combined effort of these two Indian groups to maintain gainful employment in timber resulted in the formation of an Indian settlement in Liberty County known as Woods.

Some descendants of the Woods area Oxendine family today live in Jackson County in the Marianna and Cottondale areas, along with many descendants of Noah Hill, who was identified as "Citizen-Indian" on his 1918 military enlistment, included in this volume. In order to understand the way the residents of Woods lived their daily lives, it is necessary to understand the Jim Crow environment of Georgia and Florida at that time. Malinda Maynor Lowery, in her excellent article "People and Place: Croatan Indians in Jim Crow Georgia, 1890-1920,", published in the *American Indian Culture and Research Journal*, gives a detailed study of a settlement of Lumbee Indians who migrated to Bulloch County, Georgia to work the timber in 1890. (Lowery, p. 41)These Lumbee remained there until about 1920 when the industry moved south to Florida. On July 27, 1899 the *Bulloch Herald* reported on the interest of their timber companies in the possibility of making good money in northwest Florida: "manufacturers were elated by what they saw in the way of turpentine and timber prospects in Florida and reported that they may invest some money down that way." (Lowery, p. 45) Many Lumbee from Bulloch followed the timber down to Liberty in the late 1800s and the early 1900s. Undoubtedly the same racial attitudes that these mixed-blood Indians faced in Georgia would also follow them down to Florida. One example of the conditions faced by the inhabitants of Woods is demonstrated by a 1901 article which appeared in the May 24, 1901 *Statesboro News*. This article made mention of a young boy who had been murdered at a timber camp: "The boy was about sixteen years old, and it is said was a part Indian. And like other good Indians, he is now dead. " (Lowery, p. 62)

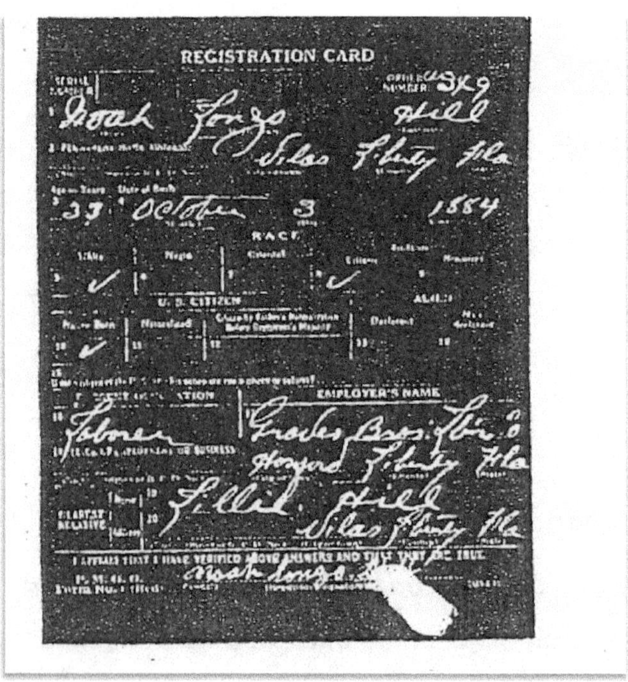

FIGURE 41 DOCUMENT: NOAH HILL'S WWI 1918 MILITARY DRAFT REGISTRATION CARD DOCUMENTING HIS RACIAL CATEGORY AS "WHITE" AND "CITIZEN-INDIAN"

Southbound

With the exhaustion of the timber along the Apalachicola in the late nineteen thirties, the majority of the Woods community's inhabitants spread out to individual homesteads in western Liberty and other surrounding counties. This was also occurring to a similar degree in the larger related Indian settlements of Scott Town and Scott's Ferry, just across the river. This dispersion of population from the clustered settlements would only accelerate in the decades to come with desegregation. In the documentary record, several Indian men, including Noah Hill from the Woods Community, are recorded on their WW I Civil Enlistment/Draft Registration cards under the race block as "Caucasian" and "Indian," with the checkmark being in the "citizen" rather than the "non-citizen" box under the Indian racial category. In his recent book *Those Who Remain; A Photographers Memoir of South Carolina Indians,* Gene J. Crediford stated:

> *"On June 2, 1924, Congress passed the Citizenship Act of 1924, which states that "all non-citizen Indians born within the territorial limits of the United States be, and they are hereby, declared to be citizens of the United States: provided that the granting of such citizenship shall not in any manner impair or otherwise affect the right of any Indian to tribal or other property" (U.S. Code, Title 8, sec. 1401 [a][2]). In this context a non-citizen Indian means, as I understand it, a person who is*

a member of a federally recognized tribe; in other words "citizen Indians" were at the mercy of state laws in that era." (Crediford, 2009, p. 103)

As we have seen from the many court cases and social incidents regarding the school and military enlistment situations in the first half of the twentieth century , north Florida's Indian people were definitely at the "mercy of state laws" of the time, as dozens of race based court cases from the time show. As can be seen on Noah Hill's 1918 Civil Enlistment, his race is Caucasian and Indian, with the "citizen" box checked. Members of the Indian settlements had to walk a fine line, resisting the local White power structure's attempts to define them as part of the Negro community.

Dozens of other men from the nearby Indian settlements of Scott's Ferry, located across the river, and Scott Town, in the next county over, and were identified as "Indian" on the civil enlistments from 1918. Many Indian men had served in the military and upon coming home were looking for a better life than allowed by the narrow restrictions imposed on their communities' identity in past generations, due to outsiders' perceptions of them as a people of racially mixed and uncertain origins.

As the historical documentation shows, many of the Indian communities' men had fought the military racial classification system when trying to enlist, including men like

Noah Hill, Sandy Scott, Willie Porter, Armand Copeland and Franklin Whitfield.

On several occasions the military sent investigators to inquire into this strange circumstance regarding the community's identity. Many of the men who enlisted were initially pushed to be in Negro ranks due to having attended "Negro schools," as some were funded as by the counties in which they lived, especially in Calhoun and Jackson Counties. The much smaller community of Woods in Liberty County escaped this label, although some of the children from various families moved back and forth over the years between community schools.

The often troubled relationship with educational authorities was a constant source of trouble for the communities throughout the Jim Crow era. They were often targets of social scrutiny due to their mixed race ancestry despite their continual assertions that they were Indians. During enlistments for all the conflicts, most were eventually allowed to be in white units, many fighting valiantly in European and Pacific theatres of WW II. My grandfather Ray Kever, the grandson of Catawba Indian Mary Brown, was one such veteran.

FIGURE 42 PHOTO: RAY KEVER IN US MARINES UNIFORM, WOODS FLORIDA 1947

Similar situations occurred and were documented by the men from Indian settlements enlisting to fight in World War I and in the Civil War as well, including the case of Rueben Blanchard, the next door neighbor of my own ancestor Sarah Scott Etheridge in Scotts Ferry in 1870. His application for his Confederate pension is one of the longest in the country, and despite harassment and racism, he did eventually receive his pension. The Indian settlements suffered the worst of the many evils of segregation, due to small numbers and self-imposed minimization of contacts with outside people and institutions.

Blanchard had served with honor his community in the difficult times of the Civil War. Like other mixed bloods from the Indian settlements in September of 1862, he enlisted with the Confederate Army in Company E, 10th Florida Infantry. Though he was soon reassigned to the Confederate Navy in 1864 and served on the ironclad gunboat "Palmetto State", he did his part until Charleston was evacuated, then found that he was re-assigned to the Confederate Army. Captured on April 6, 1865 during General Lee's retreat from Richmond, he found himself a prisoner of war, and history has documented the horrors of this situation during the Civil War on both sides.

Blanchard was remanded to the Point Lookout prison in Maryland. Records show there were 50,000 soldiers held in the army prison camp, mostly housed in tents. Lookout Point Prison records indicate that between 1863 and 1865, according to the Maryland Department of Natural Resources, nearly 4,000 died. Though originally built to hold 10,000 men, the camps population swelled to between 12,000 and 20,000 internees after the exchange of prisoners between armies was placed on hold. The terrible result for the men in their camp was crowded conditions with up to sixteen men to a tent in poor sanitary conditions, and was the largest Union-run prison camp. History indicates that its reputation as being one of the worst was not without grounds. Fortunately for Blanchard, he was interned for two months and released.

Ruben was initially denied a Florida Confederate Pension in 1908 . This travesty occurred despite his admirable loyal service to the Confederate cause. Local authorities refused to approve the pension application of Blanchard, and took the further step to write personal letters to the pension board to accuse Blanchard of being "mixed blooded". They further attempted to defame this hero by groundlessly accusing him of having joined the Union Blockade Fleet! Despite clearly documented records produced that Blanchard had served in the Confederate military, the pension board continued its persecution of him.

They declined to approve Blanchard's pension stating, "Negroes were not enlisted and are not entitled to pensions." Only after Blanchard retained the services of Jackson County law firm Calhoun & Campbell, was he was approved for the meager pension. A support letter written by W.M. Ayers stated that Ayers had known Blanchard for over 45 years, and that they had served together during the War. This is one of many examples of the local Indian people supporting one another in countless court cases over a hundred year period. The travails of individuals such as Ruben Blanchard and Frances Hill being legally attacked and socially marginalized are just small examples of what many individuals from the Indian settlements went through during segregation times. While they were being subjected to stifling social restrictions and often were legally persecuted, they would withdraw into themselves and their communities for strength. They were often erroneously labeled as Mulattoes or Negroes by the local authorities, despite very little African American lineage in the community's bloodlines. The substantial numbers and solid institutional structures provided leaders in the Black community of the times some power in negotiating White-Negro community relations, an advantage that Indians did not have, due to their small population and cultural traditions of independence and resistance to assimilation. In the "boom years" after WW II, many family headmen were visiting places where there were greater economic opportunities, and often took their families with them.

In light of the economic benefits of moving as well as less stigma of being from the "Mulatto settlements," as the Indian hamlets were often defined, many families broke ties with relatives and never returned, as stated in Anthony Parades pioneering anthropological work among several of these settlements during the 1960s and 70s. [74]The families who remained in the Indian settlements began to reorient themselves to new social realities. Hamlets like Scott Town, Scotts Ferry, Mount Zion, Bruce, and Woods found themselves free for the first time in generations to choose their own destinies.

One result of the end of forced segregation was an immediate drop in the number of marriages within the tribal

---

[74] (Paredes, 1974, pp. 63-80)

community as eligible marriage partners left for greener pastures, an event that impacted some communities more than others. My own grandmother Voncille was a part of this trend. Although her parents and grandparents were all intermarried community members of Creek ancestry for the most part, she married James Manning, a mixed blood man from a nearby community of Blountstown, and the grandson of Sarah Scott of Catawba stock of Scotts Ferry. In her generation the isolation and ways of life the family had sustained since the removal came to an end, and modernity arrived.

In the following few decades after desegregation, the people of the formerly socially isolated Indian hamlets of southern Alabama and north Florida faced the challenge of finding a new way to define "community," one that was not imposed from without, but came from within. In the new social order of the South, they were mainly ignored and the widespread attitude of most Southerners was that Native Americans in the South were extinct. This view held that these brown-skinned neighbors couldn't be "real Indians" since they didn't wear long hair, hunt buffalo, or live in teepees. In the past, you were part of the Indian community as much by the laws and attitudes of the outside society 'keeping you in your place' as by your own choosing.

Many chose to remain close to home, despite the ones whose skin was light enough to pass as white, according to elders stories. Through the century of segregation, some of those who could "pass" as White often did, and would leave, some never to be heard from again. Those with the darkest skin tones were the most racist in some cases, with shame and generations of struggle to overcome. This is not something only in the past but is a phenomenon still found among some Eastern Creeks in Blountstown and in Atmore, Alabama, as we learned firsthand during interviews of elders.

While some were crushed by the social pressure they lived under, others worked to preserve the community cohesion and their darker-skinned relatives' small amount of opportunity in the extremely limited social structure of these times. With the advent of the civil rights era and end of the old Southern social order, tribal members had a real choice about whether they wanted to be a part of their parents' and grandparents' community or not. Even as some community members moved away for better jobs or opportunity, others redoubled efforts to gain political power for Indians in the fast changing social environment and organized their families and settlements.

Some community leaders from among the several Indian communities across south Alabama and the Florida panhandle sought new strategies for survival, a few joining in the renaissance of Indian culture, and the emergence of the pan-Indian politics that picked up pace in the 1960s and 70s and would eventually blossom into federal and state recognition for some of these communities and tribes. The close of the policy of segregation found in most southern states ended the imposed social isolation responsible for the precarious "third race" social status of the various communities of south Alabama Indians and other Indians in the Southern states.

Many new challenges of identity and community survival arose, and with the integration of Indian children into larger schools, community intermarriage between Indians began to decline precipitously within a few years. Desegregation and the striking down of notorious "Jim Crow" and miscegenation (race-mixing) laws caused community dynamics within the Indian settlements that had had been in effect since the Civil War to begin to change quickly . Segregation was a powerful force that had compelled unity and cohesion for over a century. As a result of the end of the established social order, many individuals and families tried to escape their past by moving away from the settlements to areas where no one knew their families' origins.

One such family move was that of Jim Scott, who was born and reared in Scott Town in Jackson County, Florida but would move his family to Escambia County, where his son Wesley Scott would establish his family. As in many families the bloodlines of many groups would intertwine in a new generation, as Wesley Scott's son Dale would marry a descendant of the McIntosh family, Suzette. Their son Matthew

(Coweta Fixico) would be a Corn Dance leader at Kunfuskee (Koweta) Ceremonial Grounds, located only a few miles from the Poarch Creek Indian Reservation.

A new generation would value their Native background more than some had in the past. Such cases involved dozens of families that would find themselves back in Native communities despite their parents' efforts to leave their heritage behind. Moving to places like New Mexico, to Oklahoma, to the Seminole reservation in South Florida, descendants of the old hamlets who were determined to maintain their Indian identity would find places to re-establish their Native roots. But in the aftermath of desegregation, many were trying to get as far from their families' past as they could.

Some moved away to nearby areas like Pensacola, and Mobile. Others found homes in Texas, Colorado, and even as far away as California. Families moved to other areas hoping to put the pain of their ancestors' racial identity struggles behind them, and many never looked back. Others, especially in the Atmore, Alabama area turned to the emerging Creek political identity and social movement emerging in the panhandle of Florida, Alabama, and Georgia. By the turn of the twenty-first century tens of thousands of people across the South would embrace their real or perceived Native heritage and a people who were almost invisible a half century earlier would be making headlines in their efforts to celebrate Native pride.

Chapter 4 Westward

As discussed in the previous chapter, the descendants of the Doyle sisters who moved south would face many challenges. Life for people of mixed racial origins in the stifling social climate of the Deep South would create an insularity that led to an increased amount of cousin to cousin marriages among Creek and Lumbee people across lower Alabama and Georgia and the Florida panhandle. This pattern would only shift within the last few generations among Eastern Creek Indians. Conversely many descendants of Nimrod's children Amanda, Jackson, Muscogee, Winchester and others would not intermarry with cousins or even other Native Americans. Though Amanda and her children would maintain ties to the Creek Nation despite living at times in Texas, there would be many who would make their mark.

Amanda Doyle and her son and granddaughter Samuel and Alice Callahan

Amanda would share her life with several husbands and in many localities in the West. Though she does appear in an 1829 article in the *Cherokee Phoenix* which records the grandeur and fanfare of her wedding to James Hill (on the same day and place as her sisters wed brothers, George and Alexander Hill) this relationship only survived a short time.

Within three years of marrying James Hill at Fort Mitchell in 1829, she would appear on the 1832 Parsons and Abbott Roll living in Cussetah Tribal town with her new husband James Callahan, an American of Irish descent and an architect from Boston, interestingly where he father Nimrod Doyle was from. Callahan would unfortunately pass away on the family's journey to the West, but not before they had a son, Samuel, who would grow up to play a major role in the Creek Nation during the Civil War. In the mid 1830's, the family left the East for Texas.

FIGURE 43 PHOTO: WILLIAM DECATUER HILL

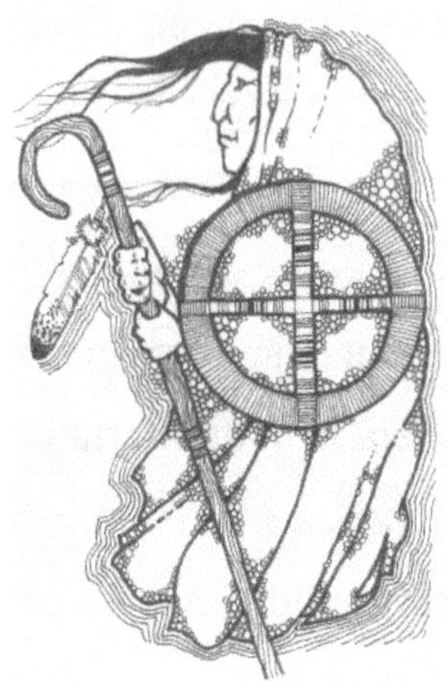

FIGURE 44 ARTWORK: TRAIL OF TEARS WALKER

Amanda Doyle Hill Callahan Davis (1810-1903)

Amanda was most likely born around 1810, according to available records. She married James Hill in March 1829 at Fort Mitchell, Creek Nation and was a student at the Asbury Missionary Institute there at that time. She is listed a half century later in Creek Nation rolls as Amanda Davis and appears on Creek Indian census card 439 on which she is shown as 1/4 Indian blood. Her father is enumerated as Nimrod Doyle, and her mother named as Mary Doyle. After a long life that spanned much of the nineteenth century, Amanda died June 1, 1902 in the Indian Territory, only five years before the creation of Oklahoma, a name which ironically means "Land of the Red Man" in Choctaw. At statehood in 1907 "Red men" would only make up a small percentage of its residents, after numerous land runs and schemes to dispossess Indians of the little lands they had left. Amanda's long life would span three quarters of the nineteenth century, and she would live through one of the greatest periods of transition that the Creek people would ever experience.

She appears on the 1832 Parsons and Abbott roll in Cussetah Town, listed as "wife of James Callahan", whom she had married after James Hill.[75] Together they would journey west but Callahan would pass on, and Amanda would once again find herself alone. Eventually she would remarry, this time to Dr. Owen J. Davis, and they would do well in Texas together. They settled in northeast Texas, and in 1849 were founders of the small community of Sulphur Springs, which was initially called Bright Star.

She is listed on the 1850 census in Hopkins, Texas as 38 years old, living with her husband Owen J Davis and son Samuel (Callahan) Davis, who is 17. She is listed as born in Georgia. Though she would spend many years in Texas she would present information later on to the authorities in Creek Nation that her family had immigrated directly to Creek Nation. Her sister Muscogee and brother Jackson Doyle would do the same in their testimonies to the board of the 1870 self-emigrant

[75] http://www.accessgenealogy.com/native/1832-creek-census-cussetaw-town.htm

roll, not disclosing the amount of time that they all had spent in Texas. The Creek Nation "self-emigrant" roll was compiled between May of 1870 and December of 1871. The ages listed on this roll are most likely correct as of 1870-71 but could also be the ages at the time of emigration in some cases. The information on this roll is valuable in reflecting how many Creek people did not initially come during the removal but in the decades to follow, as they wandered in from all over the country seeking allotments.

In the year 1886 this roll along with the many eliminations and corrections required was finalized by G.W. Stidham and was used as the basis for payments to the Creek "self-emigrants" and their heirs. Amanda, Muscogee, and Jackson (listed as A.J. Doyle) all appear on this roll, though all had been in Texas for much of the past three decades but did maintain ties to Creek Nation as the documentary record shows.

This roll enumerated the "names of Creek Indians who emigrated themselves and others from the old Creek Nation in Alabama to the Creek Nation, Indian Territory, west of Arkansas, at their own charges and expenses, and who subsisted themselves 12 months after their arrival."[76] Interestingly, an 1870 Roll of "Self-Emigrants" to Creek Nation listed Amanda (Callahan); her children Samuel and Josephine Callahan had

---

[76] http://freepages.genealogy.rootsweb.ancestry.com/~texlance/emigrants/1870s elfemigrants1.htm

emigrated in the summer of 1837 to Creek Nation in Indian Territory along with the party of Alexander Fitzgerald:

> Alexander Fitzgerald 38, Polly Fitzgerald 32, Amanda Fitzgerald 5, Sarah A Fitzgerald 1, Susey 18 (servant), Lucy 19 (servant), Mary Barnett 45 Amanda Callahan 29, Sam'l Callahan 4, Josephine Callahan 1
>
> Emigrated from Alabama to the Creek Nation Indian Territory; the Spring & Summer of 1837 - furnished transportation and subsistence, & subsistence for 12 months after their arrival - claims remuneration under treaty of 1832.
>
> Polly Fitzgerald, heir (Nation, 1870)

The "Mary Barnett" listed above is Amanda's mother, with Amanda and her children Samuel and Josephine following. The ages listed are what they were on arrival, not at the time of this roll. Despite the information on the above Roll of Self-Emigrants taken in 1870 in Creek Nation, Amanda is found on other documents to be in Texas before journeying on to Creek Nation in her elder years after her husband's death. The Self-Emigrant rolls were compiled regarding the thousands of Creeks who didn't remove with the major body of Creeks at government expense, but removed to the West themselves in subsequent years at their own expense.

We see Amanda on the 1850, 1860, and 1870 censuses as residing in Texas, so the actual situation of not only Amanda but of all of Nimrod's children (and grandchildren) who had settled in north Texas was probably complex and varied at times. One thing is clear however; Amanda maintained strong ties to Creek Nation and would eventually move there, and is where she died as her obituary shows.

Below is a transcription of the obituary of Amanda (Sybil Doyle Hill Callahan) Davis:

DEATH OF AMANDA SYBIL DAVIS

"Amanda Sybil Davis died yesterday at the residence of her grandson; Dr. J. O. Callahan. She was born in 1815 in Alabama, and was the mother of Capt. S. B. Callahan, this city, and grandmother of Dr. J. O. Callahan and Mrs. H. B. Spaulding.

The deceased was one of the original Creeks who came here from Alabama. She remembered La Fayett's visit to this country and also remembered the day and date she met him. She was a devout Christian, and her children and grandchildren and great grandchildren show the training, show the blood that was in the family, inherited through generations of right living.

The funeral services will take place this afternoon at 2 o'clock from the residence of Dr. J. O. Callahan, Callahan Street. Rev. M. L. Butler will officiate at the house and at the Green Hill cemetery, where interment will take place". From the Front Page of the *Muskogee Phoenix, June 1, 1902 [sic]*[77]

Doyle's Other Children

Muscogee Doyle Hardage Sutbury (1824-1884)

Another of Nimrod's daughters who would make the journey west to Texas with him and was a party to the Treaty of Fort Jackson was Muscogee Doyle. She was born around 1820 in the Creek Nation (East). As a small child her father would have her included for a land allotment as a part of the Treaty of Fort Jackson. Several years later after the subsequent removal of the Creeks to the West, the dealings concerning allotments in the East and the Doyle family would be investigated. The fraudulent claiming of himself (a White man) and his two children (half-blood children claimed as adults) would lead to authorities holding hearings about the circumstances.

Some land that had been allotted to Muscogee Doyle in 1832 would become present-day Fredonia, Alabama. Whatever their situation that occurred in the East before the families departure, Nimrod and his children would journey to the West and settle in northeastern Texas. It was here that Muscogee married Joseph Hardage on May 24, 1843 in Nacogdoches district, Republic of Texas, in present day Rusk

---

[77] (Phoenix, 1902)

County. She had a son Seaborn Hardage, born around 1845, and a daughter Mary Muscogee Hardage, born in December 1848. Later on, Muscogee married P. H. Sudberry (Sutbury) on 24 April 1865 in Sulphur Springs Texas, in Hopkins County.

Despite living in Texas, like her siblings Amanda and Jackson, Muscogee would claim to authorities in Creek Nation that she had resided there after removing from the East. This wasn't an uncommon situation leading up to the allotment of Creek Nation, as Creeks who were living in other areas were drawn back closer to claim allotments before the eligibility to do so was closed. A reference to Muscogee appears on roll of self-emigrants taken in 1871 at Okfuskee, Creek Nation, I.T. which is included below.

Muscogee Doyle Sudbury, excerpt from 1871 self-emigrant roll, Okfuskee Town

> Emigrated from Ala. to Texas in 1838. Her father & mother died in Texas. She emigrated from Texas to the Creek Nation, I. T. in the year 1848, bringing Archie Doyle, Susan the servant and her two children born in Texas - Seaborne and Mary Hardage.[78]

Below is an excerpt from sworn statements taken to compensate Creeks who immigrated to Creek Nation Indian

---

[78]

http://freepages.genealogy.rootsweb.ancestry.com/~texlance/emigrants/1870s elfemigrants1.htm territory at their own expense. Included is Muscogee Doyle Sutbury.

Roll of Creek Self-Emigrants, 1886

Exhibit A A.

G. W. STIDHAM, being duly sworn, testifies as follows:

I reside in the Indian Territory, Creek Nation, Nitchito Town, and am sixty-nine years of age. I prepared the corrected list of self-emigrants which is now before me, and find a mistake in the enrollment of Mary Ann Jones. The date of emigration is fixed at 1837, and it should be 1847. She is entitled to transportation and subsistence for twelve months after her arrival. Her age is correctly stated in said list, and she is now dead. I remember distinctly when she came into the Territory.

I also knew Arche-wi-che, enrolled in Oke-te-Yak-ney Town, and I knew that he arrived in the Territory in 1833, and he paid his own expenses and is entitled to transportation and subsistence under the treaty.

I knew John Shepherd, of Nichito Town. He was left a small boy in Alabama, and came west and found his own mother, by whom he was identified.

His date of arrival in the Territory is correctly stated in the list by me - that is, the corrected list. He paid his expenses, and is entitled to transportation and subsistence under the treaty.

I also knew the facts as stated as to the emigration of Elijah Beaver, in Coweta Town, to be correct, and I verify the statement in the list prepared by me.

I also know **Muscogee Sutbury and her family, four in number, which are set out in the revised list prepared by me. Their age, sex, and date of emigration are correctly stated, and they are enrolled in Broken Arrow Town, Creek Nation**, Indian Territory. They are entitled to transportation and subsistence.

I also know the Wadsworth family, of which Lewina Wadsworth is put down at the head in my revised list their age, sex, and date of emigration are correctly stated on said list, and they are entitled to transportation and subsistence.

I also knew Thomas Morris, Nitchito Town, Creek Nation, Indian Territory His name is correctly stated, and his date of arrival also to the Indian Territory. He is entitled to transportation and subsistence.

I also know Thomas Grayson, of Nillabee Town; his family is correctly stated, viz, Thomas Grayson, Levy Grayson, Samson Grayson, Millie Grayson, Lizzie Grayson, and David Grayson, in all six persons. As stated in my revised list, these people immigrated to the Creek Nation, Indian Territory, in 1830, and are entitled to transportation and subsistence for twelve months after their arrival. They were never paid by the United States Government their transportation or furnished subsistence under the treaty.

I also state that **A. J. Doyle emigrated himself in 1836 and paid his own expenses.** He is entitled to transportation and subsistence for twelve months after his arrival in the Creek Nation, Indian Territory.

G. W. STIDHAM,

Sworn to and subscribed before me, October 8, 1886.

ROBT. L. OWEN,
Indian Agent[79]

---

[79] http://freepages.genealogy.rootsweb.ancestry.com/~texlance/emigrants/stidhamroll2.htm

Muscogee would pass away a few years after appearing on the Self-Emigrant Roll, and twenty years before her sister Amanda. Listed below is Muscogee Doyle's Obituary:

Death at Eufaula

Eufaula, April 4, 1884

Died at Eufaula, April 4th, at 1 O'clock, at the residence of Mrs. Mary Coody, Mrs. Muskogee Sutbury, aged 64 years, after a painful illness of several weeks. It is with feelings of deepest sympathy we chronicle this last sad bereavement of Mrs. Coody (her only daughter) who in a little over a year has been bereft of a husband and a mother. Mrs. Sutbury was a de voted mother and spent her entire time and energies in the interest of her widowed daughter and welfare of her little fatherless grandchildren and they will sadly miss her loving presence and tender care. She was a member of the Baptist church and led an exemplary and Christian life. May God comfort and help her bereaved child. The funeral services were held in the Methodist Church and conducted by Rev. Mr. Clar, assisted by Re v. R.C. McGee. The remains were laid to rest in the family burying ground near her late home. There is still a good deal of sickness in the community. Indian Territory newspaper dated April 10, 1884. [Family ties 1B.FTW][80]

Nimrod and several of his children moved to the Republic of Texas after the removal, and he would live for several years after the resettlement of the family in Texas. Some land that was settled by this family would grow into today's modern community of Sulphur Springs, Texas.

Once again in Texas Nimrod would mount up for conflict. In 1839 Nimrod Doyle served as a Captain with the Volunteer Texas Rangers, in Robertson County from March to June of 1839, according to *A Partial List of TX Ranger Company and Unit Commanders*, compiled by Christina Stopka of the Texas Ranger Research Center. The social situation on the Texas frontier was different from that the family had left behind in Alabama, and his children would face challenges in finding permanent peace. Many would face the difficulties of the decade ahead as the United States would be torn apart by the Civil War. Some records of the struggle by Nimrod's children to get on their feet in Texas are found in the archival records.

In the 1843*Session Laws* of Texas, there is recorded "an act for the relief of Winchester Doyle, Jackson Doyle, and Muscogee Doyle, children of Nimrod Doyle" which was approved by the legislature on January 16 1843, that "invests said children with all the rights and privileges of free citizens of the republic," [81] which shows they found a place in Texas, and

---

[80] (Sourced from Dorothea Tufte, 'Audd Family Footprints' database on the World Wide Web)(NOTE NEEDS WEB ADDRESS)

[81] (Society, Alabama Historical Reporter, 1879, p. 56)

that they were considered 'white' and enjoyed the freedoms that came with that status. The same can't be said for other of Doyle's descendants, who were recorded the same year as *"the free Negro children of Nimrod Doyle"* petitioned through a bill (no. 2719, file 29, 7th congress) in the same Texas legislature for *"the right to hold property and other rights of free persons,"* a request which failed. The Doyle children found relief under what was known as *"The Ashworth Act."* "This act named for the "Redbone" Ashworth Family who along with other families associated with the Mixed Blood clan passed by the Texas Congress on December 12, 1840.

This came in response to an act passed on February 5, 1840, which prohibited the immigration of free blacks and ordered all free black residents to vacate the Republic of Texas within two years or be sold into slavery. The earlier act was designed to make color the standard mark of servitude in Texas by eliminating the free black population. It repealed all laws contrary to its provisions and nullified the act of June 5, 1837, which permitted the residence of free blacks living in Texas before the Texas Declaration of Independence. On November 9, 1840, the Hardin and Richardson petitions were referred to the Committee on the State of the Republic. A bill exempting Samuel McCulloch, Jr., and some of his relatives passed its first reading the same day. Though their initial request failed the first reading, as with the families known as Redbone, and on

November 10, 1840, the Ashworth bill passed the House, and the McCulloch bill was read a second time. At the reading attempts were made to amend the bill by adding the names of William Goyens, who was supported by Thomas J. Rusk, and other parties but in the later resolution of:

"PRIVATE ACTS AND JOINT RESOLUTIONS PASSED BY THE SEVENTH CONGRESS. "

> **A** "An act for the relief of William Ashworth, and others," passed January 16th, 1843-directs the Commissioner of the General Land Office to issue patents, on certain conditions, to William Ashworth, Abner Ashworth, Aaron Ashworth, the heirs of Moses Ashworth, deceased, Henry Bird, John Bird and Aaron Nelson. **D** "An act for the relief of Winchester Doyle, Jackson Doyle, and Muscogee Doyle, children of Nimrod Doyle," approved January 16th, 1843-invests the said children with all the rights and privileges of free citizens of the Republic. The amendments lost, but the original bill passed." [82]

The identities of these "free Negro" children of Doyle are not known except from this reference, one of several still unknown aspects of his life, although research continues. Eventually Doyle would age and slow down, but we do find in the archival record one more fascinating surprise from him.

---

[82] (Webb, 2005)

Reported in an edition of the *Alabama Historical Quarterly* from 1879 was an interesting incident from near the end of Doyle's long and colorful life.

"…of this same Nimrod Doyle, mentioned above, Gen. Blake related to me an event illustrative of the remarkable faculty of Henry Clay in recollecting names and faces, General Blake said that he was at Fort Gibson on the head waters of the Arkansas River, where he met an old trapper by the name of Nimrod Doyle, who expressed a wish to go to Washington City with Blake to see once more Henry Clay before he (Doyle) died; said that he and Harry had gone together from Virginia to Kentucky, he to make hats and Clay to practice law. That he left Kentucky and went to the West, and had led the life of a trapper and had not seen Mr. Clay for 25 years. Blake took Doyle with him to Washington City and carried him to the lobby of the senate chamber and asked him to point out Mr. Clay. Doyle's eye rested first on the seat of Mr. Webster and asked Blake if that was not Daniel Webster. Blake told him it was and asked him how he knew it was Webster. Doyle reported that he had heard an officer at Fort Gibson read a speech made by Mr. Webster, and he did not think but anybody but such a looking man as Webster could make "such a solid and heavy speech." Doyle soon discovered Mr. Clay, and said that he would 'like to have a little chat with Harry…[83]

In 1846, he appears in Nacogdoches, Texas, near the time of his death. Doyle is mentioned in *Women of the American South: a Multicultural Reader"* by Christie Farnham, in the following excerpt,

> *"…Will of Nimrod Doyle, probated November term 1846, Record of Wills, Nacogdoches Texas."*[84] **Abstract:** *"Spruce M. Baird and Jackson Doyle ask that they be appointed executors of the estate of the late Nimrod Doyle in accordance with Doyle's will. According to related documents, the estate included eleven slaves.* Doyle's will includes the following explanation for a bequest of a slave named Susy to his daughter Muscogee*: "my reason for doing so is that I gave my other children, that is to say Jackson and Winchester Education but gave my said Daughter none."*

On 20 January 1847, the newly-appointed executors petition for permission to sell a portion of the estate. Keeping in accordance with his progressive thinking Nimrod also broke many traditional White customs of his period by leaving his daughter, in the spirit of fairness, also bequeathed *"that she should also receive my home"* and that he had previously given to his two

---

[83] (Society, 1879)
[84] (Archives)

sons, *"land with its title"* According to *Family Life In A Borderland Community Nacogdoches, 1779-1861.*

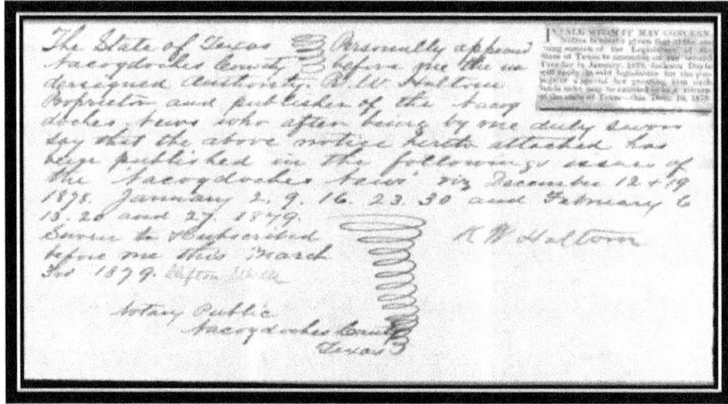

FIGURE 45 DOCUMENT: JACKSON DOYLE LAND
APPLICATION NACOGDOCHES, TEXAS 1879

Doyle would live through one of the most transitional times in America's history and play a role in several conflicts and events that were crossroads in American history. Although he appears to have been controversial in some of his decisions and actions, he was obviously a man of courage and strength. His descendants, in both Indian Territory and Florida, would forge ahead into times of continued change and challenge. Some would continue to struggle to maintain ties to the Muscogee Creek identity of his wives; others would merge into the mainstream "White" identity that he came from. As Texas records indicate, his descendants most likely were African American as well. We most likely will never know much about

266

his life and all of his descendants, but from what we do know he was an amazing character indeed.

FIGURE 46 PHOTO: JACKSON, SON OF NIMROD AND SUSAN ISLANDS DOYLE

FIGURE 47 PHOTO: SAMUEL CALLAHAN, CREEK NATION, CIRCA 1880S

Samuel Benton Callahan

Two of the grandsons of Nimrod Doyle would play crucial roles in the unfolding fate of the Creek people. One was George W. Hill, the youngest son of Nancy Doyle, who would become an appointed Chief of Creek Nation in the 1920s. The other was Amanda Doyle Callahan Davis's son Samuel Callahan, who would serve in several capacities of Creek Nation leadership during the mid and late 1800s. Samuel Benton Callahan was born in Mobile, Alabama on January 26th 1833, the son of the (Cussetah) Muscogee Creek Indian Amanda Sybil Doyle and her non-Indian husband, James Oliver Callahan, a well-known architect and ship builder from the Northeast.[85] Throughout his long and eventful life, Samuel was to move between the white and Indian worlds frequently. His parents are listed as residents of "Cusseta Town" of the Lower Creeks on the 1832 Abbot-Parsons roll, which would soon be removed to the West along with the other established Creek the West communities as a part of the infamous "Indian removal" policy of the Jackson administration.

Samuel was born during this time of difficulty and transition, and as a young child his family would leave for the West, going to Texas rather than the Indian Territory. On this journey to a new life, his father James Callahan would pass away.[86] For Samuel's mother Amanda Doyle this was the second husband she had lost in a half dozen years, having married James Hill in 1829 at Fort Mitchell Creek Nation in March of 1829, and marrying Samuel's father a year later after James Hill's death. Amanda's two half-sisters Nancy and Sarah

---

[85] <u>Wynema</u> by S. Alice Callahan
[86] A History of the State of Oklahoma by Luther Hill

Doyle would marry James Hill's brothers, George Wesley and Alexander, at the same time and place.[87]*The 1870 Creek Nation Self-Emigrant Roll* states that the family "Emigrated from Alabama to the Creek Nation Indian Territory the spring & summer of 1837 - furnished transportation and subsistence, & subsistence for 12 months after their arrival."[88]

Despite the above testimony to the contrary, Samuel and his mother would land in the area of Sulphur Springs, Texas, along with his grandfather Nimrod Doyle, aunts and uncles, and others of the family. Samuel's grandfather Nimrod Doyle's involvement in fraudulent land deals in Alabama during the Creek removal, and the subsequent investigation[89] of these events was the most likely cause of the family's relocation

---

[87] Milledgeville, Georgia Newspaper Clippings (Southern Recorder), Volume II 1828-1832 states:

"HILL, Mr. James of the US Army m. DOYLE, Miss Amanda, a Creek pupil of the Asbury Missionary Institution near Fort Mitchell Creek Nation, m. there 3-3-1829 by Rev. Mr. Hill. AC 3-18-1829; CP 4-29-1829; A th 4-7-1929; SP 3-21-1829; SR 4-21-1829. DG 4-19-1829 gives wedding date as 4-3-1829"
"HILL, Alexander of the US Army m. DOYLE, Miss Sarah, a belle of the Creek Nation, m. there 3-3-1829 State of Georgia CP 4-29-1829"
"HILL, George W. of the US Army m. DOYLE, Miss Nancy, a belle of the Creek Nation, m. there 3-3-1829 State of Georgia CP 4-29-1829"
[88] *1870-71 Self-Emigrant Roll of the Creek Nation*; This Creek "self-emigrant" roll was compiled between May 1870 and Dec. 1871. The ages listed on this roll are presumably the ages as of 1870-71 but could also be the ages at the time of emigration. In 1886 this roll with many eliminations and corrections was finalized by G.W. Stidham and used as the basis for payments to the Creek "self-emigrants" and their heirs.
[89] SENATE DOCUMENT # 151, 23d Congress, 2d Session

(outside the reach of American authorities at that time.) On the family's arrival in the Republic of Texas, his mother would soon marry a physician named Owen Simpson Davis, who would raise Samuel and instill in him an appreciation for education and civic mindedness. On the dusty plains of Texas young Samuel got his education in the public schools of Hopkins County, and later attended McKenzie College in Cloutsville, evidence of an appreciation for learning that would show itself more in the years to come.

After leaving his educational pursuits at McKenzie in 1856, he edited the *Sulphur Springs Gazette*, the start of a lifelong interest in newspapers, education, and community and self-development. In 1858 he, like his mother before him, married a non-Indian, Sarah Elizabeth McAllester, and the next year he moved the young family to the Creek Nation in Indian Territory, several hundred miles north. Here he would reconnect with his Muscogee Creek ancestry and community and begin a new life among his *Mvskvlke*[90] by establishing a ranching operation near Okmulgee, the capital of the Nation. Though raised among Non-Indian people, Samuel displayed a deep and lifelong commitment to the survival and betterment of the Creek people. Though of "Mixed Blood," Samuel like many others of his class was considered "fully" Muscogee Creek Indian, traditionally speaking, in the Creek Nation, since as a society the

---

[90] The Creek People

Creeks were a matriarchal people, who traced ancestry and identity through the mother's line.

Samuel was a part of a large class of Mixed Bloods who used their place in the world as a bridge between the American and Muscogee Creek worlds and cultures. Best-known among this small but influential group of Creeks was Chief William McIntosh, a chief of Coweta who had signed the treaty of Indian Springs and was later executed for violating the Creek Nation law concerning individuals selling Creek communal lands. Throughout Samuel's life he would walk the difficult road of the Mixed Blood, negotiating his way through the perilous days ahead with dignity and courage, using the aspects of American culture which could not be escaped to negotiate a better future for his people.

Samuel and Sarah would in time have eight children together, including Josephine Callahan (Spaulding), (Dr.) James Owen, Jan Evylin Callahan (Shaw), Samuel Benton Callahan Jr., Sophia Alice Callahan, (who would later write the important book *Wynema,* before her untimely death), Emma Price (Adair), (Dr.) Walter McKenzie Callahan, and Edwin Thornburg Callahan. Many of their children would grow up to be very successful members of society but early on the family's fortunes were dubious at best, with heartache and danger soon to make their lives and futures a contest.

As for Indians everywhere, the future in the mid nineteenth century was all but rosy, with the forces of history once again closing in on the family. In the Indian Territory, Samuel's ranching operation expanded and he grew his connections and interests in the nation in the years building up to the bloody Civil War. The conflict would once again tear the Creek people apart, with many of the traditional "full blood" people staying loyal to the treaties and agreements with the United States, while other Creek people, mainly the wealthier and more assimilated "Mixed Bloods," sided with the Confederacy.

Lines of hostility among the Creeks that went back to the pre-removal days would emerge once again in the coming conflict between two very different world views. Many who served in the Confederate ranks came from the tribal town families of Coweta, Cussetah, and others, long more assimilated and identifying with the fortunes of fellow Southerners.[91] In 1861 Samuel, like many of the more affluent class of Mixed Bloods, left his ranching operation to enlist in the Confederate cause. Not long after his departure for service, a band of Union marauders attacked his ranch, burning his trading house and stripping his home entirely.

His wife, two young children, and a slave nurse fled back to Sulphur Springs, Texas for the duration of the war, and for

---

[91] Andrew K Frank, "Creeks and Southerners"

years afterward Sarah did not return to the Indian Territory. Samuel had joined the First Creek Regiment of the Confederate Army, which was commanded by Colonel Daniel N. McIntosh. This unit was assigned to the First Indian Cavalry Brigade, along with the Second Cherokee regiment commanded by Major William Adair, Major Joseph Scales's Cherokee Battalion, Colonel Chilly McIntosh's Second Creek Regiment, Captain Kenard's Creek Squadron, Lt. Colonel John Jumper's Seminole Battalion, and the First Osage Battalion commanded by Major Broke Arm.

Fighting between groups loyal to the Confederate and Union forces was fierce during the war, with the First Creek Regiment frequently seeing action along with the other units, with significant actions at Pleasant Bluff and other engagements (name some). Its most vaunted victory was on September 19th 1864, when along with forces from Texas, the Indian soldiers captured a supply train of the Union, worth 1.5 million dollars. The Indian brigade was thanked by the Confederate Congress and General Kirby, the Supreme Commander of the trans-Mississippi forces of the Confederate Army.

He stated that the action was "The most brilliant of the war." [92] Samuel would play an important role in his unit, and was an inspired leader and courageous warrior on the field of battle as well as being shrewd in politics. He was commissioned

---

[92] (Ryan M. , 2007)

274

first Lieutenant of his company and was elevated eventually to adjutant of his regiment during his first year. During the second year of the conflict he re-enlisted in the volunteer regiment and assisted with the reorganization of the command, serving on the front as Captain of Company K of the First Creek Regiment. In 1863 he left his service in the Confederate Army to serve as a congressman in the Confederate Congress in Richmond, Virginia, a position which he held until 2 weeks before General Lee's surrender of the Confederate forces.

Despite Samuel's units' victories during the war, they were ill supplied and often lacking in even the basic supplies, with many of the warriors riding their own Indian ponies and using supplies given by sympathizers and plundered from Unionist homes. The unit was often ragged and hungry, with some of the men using antiquated flintlocks that had been brought on the Trail of Tears from the old country. Most had only common sporting rifles. . Undaunted by these challenges, the unit would fight with vigor and courage. Ultimately the news capture of Robert E. Lee and the abdication of the Confederate government would reach the wilds of the Indian Territory and the long and bloody conflict would find its end with the surrender of the unit's supreme leader Lone Watie and his forces at Doaksville on June 23rd 1865; he was the last Confederate general to surrender.[93]

---

[93] Allen C. Ashcraft, "Confederate Conditions in Indian Territory, 1865," *The Chronicles of Oklahoma* 42 (Winter 1964-65). Allen C. Ashcraft,

With the end of the conflict, the Creek Nation, like many other parts of the South was in burnt ruins and the crippled and broken were in multitudes. Unlike other parts of the South, the war in Indian Territory would "slowly grind to a halt" with killings and atrocities continuing for some time after the war as old scores were settled. (Ryan M. , 2007, pp. 23-45, 67)

With the end of the conflict, Samuel went to Texas to reunite with his wife and children and try his hand in the mercantile business for a short time. However, he was soon back in Indian territory, locating a new stock raising enterprise near the city of Muskogee, while his family remained in Sulphur Springs, Texas. Once again his interest in politics led to him become involved in the rebuilding of the Nation, being chosen as the Clerk of the territorial Senate of the Creek Nation's legislature, the House of Kings. He held that position for four years from 1868 to 1872, living in the tribal capital of Okmulgee to be close to his work, even while maintaining his ranch holdings. He then became a Clerk of the Creek Nations Supreme

---

"Confederate Indian Troop Conditions in 1864," *The Chronicles of Oklahoma* 41 (Winter 1963-64). Allen C. Ashcraft, "Confederate Indian Department Conditions in August, 1864," *The Chronicles of Oklahoma* 41 (Autumn 1963). Wilfred Knight, *Red Fox: Stand Watie and the Confederate Indian Nations During the Civil War Years in Indian Territory* (Glendale, Calif.: Arthur H. Clark, 1988). Lary C. Rampp and Donald L. Rampp, *The Civil War in the Indian Territory* (Austin: Presidial Press, 1975). Marvin J. Hancock, "The Second Battle of Cabin Creek," *The Chronicles of Oklahoma* 39 (Winter 1961-62). Lary C. Rampp, "Confederate Indian Sinking of the *J. R. Williams*," *Journal of the West* 11 (January 1972).

Court, and in 1896 was chosen as a delegate of the Creek Nation to confer with President Grover Cleveland.[94]

In 1901 Samuel was appointed to the honored position of Justice of the Creek Nation Supreme Court. He was also involved in efforts by many in the Creek Nation to establish schools, serving as a superintendent of the Wealaka Boarding School, a Methodist mission school located on the Arkansas River in the Coweta District of Creek Nation, from 1892 to 1894. He was also a secretary to Creek Principal Chiefs Samuel Checote, Roly McIntosh, and Isparheche.

In 1885, he moved his family from Texas to the Indian Territory, purchasing a hotel in Okmulgee. The *Indian Journal*, a local newspaper based in Eufaula, reported in the November 5, 1885 edition that his establishment was crowded with guests during the session season when the Creek Nation legislative council was meeting. [95] Soon afterwards, Samuel became editor of the paper and the family moved to Eufala in 1887. He would serve the Creek Nation's people in many capacities and undertake many trips to Washington D.C., representing his people to the authorities there.

When Samuel Benton Callahan died on February 17th 1911, he was buried in his sixty year old Confederate soldier's

---

[94] This would be a position of considerable importance due to the impending enforcement of the Allotment Act and land runs to come, all leading to the loss of the Creek Nation's sovereign status for generations.
[95] (Rogers, 1995)

uniform, and was the last living member of the Confederate Congress.[96] Much like his grandfather Nimrod Doyle, Samuel Benton Callahan faced many changes and challenges, for himself and the Creek Nation which he loved as proven by his many years of service on its behalf. Although he had only a small amount of Creek blood, his heart was that of a Muscogee warrior of old, and his hands helped to build the Creek nation we have inherited today. As the historic record shows, Samuel met these challenges with courage and ingenuity. His daughter Alice would be cut from the same cloth, and make her own distinct mark on the world.

---

[96] "Capt. Callahan Dies Here Today" 17 February 1911 -*Muskogkee Times Democrat*

FIGURE 48 PHOTO: ALICE CALLAHAN, CREEK NATION CIRCA 1880S

Alice Callahan

Another distinguished descendant of Nimrod Doyle is his great granddaughter Alice Callahan. During her short life of only 26 years she did much to better herself and her people's position in this world, which is exemplified by her novel advocating for Native American and women's rights called *Wynema*, the first novel written by a Native American (Ryan M. , 2007)Although she grew up in Texas she spent most of the few years of her adult life in Creek Nation Indian Territory, working steadily to better the lives of Creek children, with several years of teaching school and being involved in efforts to promote social issues there. Much like her relatives before her she was a dedicated Methodist. She worked at Wealaka Boarding School, a situation harkening back to her Grandmother Amanda Doyle's first marriage, to James Hill in 1829 while Amanda was a student at the Methodist boarding and mission school, the Asbury Missionary Institute at Fort Mitchell in the (old) Creek Nation[97]

Sadly her grandfather James O. Callahan died en route to Texas. Her father Samuel, who is listed on the Dawes Roll as having one-eighth Indian blood, grew to adulthood in Sulphur Springs, a town his parents founded, as did his daughter Alice. Both of their lives were filled with hard work and struggle, for their own benefit as well as service to the Creek people. Both strove to better themselves and their community.

Sophia Alice Callahan was the daughter of Samuel Benton Callahan and Sarah Elizabeth McAllester, and the granddaughter of Amanda Doyle. She went simply by 'Alice' and was an energetic and charming young woman who lived

---

[97] previous to Amanda's marriage in 1830 to Alice's grandfather James O. Callahan and their subsequent emigration west

earnestly and worked hard to be a good example to those around her and exemplify the values of her Christian faith, which like the values of educational self-betterment and excellence were a guiding light for her. She was born in 1868 in Sulphur Springs, Texas where her grandmother and father, led by her great-grandfather Nimrod Doyle, had settled upon emigrating from the South during the Indian Removal. Alice grew to adulthood in this small but vibrant north Texas community.

As an eighteen year old fresh faced girl, she began her lifelong work of service to others, and moved north to Creek Nation in the Indian Territory, which was just beginning to recover from the destruction and dysfunction resulting from the years of killing during the War Between the States, which had ended two decades earlier. Although the war had been over for years, the emotional scars on the land and its people were deep and slow to heal.

In 1886 she was teaching in Okmulgee, Creek Nation, Indian Territory where the small school was said to be in *"a flourishing condition"* under (whose?) leadership according to the *Indian Journal* on May 20, 1886. In 1888 she went to ten months of teacher training at the Wesleyan Female Institute located in Staunton, Virginia, It was a small liberal arts educational institute where she would get her initial grounding for working as a teacher, and on returning to Indian Territory in June of 1888 she put this to use.

The Wesleyan Female Institute was founded in 1846 and remained in operation until 1900, like several other educational institutes of the time focused on training young women for teaching, one of the few employments socially acceptable for a female on the rough and tumble frontier. In an announcement concerning her and a fellow student's arrival back in Creek Nation, the *Indian Journal* wrote on June 21, 1888 that "These young ladies won honors of rare merit in that institute as a reward of persevering effort and close application, for which they deserved the congratulations of parents and friends." [98] In 1891 Callahan began work as a teacher at the Harrell International Institute in Muskogee, Indian Territory.

This was a private Methodist high school that the Creek National Council established in 1882 to help educate young Creek people for the sorely needed work of nation building... Some of its stated goals were to teach young people the "elements of sciences and agriculture and mechanical arts." (Littlefield, 1984).

The Harrell International Institute was named in honor of the Reverend John Harrell, a Methodist missionary among the Creeks. Like its predecessor the Asbury Missionary Institute where her forebears had attended school a half century earlier, it was rooted in the values and perspectives of the Christian faith with an underlying goal of spreading these to the Indian people

---

[98] (Rogers, 1995)

through education and improved standard of living. In the year 1882 Ms. Callahan took the task of editing a journal affiliated with the Harrell International Institute called *Our Red Brother*, a Methodist publication that was progressive in nature and which often had news relating to the women's rights and the temperance movement (Littlefield, 1984)To add more to a very busy and difficult year in her short life, Alice Callahan also completed her work on her novel, *Wynema.* An announcement concerning the book's publication was posted in June.

In this article it was stated that Callahan "is an intelligent Christian Lady and we look forward with pleasure to a time when our other duties will permit us to read the book. It is certainly cheap at 25 cents a copy." (Callahan, 1891)Although a groundbreaking book for the time, it received little coverage. It was the first novel written by a Native American woman. Although it used many stereotypes and was written to appeal to a non-Indian audience, her work was unique in its focus and advocacy for Native, women's and educational issues and its emphasis on women's roles during a time when these issues were swiftly growing in the consciousness of American society. Alice's mother died on October 6th of the same year, a difficult blow that may have played a part in her increased activities at the Muskogee Methodist Church and deepening commitment to her faith and practice that she expressed in her letters to friends at the time.

During 1892 and 1893, sadly the last years of her short life, Alice was engaged to teach at the Wealaka Boarding School. With over one hundred students, it was larger than any of her previous postings as an instructor. It was an expansive and roomy establishment, with three stories and plenty of room. Wealaka Boarding School was a mission school run by the Methodist conference located in the Coweta District of Creek Nation. During the years that Alice taught there her father Samuel was the Superintendent of the school, which probably pleased Alice, having her father near.

The Wealaka School was built to replace the old Tullahassee Mission which had burned down and had been an important institution in the northern part of Creek Nation. In an 1893 letter she expressed her interest in returning to Staunton to finish her education, was involved in local and national women's issues, and expressed strong interest in eventually founding her own school. This last year of her life found her busy and active in her lifelong pursuit of being a useful and worthy person, contributing and making a difference. On January 7, 1894 Alice Callahan passed away from an extended illness related to an attack of Pleurisy. Though her novel did not receive much attention when it was published it was groundbreaking for its time and is a testament to her great concern for Native American struggles as well as women's issues of her era.

As an aspiring historian and writer seeking to document tribal life myself, I would think of this distant relative as I worked with my cousin S. Pony Hill in years past to complete our 2010 book *The Indians of North Florida*, a work which also was focused on Native and Identity issues, much like Alice Callahan's book. As someone whose Creek blood quantum was one-sixteenth and who could have easily done other things in life, she was very committed to bettering the lives of the Creek people and their futures through education.

I find this commendable, inspiring, and rooted in traditional Creek values and worldview as I look back on her life and work now more than a century later. I am often reminded of letters from the 1940s written by another cousin seeking to better herself and her people's hardscrabble lives, Mary Francis Porter from Scott Town, Florida. The daughter of community leader Mathias Porter, she was trying to secure her own education a half century ago. While she was a student at the Cherokee Indian Normal School in Robeson County, North Carolina, she wrote in a letter to the Mr. Lowery, Dean of this school, of her desire "bring the light of education back" to her people's dark existence as Native persons trapped in a changing world full of challenges and a deck stacked against their own success.

Unlike in Oklahoma, where under the state constitution Native people were socially considered "White" versus Negro,

Mary Francis Porter and her relatives in the isolated and scattered Indian settlements in Florida were often treated socially as "black" or "Mulatto" by county governments. Unlike relatives in the Jim Crow South, Alice had the benefit of her father Samuel's involvement in tribal politics of the federally recognized the Creek Nation to help her on her goals and aspirations to be a light to those around her.

In a life cut short but still full, Alice was a witness to the oppression and injustice endured by Native Americans as well as women in her time. Due to her family being one of the more fortunate among the Mixed Blood elite, she could well have lived a life of leisure and idleness. Instead each year of her life was one of steady work to improve her personhood and help people around her as well. Due to her education, status as a "thin-blood," and family's privileged lifestyle, she was at once deeply involved in, yet separate from, the Creek language, culture and religion of her ancestors.

As a descendant of noted families among the Creeks such as the McIntosh, Islands, and Doyle lines, Alice Callahan's life, much like her father's, reflected the rich heritage of civic and tribal participation in the social life of Creek Nation, even as the family's repeated marriages to outsiders led to a steady diminishment of their blood quantum. The dedication of her book *Wynema* is "to the Indian tribes of North America, who have felt the wrongs and oppression of their pale-faced brother."

(Callahan, 1891)For someone reared in Texas, with a nominal amount of Native blood or knowledge of the Creek language and lifestyle, this is clearly an indication of the respect and regard she had for her family's heritage. The advocacy for women's issues expressed in her work is solidly in line with the most ancient and beloved roots of the Muscogee world, the matriarchy and feminine perspectives which are at the root of the *Nene Mvskoke*.

George W. Hill

George W. Hill was one of the members of my grandmothers family who I remember hearing about at times as a child. Though he lived before my or my parent's time, my grandparents had heard of him and he lived on through their tales. My grandfather would sometimes say, "I may be Indian myself, son but your grandma is related to a Chief!" My grandmother's great Uncle, George W. Hill was the relative that bridged the two branches of descendants, east and west. Though born in the East decades after removal, he would journey to Indian Territory and play a role in the events of the allotment and loss of Creek Nation's self-determination for two generations. Nancy Doyle Hill had many children. The youngest of her thirteen children, George W. Hill, was born at Spring Creek on the Florida-Georgia state line in 1856, the year of her death, which may have been related to his birth. The family had moved to Spring Creek a couple of years after the removal.

FIGURE 49 PHOTO: MARTHA EMMA HILL WITH SON DANIEL MINTON AND FAMILY

Nancy's husband George Robert Wesley Hill took their children and moved across the state line soon after her death. In the 1860 census of Jackson County, Florida young George is four years old living in his father's home, and again in 1870 they are still living in the same community. Soon after, he was married to Caroline Conyers on the 2nd of February in 1872, while in his late teens. They had 2 children, James Wesley and Martha, and all are identified as resident in Jackson County in the 1880 census. Their union, however, wasn't destined to last.

Soon after the end of this marriage he would leave for the West, where many of his mother's relatives had already gone, including his grandfather Nimrod Doyle, his aunts Amanda and Muscogee, and his uncles Jackson and Winchester Doyle. George moved to the Creek Nation in Indian Territory, where he would be married twice, once to an unknown full blood, with whom he had a daughter Melissa, and later to Lucinda Grayson, from the prestigious Grayson family, long leaders in Creek Nation. She was the daughter of George Washington Grayson, whose other children included William McKinley, Helen, and Alice. His many children with several women are known either through the documented record or from oral history interviews in 1995 with his descendant Wiley "Grandpa Bill" Sampson of Okmulgee, Oklahoma.

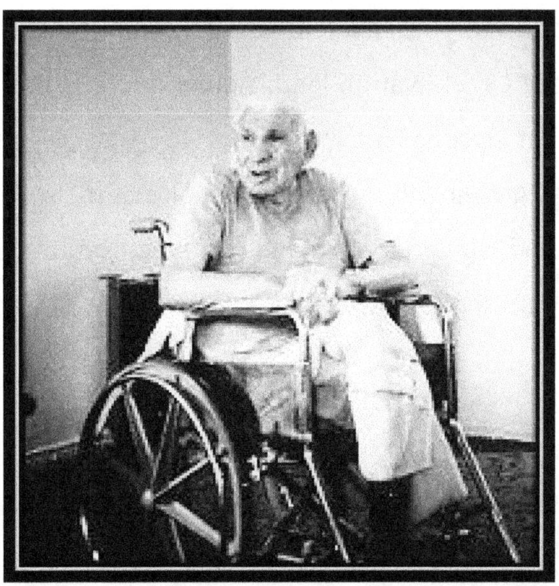

FIGURE 50 PHOTO: WILEY "GRANDPA BILL" SAMPSON, OKMULGEE OKLAHOMA 1995

Wylie was the son of Solomon "Wash" Sampson and 'Cinda (Lucinda) Hill. He was married to Mabel Lewis. The descendants of 'Cinda Hill hold a large family reunion in

Okmulgee which family members from the East have visited several times, and George's descendants there always had plenty to say about him. Grandpa Bill was always glad to share. He was born on August 13, 1904 and he died May 28, 2001.

He was born in the Creek Nation, which would be forcibly allotted and subsumed by the new state of Oklahoma within a couple of years. Grandpa Bill would be an elder and deacon of Graves Creek Indian Church in Hitchita, Oklahoma for many years. When he passed away he had 35 great-great grandchildren! Grandpa Bill was named a "treasure of the Muscogee Creek Nation" in his elder hood. He told me about letters that George Hill would receive from "his sisters in Georgia" and how he sometimes spoke of them. Grandpa Bill said he had wanted to meet his relatives from the East that George had spoken of.

FIGURE 51 PHOTO: WILL "SONNY" SAMPSON

Grandpa Bill's son Will is well known for his groundbreaking roles in Hollywood as an actor. Will "Sonny" Sampson (1933-1987) grew up hearing from his father about his ancestors' struggle to survive and their pride in being Indian, and came to manhood during a time when Indian people were just beginning to reassert the right to self-determination. Sonny would bring this strength and pride to the roles he played in over 27 movies. He would inspire many and be the face of native America to a generation of moviegoers.

His groundbreaking role in "One Flew over the Cuckoo's Nest" was the first time in cinematic history that a Native person had played a role that was not "stereotypical." It was the first time an Indian played a major role in a major motion picture. Aunt Norma Bible said that through the years even when Sonny had a big house and exciting life in Hollywood he would fly in overnight just to ease off to the stomp dance or spend time with family at a local powwow before heading back to California the next day. His nephew, our cousin Rusty, would tell us of Sonny's conversion to the Christian faith later in life, and his sharing of his spirituality with friend and stranger alike. Today he is buried in the graveyard at Graves Creek Church among his people, far from the bright lights and busy streets of Hollywood which he trod in life.

My cousin S. Pony Hill and I would travel to spend time with Grandpa Bill's daughter Norma and gather stories from the past about the family's struggles on the Oklahoma prairies in Creek Nation. Grandpa Bill's sister Alice (Freeman) is a well-known elder, admired for her great knowledge and heart. The family is all respected throughout the community and a younger generation is now coming of age and shouldering the heritage of their family in working for the Creek people. Peggy Powell is one such family member. While times are better than they once were in the Creek Nation there are still hard times faced by many poorer full blood Creek people in the small communities that dot the Nation.

FIGURE 52 PHOTO: NORMA BIBLE IN OKMULGEE OKLAHOMA

These many descendants of George Hill; Wylie Sampson, Sonny Sampson, and Alice Freeman would carry on his tradition of service to the Muscogee Creek people. On arriving in the Creek Nation, George Hill would start a new life among his people. George did well in the West. He was involved with ranching and later politics in a big way. One story shared by Grandpa Bill was that George had the first car in the neighborhood where he lived, and would show off at times. He would even drive his car the quarter mile down to the road just to check his mail. He said that one time George went to check the mail and was on his way back, still fairly new to the automobile. Relatives were on the front porch of the house when up the drive came George barreling along on his automobile at high speed, yelling "Whooh, Whooh!" He crashed the auto into the side of the house! Another story Grandpa Bill related was that one of George's pastimes was to go to Tiger Mountain and search for a lost payload of gold coins that was supposed to have been buried there by Creek Confederates who had raided homes of Union sympathizers in the area. Needless to say he never found it nor has anyone else. According to Grandpa Bill's family lore, although George was a Christian and involved in politics, it wasn't unknown for him to slip off the ceremonial grounds to the all-night stomp dances. He said that George would usually go to Tvlwv Rakko (Apalachicola) grounds, where he had relatives. This tribal town was removed from the Florida panhandle from the same area George grew up in and was a leading town of the Lower Creeks historically before it was stripped of its status due to a massacre that was allowed to occur there.

This was unheard of as it was a "Peace Town" and was supposed to be a place of refuge. As punishment the Creek National Council stripped it of its status as a lead town. Its citizens were removed to Texas among the Alabama and Coushatta there initially, but many of the Apalachicola would soon journey on to Indian Territory. A few families would remain in Texas. A small remnant of the Apalachicola would remain behind in the East and contribute descendants to the

Seminole and Eastern Creeks as well. Grandpa Bill shared many stories with us about the older times in the Nation. Wiley "Bill" Sampson died May 28, 2001, at Leisure Manor in Okmulgee. He was born August 13, 1904 according to records. Gravecreek Baptist Church is his final resting place, with Rev. Alex Lowe and Rev. Mitchell Taylor officiating at his burial at Gravecreek Cemetery. He was a retired laborer and farmer. Proudly he had served as deacon at the Gravecreek church for many years. He had many children, as well as 23 grandchildren, 43 great-grandchildren, and 35 great-great-grandchildren. He was a treasurer of the Creek Nation without doubt.

FIGURE 53 PHOTO: CHIEF GEORGE W. HILL, MUSKOGEE OKLAHOMA

Most of the stories we heard from Grandpa Bill were about Chief George W. Hill. George would be involved in business and ranching in Creek Nation and do well for himself. His Creek Nation enrollment card shows his enrollment in 1890 (in his mid-30's), and his residence as Osoche Town (interestingly a tribal town in Creek Nation founded by the remnants Florida Calusa). His father is listed as a "White non-citizen" and mother (listed as an unknown full-blood) as having "died before the Civil War..."[99]

---

[99] In an interview with Wylie Sampson in 1995, He stated that his grandfather George Hill said that he didn't know who his mother was as part of his political approach to life. He had earned his way up from the bottom upon his arrival in Creek Nation in the late 1800's and due to his having no (known) ties to the established parties and factions within Creek Nation he was able to chart a path through the factionalized politics of the era to attain eventually the highest political office, that of Principal Chief, in 1923.

FIGURE 54 PHOTO: GEORGE HILL ON CREEK NATION
SCHOOL BOARD 1905

He is present in the 1910 census in McDaniel, McIntosh County, Oklahoma with his wife Lucy and their children, and is again listed there in the 1920 federal census. The 1910 census states that he has been married three times, and is one-half Creek Indian. It also says he received his allotment in 1899. In some of the last documentation from his lifetime, he appears in the 1920 federal census; we find his grandchildren Lucille and Clarence Hardridge, young teenagers, present in his home in Muskogee, along with his own children.

After the (illegal and forcible) dissolution of the Creek Nation's national government at Oklahoma statehood in 1907, only enough of a "governmental structure" was left intact as thought necessary to "clean up" any remaining affairs of the Creeks. Chiefs from statehood until the reorganization of Creek Nation in the 1970s were appointed by the US president. In 1923 George W. Hill was appointed by President Calvin Coolidge, and served until 1928. Grandpa Sampson said that his grandfather George Hill was chosen because of his neutrality among the several competing parties in the Creek Nation politics of the time.

The fact that he was appointed as chief of Creek Nation by the president of the United States was not as prestigious as it sounds, since hindsight has shown that many of the chiefs who were appointed during that era were not acting in the best interest of the Creek people. He died soon after his retirement from the post in 1928. His and Cinda Hill's descendants have a large gathering yearly where the rich heritage of this family is remembered and celebrated.

FIGURE 55 ARTWORK: BY THE AUTHOR SCOTT SEWELL, TITLED:
INDIAN FACES OLD FIXICO

FIGURE 56 ARTWORK: TITLED: STOMP DANCE SHELL SHAKER GIRL

Chapter 5 Now

My grandfathers used to tell me stories of our family's roots, some of these tales of days past reaching as far back as the "War between the States." Often these stories would begin, "Back when grandma's grandma was living in Carolina," or "back when Uncle Hugh Oxendine was with us...." These stories would fuel my young imagination with a desire to know more about the people and places in these oral histories than the storyteller could supply, since they would "sell it to you like I bought it..." The desire to know more about my ancestors and community eventually led to decades of research and travel in a half dozen states to find the origins and trail across the years and miles that led to the sleepy little hamlet of Woods on the

Apalachicola River in which my grandfather and I would pass our too few days together during my childhood.

Figure 57 Photo: Ray Kever (Catawba) Woods, Florida
1988

We would ride the roads of this isolated and rural area, most of it forested and unpopulated. Located in Liberty County, in the central panhandle, the settlement of Woods was never big to begin with but in the opening decades of the twentieth century was much more of a going concern than the sleepy collection of houses it had dwindled to by the end of the century. Liberty County is the least populated county in the state of Florida and one of the newest. Over 80% of it is composed of the Apalachicola National Forest and it was originally part of the "Forbes Purchase," so it has always had the lowest population and population density of any county. It is still the smallest in population, with only a little over 8,000 people today. It has the highest percentage of Native American residents of any county in Florida as of the 2000 census, both Lumbee and Eastern Creek. This isn't really because there are so many Indians per se, but because there are so few people!

When I was as a boy, my grandparents would point out the old "home-places" of the many families who were our relatives, some of whose surnames were already gone from the county by my time. The former sites of homes of Oxendine, Jacobs, and Hill family members still draws my attention as I pass by even today. As we rode slowly down the winding deserted roads, the names of the people who had carved out a raw and rambling settlement generations ago would come near as my grandfather shared stories he had heard from his own parents and community elders, tales of the Florida past before the tourists, electricity, or outsiders moving in and our people moving away.

FIGURE 58 PHOTO: NOAH HILL

The Woods settlement of my grandmother's youth three-quarters of a century ago was one of hog-killings, chicken fights, and a yearly trip "to town" a dozen miles away, if you were lucky. One of the ever-present facets of these storytelling sessions was the migration of a half dozen of the families from the Carolinas to the then almost unsettled lowlands along the Apalachicola's wide ranging and meandering path through the heart of the central panhandle.

As I heard the descriptions of the lives before mine or even my grandfather's and grandmother's time related to me, my mind's eye would see clearly the faces of Noah Hill, Tom Oxendine, Corva Jacobs, Cleve Conyers, and Joe Scott as they risked the dangers of the river to deadhead out valuable cypress, struggle to round up their free-ranging cattle from the river bottoms, and endure blistering heat to gather the meager offerings from their turpentine buckets along the piney trails of the "river-swamp."

Beginning in the 1950s, an awareness of their rights as Native American people began to take root among the scattered Indian settlements of the South. This movement converged with a general renaissance of interest in genealogy and ethnic identity that was becoming more pronounced in society in general. This large movement would grow to many thousands of people of Creek descent from all over the area, forming an organization which we initially called the Perdido Band of Friendly Creek Indians of Alabama and Northwest Florida, before being renamed the next year the Creek Nation East of the Mississippi. This large umbrella organization formed in 1958 was a movement led by Indians from the areas of Atmore Alabama area, Pensacola, Florida and Cairo, Georgia and was headed by Calvin McGhee of Atmore.

It grew over the next two decades, eventually separated by the late 1970s into several locally specific tribal organizations: the Lower Muskogee Creek Tribe (aka Tama tribal town) in Georgia, the Florida Tribe of Eastern Creek

Indians (aka Muscogee Nation of Florida), and the Poarch Band of Creek Indians in Alabama. It would culminate with the federal acknowledgment in 1984 of the Poarch Band of Creek Indians (PCI) in lower Alabama, and state recognition of *the (Tama) Lower Muscogee Tribe* in Georgia, the MOWA Band of Choctaw in Lower Alabama, and the still ongoing petition for federal acknowledgement by the Muscogee Nation of Florida. Known for decades as The Florida Tribe of Eastern Creek Indians, the latter group is now headquartered in the tiny central panhandle town of Bruce, but was based originally in Pensacola.

When this surge of activity began after the Second World War, many Indian people were taking their first steps outside of the small hamlets that had been home to their families for generations. Setting the stage for momentous social changes to come, many men from Indian hamlets throughout the South returned from World War II wanting to make changes for their families, and to have a better life than that of the older generations. This generation made many great leaps in the subsequent decades, as can see by the reorganization and acknowledgment of eastern Indian tribes from the Seminole and Miccosukee of Florida to the Tunica-Biloxi of Louisiana.

A dozen tribes across the Southeast who had previously slumbered in rural isolation emerged into the realm of federal acknowledgment and modern American politics in the last half of the twentieth century, the struggles for community dignity and social stability of the previous century behind them. For the federally unacknowledged communities such as those in the Florida panhandle, the MOWA Choctaw of lower Alabama, the Lumbee and Tuscarora in North Carolina, and a dozen other tribal communities across the South, the fight for native power was still a daily struggle with local realities and ever present racism and assertion of White privilege. Without the protective mantle of federal recognition, these settlements were still at the mercy of local and state authorities and racist attitudes of many Southerners.

Nevertheless, with the determination characteristic of the "greatest generation," the returning veterans of WW II throughout these Indian communities led them into a new era of expanded civil rights and opportunity. This all was occurring within Indian communities even as the legal, political, and social face of the entire Southern society changed. The social dialogue within what remained of the swiftly eroding population base of the communities grew, and leaders of non-federally acknowledged groups became cognizant of the need to refocus community self-awareness, activity, and identity on the common past versus an uncertain future. Using the experiences and guidance of key elders such as Buck Bryant and Andrew Ramsey in Blountstown as a point of tribal unity, they encouraged Indian pride as a legitimate feeling and expression of love of self and community.

For some of the older generation who had experienced the racism of the old social order, they had a difficult time embracing the new "popularity" of being Indian that swept the South in the 1970s. This was understandable after having been attacked on all sides for a good part of their lives, simply for not looking "white" enough.

The newly emerging Indian identities that developed were hard to understand for some elders, especially the reclusive "core" Indian families in communities like Poarch, Scott Town, and McIntosh. Especially controversial were some newly declared "Creek Indians" who were popping up all over the tristate area and wanting their "Indian Money," some of them grandchildren of the same authorities who had persecuted the settlement Indians as "Mulattos and Negroes" in decades and centuries past!

FIGURE 59 PHOTO: SCOTT TOWN GROUP JACKSON COUNTY, FLORIDA CIRCA 1940 L TO R: MATHIES PORTER, TOM SCOTT HOLDING MITCHELL SCOTT, SHARON AND JACKIE SCOTT, INEZ

SCOTT, DAISEY PORTER SCOTT, ELLEN PORTER (BEHIND HER
LEFT SHOULDER) BESSIE PORTER, PAULINE SCOTT, NELLIE
SCOTT (REAR), RUBY SCOTT, EDNA MAE PORTER

Difficult as the years after the civil rights era were, they were better than they had been in a long, long time. At long last, the power to define their community was now in their own hands, but as before, they would face opposition from others when they would assert their Indian identity. These tribal communities were isolated and self-reliant, tribal members taking care of each other and often times the less fortunate of any race who wound up among them (Sider 1993). (Sider, 1994, p. 67)

The schools in the Indian communities during the segregation era were often classified and funded by the county as "Negro" or "Colored," despite the people attending them looking decidedly Indian and identifying themselves as Indian in the board of education correspondence records, military enlistments, and other county, state and federal documents. A few were able to gain traction as Indian but several would be dogged by racist perceptions of the identity of the children attending these schools, especially those in the panhandle with children of Lumbee origin.

Now

Eastern Creeks:

The Indian Claims Commission and the Creek Land Claims Dockets

A big force behind the reawakening of the identity of some of the many thousands of people in the late 1960s and early 1970s who were appearing publicly as "Creek Indians" (and especially "Creek Chiefs" in gaudy pink and green plains Indian headdresses) was the anticipated payout of Indian land claims funds to all descendants of Creek Indians who would submit to the federal government documentation of their descent from a Creek Indian who appeared on the rolls during the removal. In the twenty-first century, one finds the South littered with tens of thousands of descendants of the Creek Nation who identify with the mainstream culture and an Anglo identity. Many first became aware of their Indian ancestor as part of the push to sign people up for "Indian money."

The Indian Claims Commission was established in 1946 as a venue for redress for Native Americans of past frauds, treaty violations, and losses, of which there were many. Its mandate was to provide monetary compensation for such past wrongs as proved to the commission, but it was not empowered to return lost lands or territory. It also encouraged "neglected groups" in the South, northeast, and California to pursue claims. Efforts from the 1950s through the 1970s to secure documentation to support claims of the descendants of the historic Creek Nation to reparations led to the organization of several Creek groups in the Southeast and the federal acknowledgment of the Poarch Band of Creek Indians on August 11, 1984. Tens of thousands of people across Alabama, Georgia, Florida, Oklahoma, and several other states received small checks as a part of the settlement. Ultimately, activities surrounding the Indian Claims Commission were deemed to have accomplished much of the work it had been tasked with, and it was decommissioned in 1978, having completed 546 docket cases and awarded $818,172,606 dollars in judgments.

This same year saw the creation and implementation of a process for petitioning for federal acknowledgment set up by the Bureau of Indian Affairs as a result of the work of the Indians Claims Commission. Because of the potential for economic gain that was broadcast far and wide in the period leading up to the Creek land claims settlements, tens of thousands of persons who had not been in anyway identified with Native ancestry or the surviving intact communities of Native people in many generations became involved in the search for Creek Indian ancestors.

Many of these distant ancestors of mainstream Southerners originated during the period of heaviest intermarriage between Choctaw, Cherokee and Muscogee women and white "Indian countrymen" which occurred in the early 1800's and late 1700's. Admittedly, only a small portion had any degree of intermarriage after the initial singular Indian ancestor during the removal. Only some even knew of their Creek ancestry before the push by Indian descent organizations to sign up members for a push to establish a "Creek Nation" in the East.

As a result of this unique period in Creek history, there are many hundreds of thousands of people today who can document direct descent from the historic Creek Nation. The descendants of the powerful confederacy of Muscogee and allied tribal towns that became known as the Creek Nation during the colonial era are today of many colors, languages, and cultures. At the end of the twentieth century several tribes traced their political history back to this group, including the Seminole and Miccosukee tribes of Florida, Coushatta tribes in Louisiana and Texas, The Poarch Band of Creeks in Alabama and Florida, and dozens of state recognized tribal groups found throughout the South. There are also several 'unacknowledged' tribal groups such as the Independent Seminole in south Florida and several communities of Creeks in the panhandle of Florida.

FIGURE 60 PHOTO: ESSIE HILL

Most of the tens of thousands who applied for and
received payments as parties to the small compensation the ICC
disbursed have returned to the lives as mainstream White
Southerners, and thankfully so for the traditional Creek folks of
the panhandle. The crowds of the 1970s are gone, and once more
the tribal meetings are small, the ceremonial grounds at Ekvn
Hvtke and Kunfuskee attended by the small membership

marking another Green Corn as they always have; the few hundred dollars the ICC offered as compensation was not applied for by most of them.

In the West, the Muscogee Creek Nation of today charts a bright course into the future. In the 2011, Principal Chief of the Muscogee (Creek) Nation, A. D. Ellis reported at the annual "State of the Nation" address that current enrollment number for the tribe was over seventy thousand, of whom less than eighteen hundred were identified as "full-blood" Indian. It is said by several tribal leaders that there are less than a half dozen "pure-blood Creek" remaining, but this is difficult to document.

The December edition of the *Muscogee Nation News*, a semi-monthly publication of news from the Muscogee (Creek) Nation, stated that in January of 2004, the first year of the administration of Chief Ellis, Muscogee (Creek) Nation's enrollment was at 53,471 enrolled members. The growth in population has come from many Creeks who left a generation before returning to the wind-blown and economically struggling part of Oklahoma that the Creeks settled so long ago. One can see in this narrative how it occurs that so many people in this country share a common heritage, the descendants of the Doyle sisters being an example.

FIGURE 61 ELAINE HILL FOWLER

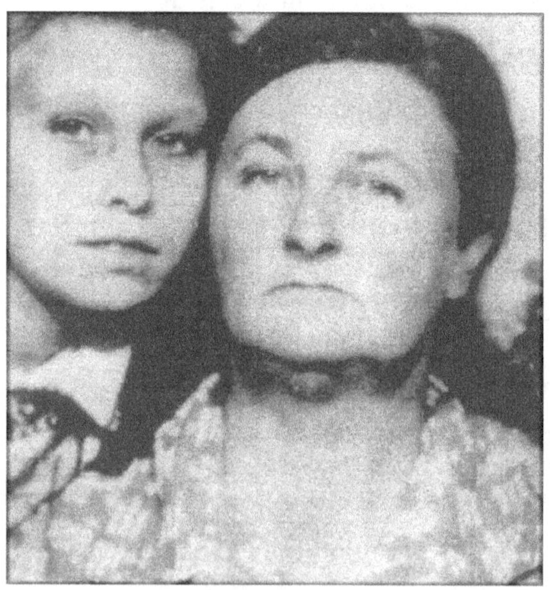

FIGURE 62 PHOTO: MECK HILL CONYERS WITH DAUGHTER VONCILLE 1940'S

The years from the end of the Civil War to the civil rights era were difficult times, and the community members were socially persecuted and subjected to undue harassment often as documented by Frank G. Speck, (1941) probably the most important researcher of the early twentieth century regarding Native Americans of the times. (Speck, 1947, pp. 195-198)In my studies and travels I have observed that the social existence and uniqueness of these communities is unappreciated and mostly unknown by the majority of contemporary academic authorities on Southern Indians, especially so with the communities still without federal recognition. The Indian struggle for self-determination can be seen in the many legal records that have been collected in various archives, reflecting the last one hundred and eighty years of interaction with outside authorities by tribal members and communities.

I accessed thousands of documents in the telling of this story, from dozens of sources. These same records and documentation, important in that they record frequent legal prosecution for violations of race-mixing laws and oppressive social customs imposed by the local White authorities and the race-obsessed Southern society in general, are only now being fully researched. There are still entire chapters of history yet to be found, waiting to be understood. They are now being placed in their proper historical context, one long unknown outside of a few early researchers and the people themselves.

The pioneering work of anthropologists like Parades, Dysart, and Ellsworth in the 1970s and 1980s , built on the important and consequential works of earlier twentieth century researchers, both academics and those with a social interest like Frank G. Speck, Brewton Berry, and Angie Debo, we have a lot of information available, with more coming forth in this generation thanks to lay researchers like S. Pony Hill, Melinda Maynor Lowery, and Frank Sweet. Finally able to better place the struggles of these ancestors and their communities in the large context of southern and American history accurately, we understand more definitively the courage and strength of our forebears and of the importance they placed on heritage and community.[100]

The Evolving Native American Identity

The complexity of the American Indian identity is unknown to many modern Americans. It is unique among the many ethnicities of the increasingly complex social landscape of the United States. Native American people, unlike any other group of Americans, must prove the status that they claim using

---

[100] -"Names in South Carolina" edited by Claude Henry Neuffer.Pg.XII:41
-"South Carolina Land Grants" (1784-1830) 160, vol. 32.R A Gray Library Private Collection, Florida State Archives, Tall. Fl
-"Early South Carolina Marriages" Vol.2 (1735-1885) implied in SC Law Reports, Union County
-"North and South Carolina Marriages 1800-1885" R A Gray Library Private Collection, Florida State Archives, Tall. Fl
-Records of US Army enlistees (South Carolina) 1795-1850
-Federal Census of Georgia:1860 Decatur County1870 Decatur County
-Federal Census of Florida:1860 Jackson County1870 Jackson County1885 Jackson County1870 Holmes County 1885 Holmes County
-"Decatur County Past and Present" 1823-1991, compiled by the Decatur County Historical Society and the

documentation which directly comes from the very government and society that their ancestors in many cases resisted being part of. This has little similarity to the immigrant experience of the millions of newly-minted Americans or their descendants that now people the "turtle continent."

The political status as "Native Americans," fraught with multi-layered meanings and with its accompanying legal and social baggage of history, is a major factor in the creation of a spectrum of assertion of, as well as acceptance as, "Indian" which many individuals and entire communities must navigate in the modern era. The need to prove the asserted identity as an American Indian in certain social and legal situations is not a circumstance that any other persons face in identifying their ethnic identity.

This social pressure to conform to perceived expectations of the identity that many Americans believe is Native American is one common to the lives of Native persons throughout "Indian Country." From using dream catchers to having "high cheekbones," many so-called attributes of "being Indian" are simply urban (or rural) legends that are passed along from generation to generation among those who feel they are of Indian ancestry somewhere along the line but have no known ties to the tribe from whence they feel ancestors came.

Changing perceptions of the American Indian identity by the mainstream through time lead persons and communities of

Native origin to participate continually in reconstructing the definition of Indian to adhere to norms imposed from without, even as they strive to maintain the interconnections and cultural patterns of a protected and cherished interior world of tribe, community, and friends. Community ceremonials and family identity are the actual markers of those closest to the heart of the tribal identities still surviving after five centuries of inundation by other cultures, languages, and belief systems.

Because the government to government relationship delineated in the commerce clause of the United States constitution clearly defines the status of Native American tribes to the more recent occupants, and the exclusive right of the American government to conduct business with them, tribes in some ways have a clearer definition than do their members. Tribal units, especially in areas where large blocks of isolated lands have been broken up or are now in a patchwork of other peoples and communities, are difficult to see, and in places like Oklahoma may be unknown to the majority of the residents who are not of Indian extraction.

Since the treaties between tribal governments and the federal government are still in effect, the tribes as social units will have a function in centuries to come just as they did in the past; they will advance with full support by and through the federal government, despite the degree of Native ancestry which those tribes' members may or may not possess in the future. The status of tribal governments as sovereigns under American law and their power to determine their own membership based on their own customs and requisites has created a diverse patchwork of requirements and perspectives concerning who is included and excluded from the tribal rolls.

A recent report from National Public Radio highlighted the emerging struggle over identity in its reporting on the growing phenomenon of the disenrollment of tribal members based on disputes of ancestry and identity from a century or more ago. In the report, an entire family from the Confederated Tribes of the Grand Ronde is being expelled from the tribe's membership roll, relating to a dispute that goes back more than a century and a half. Despite the family' assertions that its ties to the tribal community are deep, the tribal government says that "they do not deserve their casino-generated checks."[101]

This dispute is just one of dozens that are blossoming as more and more tribes see increased income from gaming operations and investments. According to a Lumbee tribal member and professor of American Indian studies at the University of Minnesota, incidents of people being removed from the rolls once a tribe sees and increase in income are not a new occurrence. David Wilkins estimates that as many as 8,000 persons have been removed from their rolls during the last

---

[101] "For Native Americans, Losing Tribal Membership Tests Identity." By David Nogueras, Morning Edition (NPR), 04/01/2014

twenty years by tribes of which they were once members in good standing, in an increasingly common arena of contention.

FIGURE 63 PHOTO: ELAINE HILL BLOUNTSTOWN 1960

"Disenrollment could be putting tribal autonomy in jeopardy" he said to David Nogueras of NPR.[102] Close scrutiny of the growing incidents of conflict within tribal communities by

---

[102] (NPR, 2014)
http://www.npr.org/sections/codeswitch/2014/04/01/295798832/for-native-americans-losing-tribal-membership-tests-identity

the press have led to dozens of protests and campaigns by social media and community activists seeking to bring to the attention of those outside of the often socially closed and frequently secretive tribal communities and governments. Wilkins goes on, "At some point there is going to be enough clamor raised by dis-enrollees that there is going to be a congressional hearing, or there is going to be a Supreme Court decision that might seriously impinge on what is a true sine qua non of a sovereign nation- that is the power to decide who belongs."[103] Tribal communities of multi-tribal and even multi-racial origin which had been united into seemingly homogenous units decades ago are now experiencing fracturing and division based on ancestral differences among their constituencies with the advent of gaming monies and per cap pressures, with calls to tighten definitions of tribal membership.

With the advent of the modern era, an explosion of persons identifying as Native American led to exponential growth in the Indian population, as well as debates on who belongs and who doesn't. The emergence of identity politics in "Indian Country" is happening within the context of an increasingly diverse and multicultural American social landscape. A recent example of a proactive approach to the swiftly changing dynamics of the composition of the populations in the American mainstream is a Wyoming tribe joining the

---

[103] [Ibid]

NAACP. In the years since the NAACP formed to champion the rights of people of color, there have been few interactions between it and Native Americans. But a decade ago the Eastern Shoshone people purchased the $5,000 membership, the highest level of membership offered, something which had never happened before.

"They are impressed with our record of changing conditions for people of color," says the Rev. Nelson B. Rivers III, chief operating officer for the NAACP. "They believe we would be a good partner, and we agree."[104] This situation is an example of the growing cooperation between various communities of people of color as the "browning of America" grows. In the context of these changes, identities which were once very locally specific and defined by residency, blood ties, marriage, and community context are today becoming pronouncedly less so.

National organizations and identities, Pan-Indian cultural traditions, and Native-oriented social media are all increasingly shifting interactions from face to face encounters to an online environment. With an expanding urban and suburban population more than at any time in the past, tribal governments are challenged in defining relevant membership criteria. The blood quantum classification system in use since the earliest

---

[104] Lindsey, Nedra. "Wyoming Indian Tribe Purchases NAACP Membership." *Crisis* (15591573) 113.6 (2006):57 *Academic Search Premier.* Web. 15 May 2014

interactions between the United States and its aboriginal citizens is coming under increasing fire as anachronistic, irrelevant, and inefficient.

Its appropriateness and feasibility as a part of the landscape of tomorrow's Native American communities is being questioned in many corners. The place of identity in Native American communities has been a matter of debate and contention among all parties concerned for centuries, and this debate shows no sign of becoming less raucous as more and more tribes find avenues for economic development and the appeal of membership becomes less cultural, social, or spiritual, and more economic in nature. The meaning of being Native in a racially diverse society as the American mainstream is increasingly becoming multifaceted, and specific identities in the context of the larger whole are more diffuse.

Factors such as legal status, attitudes regarding race, local or regional terminology, and the composition of the surrounding population all play a part in shaping the way Natives see themselves, and how others view them. In the last several generations, all Native communities have moved deeper and deeper into a sense of a larger "Native American" identity versus the tribally specific identities espoused by community members during the pre-WWII era. Differences among tribes are decreasing as similarly among "Indians" increases in the modern world of social media and global economic integration, with identities of average Americans becoming less European in origin, and more global in their roots.

Although harder to see and sometimes more hidden by those involved, the same process of hybridity is taking place in Native American communities, but within these the identification with a common tribal history and sense of belonging is ofttimes growing stronger, even as the blood quantum on members' Certificate of Degree of Indian Blood card continues to diminish. In a multiracial America what will be the place of a tribe in the scheme of things? Where will tomorrow's Indian fit into the mix?

The Persistence of Cultural identity in Florida and Alabama

Creek traditions went on in Alabama and Florida throughout the Jim Crow years, though small and secretive in the conducting of ceremonies and tribal gatherings. Indian people from the panhandle and the Creek-speaking Seminoles north of Lake Okeechobee maintained contact and visited each other's busks. Corn Dance tradition tells of the Great Green Corn dance held yearly near Ocala where Creeks from one end of Florida to the other would journey to gather, a tradition which only ended with the advent of WWII.

After that the ties between the Creeks of the panhandle and those of the Big Cypress slowly atrophied over the next few decades as modernity took off for both groups and new forms of (non-traditional) government arose; the Creek Nation East of the

Mississippi in the panhandle and the Seminole Tribe of Florida in the South. One south Florida Indian family, that of Seminole tribal leader Euchee Billie had recent ties to the panhandle people through his grandfather Sam Story, the ancestor of the Holmes County Indian people, often called Dominickers.

Today's generation continues the work of their elders. As a 25 year old I sat on the tribal council next to a 97 year old; she was the oldest ever to sit in a council person's seat, and I the youngest. Panhandle Creek artist Dan Townsend has photos on his wall of his father in a traditional long shirt sitting in his chickee in the 1940s.[105] At the Corn Dance held every summer in Blountstown, Ekvn Hvtke tribal town leader Daniel Penton can be found addressing the people holding the 150 year old speaker's staff that has been passed to him through generation after generation of his ancestors as leaders of Creek tradition, much as his grandfather Sankey Godwin did.

---

[105] Interestingly Dan Townsend is a descendent of a Creek man who appears on the Parsons and Abbott Roll of Creek Nation from 1832 in Eufaula town named what else, Daniel Townsend!

FIGURE 64 PHOTO: THE AUTHOR'S MOTHER REGINA SMITH WITH HIS NIECE SUMMER SEWELL 2013 ESTIFFANULGA, FLORIDA

As he has for nearly a half century Dr. Andrew Ramsey leads the Creek people of Apalachicola tribal town in prayer to the Creator for another year's bounty. His presence amidst the elders and children at the annual Blountstown Indian Community Conference is a reassuring continuity in the fast paced times of our present day. Many of the elders of my youth are gone on now. The shining eyes, gentle hands and quiet words of beloved elders like Essie Hill, Sallie Kever, and Mary Francis Johns are no longer found at the Corn Dance grounds as they once were when summer's heat came to usher in the cycle of renewal and thanksgiving to the Creator once again. Now they live in the hearts of the many people whose lives they touched and in the songs and faces of their great-grandchildren and great great-grandchildren.

In the early 1980s, Chief Andrew Ramsey of Blountstown, a member of the Florida Governors Council of Indian Affairs and a well-known activist for Eastern Creek people for many years was able to secure ten acres of land near the location of the historic Apalachicola people's ceremonial grounds, on the former reservation lands at Blountstown. Here many families would gather for Corn Dance in times gone by. With the loss of the long time site for the Corn Dance near St. Marks, the sacred fire's ashes were moved to the land in Blountstown. A new cooperation between Creek families from Christian as well as traditional backgrounds, this community would inspire people from all over the panhandle to return to their roots; and within twenty years Creek ceremonial grounds would return to the Poarch Creek Indian reservation in Atmore, Alabama and the state reservation of the lower Muskogee Creeks in Tama, Georgia.

My grandmother attended the Green Corn Dance at the ceremonial grounds in Blountstown, where Andrew Ramsey was the ground's Mekko; a man from outside the community, Sakim, the Maker of Medicine for some years before being having been removed by the people of the tribal town. This 1997 article about the Apalachicola tribal town mentions me along with my cousin S. Pony Hill's grandma (and my Auntie) Essie Hill Syfrett.

FIGURE 65 PHOTO: ESSIE HILL WITH HER CHILDREN

These excerpts are from a transcription of an article printed in the Religion section of the <u>Dallas Morning News</u> on May 24 1997.

-by Jeffrey Weiss, staff writer of the Dallas Morning News)

Blountstown, Fla. - Indian blood is not primarily what ties the Pine Arbor people to each other or their history. Sure, many of them claim Creek Indian heritage. Some report blood ties to other American Indian tribes. But others with no known link to Native America are fully accepted members, even leaders of this group. What binds them is the Muscogee Way, a religion and way of life with an archeological record many thousands of years old. Those who travel the Muscogee way-and others who meet them-say they act differently from many in America's Christian mainstream.

Chris Sewell is aggressively proud of his Indian heritage. For a while he lived out west with members of the American Indian Movement and participated in ceremonies of the Western tribes. Eventually he was drawn home to North Florida and his own traditions. His Indian genes express more strongly than do those of many at Pine Arbor. With his broad features and dark complexion, he says he is sometimes mistaken for Hispanic. He has "about 500 cousins around here, most of them are double cousins." Essie Hill Syfrett, 79, is Chris Sewell's mother's aunt. She is a proud member of a Pentecostal Holiness Church and knows little of Muscogee way, but Mrs. Syfrett remembers being taught two things explicitly about her families' heritage, pride and fear. "I was taught I was an Indian before anything else," she says. She also says" Mother taught us to protect ourselves and not to tell anyone we were Indian. " Though Sakim took many liberties in the sharing of community knowledge with the visiting reporters, he was eventually to find another "spiritual home" at a new ground along with others at a new location in Gadsden County, and Chief Andrew Ramsey would reassert his hereditary leadership of Apalachicola tribal town. In 1996 the ashes of the Green Corn Dance grounds (Apalachicola) were divided by conflict and three ceremonial grounds emerged from the struggle; (New) Pine Arbor, Ekvn Hvtke, and (Coweta)

Kunfuskee. All three continue to carry on the ancient traditions of the Nene Hvtke, the "White Road" of peace. Some like Kunfuskee carry on close ties to relatives in Oklahoma, while others such as Ekvn Hvtke are closed and insular. Today half-dozen groups have started up ceremonial grounds, many with little knowledge or training in actual Muscogee Creek traditional ways. The future of these new "ceremonial ground" organizations is unknown, and if they survive the decades of future generations, only time will tell. The Blountstown Indian Community Conference, started in 1996 to preserve the efforts to organize the local Indian people, continues.

Conclusion

A long chain of generations and events lies between me and my ancestors of the Creek Nation at the time of removal. Though my own life has been rich in experiences and community rooted in our Creek heritage I find that there is always more to be done to assure the survival of these traditions. In each generation for us of the East, some felt more strongly than others their connection to the Indian people. In the panhandle of Florida where my family has lived for generations there are thousands of people who identify strongly with their Creek ancestry. There are a few hundred who live closely bound to the *Nene Hvtke*, and a few dozen for whom their commitment to our native traditions has been of the utmost lifelong importance.

Conclusion

I am one of those people, and like many of my cousins in the most recent generation I have reared my children to know and respect this inheritance from our old ones. Like many Eastern Creek Indians from southern Alabama and Georgia and northwest Florida, I originate from families which were split in the1830s, with part leaving for the sunset on "the trail where they cried" and some remaining in a social limbo which would make them strangers in their own land within a generation.

The children and grandchildren of the Creek and other Indian people who were able to avoid removal would live their lives in the tumult of the civil war years, and their grandchildren would come of age in the economically depressed and racially stratified South of the early twentieth century, which differentiated them from their brethren in Indian Territory. The South of the late 1800's was not an easy place to live. This was a raw and rugged place, where little contact with outsiders or trust of strangers was the norm for all. The South would languish in its own stew of racial strife and bigotry, even as other parts of the country would open up and move forward.

Despite the horror of the removal of the Creek Nation and the ensuing decades that followed pockets of Indian people were scattered across the Southland still, struggling to adjust to a new order, one where their identity was now in question. My family, like dozens of others, turned inwards to find that identity, finding the strength to survive from kinsmen. How the outsider perceived us was always in question; how we perceived ourselves was not.

The Civil War which unfolded thirty years after the removal did little to help the situation for Native people in the South. Most were socially invisible in the emerging reality of post-Civil War racial order. The evolution of identity in conjunction with race was to happen quickly during the post war years. Thousands of persons who had been slaves would cross the color line and become "white".[106] Before the war, ones status as free or slave would have dictated important aspects of a person's treatment by others, as individuals and communities. After the conflict a new emphasis on race as appearance would take hold, with any darker complexioned person being cast as "mulatto" or Black by the majority. Many stories of family and communities feeling the bite of the Jim Crow era's racism were passed on to me.

The reorientation of racial identities in the Jim Crow era was complex, and in this window of time many of the remaining Creek Indian and Mixed Blood families would struggle to find a foothold, as the prewar binary social structure of slave versus free faded into a more appearance oriented means of defining race. With this situation, the Indians who lived "among the whites"[107], in lower Alabama, south Georgia and the Florida

---

[106] Sweet, Frank (2005). Legal History of the Color Line. Palm Coast Florida, Backintyme Publishing
[107] To use the terminology of the Treaty of Fort Jackson

panhandle began to withdraw into small endogamous settlements in the remotest of areas, and communities like Woods, Scott Town, Scotts Ferry, and Poarch grew.

They would walk a line between the white empowered majority and disenfranchised black and brown population, with attachment to one's community often the defining factor of the public's judgment of a Mixed Blood's race. As W.E.B. Du Bois said, "The discovery of personal whiteness among the world's peoples is a very modern thing- a nineteenth and twentieth century matter, indeed…"[108] and in the lower South this was the proving ground where "whiteness" and "otherness" would lock into a struggle that would produce dozens of court cases regarding the identity of Indians in the binary social order in many of the Indian communities that remained. Catawba, Lumbee, Eastern Cherokee and Creek, and Mississippi Choctaw and other tribes would all feel the brunt of the push to force them apart and into the "colored" class in the eyes of the law and social opinion.

The racial environment faced by persons of color during the dark days was harsh and limited. One man remembered from those times that "the pressure of southern living kept me from being the kind of person I might have been."[109] This is a

---

[108] Du Bois, W.E.B. (1921) 1996. The souls of white folk. In The Oxford W.E.B. Du Bois reader, ed. Eric J. Sundquist, 497-98. New York, Oxford University Press.

[109] Wright, Richard. [1945] 1988. Black Boy (American Hunger): A record of childhood and youth. New York: HarperPerennial.

sentiment I heard from several elders during interviews for this work. All who were to survive would have to rely solely on fellow community members as well as their own internal strength for a quality of life of value. Families of Eastern Creeks such as those in Atmore, Alabama or Blountstown, Florida would learn to negotiate the slippery slope on which they found themselves, and in some cases attain success. Chief Andrew Ramsey is one such case. Born during the end of the social cancer of Jim Crowism, Andrew Ramsey would lead the Indian people of the Blountstown Indian Community for a half century towards a better future.

As scholar Don Mitchell stated, "control over the production of space-the ability to create space in particular ways-also lends to powerful groups the ability to actively create race."[110] For many of us, the ceremonial grounds are such a place, in generations passed as well as now. A sacred place where in we define ourselves in a sacred way, a time in which we renew our spiritual energy, and experience the Creator in our midst, for Indian people in the panhandle we live in a subtle and pervasive reality wherein the mainstream "norms" are left at the gate, and a "smile and a handshake" is met on arrival.

When the specter of segregation was hanging over the people of color of the South, hard times made for hard people. Intimidation was everywhere and refuges few. Families were

---

[110] Mitchell, Don. 1996. The lie of the land: Migrant workers and the California landscape. Minneapolis: University of Minnesota Press.

divided by hard choices. Outsiders' opinions cost families their peace. This is what the post Reconstruction White population did, and many Indian people of the South had new choices to make, as individuals and communities. Natives would have no protections during Jim Crow from state and local authorities by the federal government and in many cases active persecution by local authorities occurred, as hundreds of court cases regarding their racial status records show.

In the South of the late nineteenth century and early twentieth, knowing one's place was a looming and ever present part of the social fabric of the rural communities where the grandchildren and great grandchildren of those who had not been removed or assimilated lived. My family and communities were strongest in this time. As Creswell points out the position one held in the social ladder had as much to do with culture as with propinquity and location.[111] The well-known "Jackson County War,"[112] a period of severe racial strife and conflict in the area, is just one example of the intensity of racial struggle in the time.

In the aftermath of the Brown v. Topeka Board of Education decision in 1954, C. Vann Woodward wrote that "there is more to Jim Crowism practiced in the South than there are Jim Crow laws on the books."[113]These were the unwritten

---

[111] Cresswell, Tim. 1996. In place/ out of place: Geography, ideology, and transgression. Minneapolis: University of Minnesota Press.
[112] http://www.thejacksoncountywar.com
[113] Woodward, C. Vann. [1955] 1974. The strange career of Jim Crow. 3rd ed.

laws that defined our elders' existence as much as any official law enforced by the often racist courts of Jackson and Calhoun counties. Refuge from the social pressures of being brown in a White/Black social order was a luxury for the few with money or connections. "Real" Indians look for kinsmen; Brickhouse Indians would look "through" a kinsman (pretend not to see).

This was especially true along the area of the border of the panhandle of Florida and its neighbors Alabama and Georgia, and the oral histories passed on by many of my communities' elders reflect the challenges they lived through, and for some the trauma they still live with. With several communities of Indians and Mixed Blood people well established several decades before the Civil War, the post war period would push these several settlements back economically, and strip them of the fairly certain and accepted status, an "in between" identity that they had held before the conflict. This post war era would be the most difficult of times.

In Jackson, Calhoun, Holmes, Walton and other panhandle Florida counties the Indian settlements would in some part come to be defined as "Colored" socially and to a smaller degree legally by the White power structure, and the complex dynamics within and between families in the settlements would be tested at times as the generations responded to each new challenge these decades brought.

New York: Oxford University Press.

Conclusion

When some could pass as White by moving away from the Indian settlement they would, while others would maintain ties with kin and suffer the social stigma that came along with it. As Hoeschler put it, this externally defined identity which impacted many of the Mixed Blood and Indian families was "a central theme in the historical geography of the American south and other places marked by geographies of exclusion: how a dominant group was able to create a culture of segregation that extended well beyond the boundaries of its legal apparatus."[114]

---

[114] Hoelscher, Steven. 2003. Making Place, Making Race: Performances of Whiteness in the Jim Crow South. Annals of the Association of American Geographers, 93(3) 657-686

Figure 66 Photo: Old Jim Scott with James Scott

These extended boundaries shaped the lives of Jim Scott, Hugh Oxendine, Corvia Jacobs, and Noah Hill. The domination by local White authorities of the lives of persons of color who were unable to pass as "White" (as did many of the third and fourth generation of descendants of unremoved Creek people in the South) was total. Court records from Jackson and Calhoun counties reflect dozens of such struggles over a one hundred twenty year period, battles for respect, personhood, and justice in the face of social oppression. Without the great numbers that the African American community had, the Dominicker and

Conclusion

Indian people of the panhandle had fewer options but stronger ties. The subtle passageways of the heart, the hidden trails of the mind, and the spiritual nourishment of the wild fed the reclusive and skittish soul of the unremoved Indians of Poarch, Wild Fork, Scott's Ferry, and Woods.

With the WWII, hope began to break like a dawn's first rays on the horizon. White supremacy was integral to the post-war period, socially and legally speaking, though it was never completely able to seep within the heart of the isolated and ofttimes violent settlements of the mixed people. The hold on power exerted by Jim Crowism was constantly in flux and remade in response to the evolving social realities, as Melinda Maynor Lowery documents in her research on the lives of Lumbee people in Carolina and Georgia. Lumbee descended families living in Woods in Liberty County such as the Oxendines, Jacobs, and others.

The social memories which a family, a community, and a people retain in the passing generations and years is what Fentress and Wickham felt identified " a group, giving it a sense of the past, and defining its aspirations for the future. "[115]The stories and traditions I have received from my elders have done that. The journey to organize our people, obtain academic as well as traditional educations, and rear our children as invested in our Native identity has guided me and many cousins such as

---

[115] Fentress, James and Chris Wickham. 1992. Social Memory. London: Blackwell

S. Pony Hill, Angela Barrera, Matthew Livingston, and Marcus Briggs-Cloud.

FIGURE 67 PHOTO: ANGELA BARRERA, THE DAUGHTER OF ELAINE HILL, IN BLOUNTSTOWN

The heavy endogamy among the Mixed Blood and Indian settlement families which intensified in the post war years, and the oral histories and unique lifeways and occupations, were social memories we have been fortunate to inherit. Tales rich in stories of the lives past lived in the Carolinas, passed from the first generations to settle in Florida, by the many Lumbee migrant families such as the Oxendine,

Conclusion

Jacobs, and Porter families of Scott Town and Blountstown
Florida, were threads in a fabric of survival, a tapestry of place
and identity. Eastern Creek perseverance of cultural and
ceremonial traditions allowed a sense of community to root us in
our community.

In lower Alabama and the Pensacola area, family
traditions of Creek Indian ancestors' courage and fortitude to
survive and "avoid being took out to Oklahoma" were still
prevalent in the 1950s, more than a century after the witnesses
were gone. Elders such as Zera Denson, Don Sharon, Buck
Bryant, Clarence Mabry, and others would instill in us the
import of our present opportunities compared to the struggles of
their youth.

These stories and the memories from which they were
created were passed along in private, in consideration of the
family members' appearance, whether they "looked Indian" or
didn't (could pass as White or Black), and the position of their
families in the hierarchies of the small settlements' social
ladders, which old-timers called the "Old Heads." The habit to
be "notoriously selective in the exercise of historical memory"
(Fabre, 1994, p. 111)displayed by any peoples was not remiss
among the people of Hog Fork, Bell Creek, Poarch, Scott Town,
or Scott's Ferry. As the families of the original migrants
branched out across the panhandle over several generations,
some continued to marry within the cluster of interrelated

families, and would stay in the safety and security of the small settlements while others would marry local Whites and become a part of the local population centered on town. In our own time some of these old settlements are beginning to see renewal.

"I only went to town maybe three times before I was twelve years old," one elder would recall of her childhood in the 1920's.[116] That kind of isolation allowed a sense of rootedness that later generations would have to strive for. Back then, the avoidance of social situations that could lead to community members appearing on equal footing with local African Americans was an important aspect of how the community saw itself, despite local whites' view of them. "Uncle Hugh Oxendine would always walk when he would come to town, and even when white people would try to pick him up, he wouldn't take the charity" Sallie Kever would say of "Uncle Hugh" Oxendine, reputed to be the "last full blood Indian" alive in Woods in the 1940s by several elders who participated in an oral history project in the 1990s.

What is accepted as the truest version of the past as remembered by various elders is a powerful authority at work in the family lines, even today, after several generations of activity within the larger movement to reassert the historic community's

---

[116] From notes from an Oral History Interview with elder Sallie Kever for the Scott Town-Scotts Ferry-Woods Community Oral History Project as part of the Florida Tribe of Eastern Creek Indians petition for federal Acknowledgement, conducted at the Blountstown Indian Community Tribal Office, Calhoun County Courthouse, Blountstown Florida, March 1996.

identity. As George Orwell wrote in *Nineteen Eighty-Four*, "Who controls the past controls the future; who controls the present controls the past"[117] and this control of the narrative concerning the tribal past would not be without fierce contention in the century after the Civil War, or in the half century since desegregation.

The various perspectives on race, disagreements on tribal origins, community identity, and the social structure and leadership of the pre-segregation era settlements would become a political football in the struggles of the late twentieth century to define clearly the nature of the Indian settlements before their reorganization and in some cases dispersal in the 1960s, but in the long decades leading up to the twentieth century, the small inwardly focused settlements of Indians scattered across the Gulf coast were places of family, work, and acceptance in an otherwise hostile world. The Indian communities of Mississippi Choctaw, MOWA Choctaw and Poarch Creeks In Alabama, and the scattered settlements of Eastern Creek and Lumbee in south Georgia and the panhandle of Florida would survive socially through reliance on one another and physically through subsistence farming, fishing, and turpentine work, for the most part.

My own family members, like many from the small settlements, began to network with others who were reaching

---

[117] Orwell, George. [1949] 1981. Nineteen Eighty-Four. New York: New American Library

out, making connections and glimpsing new horizons which had been unavailable before. Beginning in the 1950s, the Indian Claims Commission would make attempts to compensate Native peoples for the unjust seizures of land which had occurred in the past. The Creek Nation like many others would be awarded funds, which courts ruled applied to Creek people in the East, as well as in Oklahoma. When the Eastern Creek land claims payment was organized, many thousands stepped forward to file, those who could read assisting those who couldn't in trying to gather documents on genealogy which were then hard to come by. Tribal council meetings among the "Creek Nation East of the Mississippi" as it was called brought together Indian people who had formerly been reclusive and non-political. Dreams were born, hopes soared.

By 1970 the feeling of a brighter future and a sense of Indian pride would be felt all over south Alabama and north Florida, as throughout the country. My cousin Chief Andrew Ramsey would find a seat on the Florida Governor's Council on Indian Affairs along with the leaders from the Seminole and Miccosukee tribes. In time I myself as a twenty-something would attend meetings at the state capital as well as in D.C. representing the interests of our community. Family members would step forward to contribute to the struggle. My grandmother would help with cooking for tribal meetings where our options as a tribe rather than just a community would be discussed.

In time we had limited success as some of our people, those in Escambia, Munroe, and Baldwin counties in Alabama would secure federal recognition as the Poarch Band of Creek Indians, and Creek people descended from Chief McIntosh living in South Georgia would be recognized by the state. Yet many communities would continue to struggle for acknowledgment of their long road of survival. For many years as a young man, I would talk with elders and kinsmen at Green Corn Dance about what we faced then. As a teenager I became a single father, an event which only fired me to struggle harder so that my son Harjo wouldn't know the challenges faced by my grandparents.

At times anger would cloud my mind, fears my heart. Auntie Mary Francis Johns would tell me in the quiet evenings during Green Corn, "Don't worry son we will get there." In time I would pursue my education, graduating from Rogers State University in Claremore, Cherokee Nation, Oklahoma with a BS in sociology as my son graduated from high school and found his own place in the struggle of life along with his Cheyenne/Arapaho wife. Later, I earned an MBA from St. Gregory's University in Shawnee, Oklahoma. Our thoughts are always with the elders who mightily strived before us for equality.

The constant struggle by the Indians in these small settlements back then to navigate the treacherous waters of survival as persons of color was captured in a statement by Richard Wright in 1946; "There is not a black problem in the United States, but a white problem."[118] The targeting of specific individuals within the community as colored while others were accepted as White shines a light on the often arbitrary circumstances individual community members would face, such as Rueben Blanchard, Noah Hill, Armond Copeland, Tom Scott, Mathias Porter, and Hugh Oxendine, or Jim Scott to name a few who the documentary sources record as slipping back and forth across the White/Black/Indian color line several times depending on the social situation and the decade.

Whatever the challenges of that past, today the people who are inheritors of the struggles of generations past are finding their voices, working to restore community institutions, and implementing language and cultural preservation efforts alongside much needed economic developments. The Eastern Creeks of Alabama, Florida, and Georgia are finding the twenty-first century one in which, as in the lives of distant ancestors of the removal era, the society around them is changing once again in a major way, with a new and multicultural America coming to

---

[118] Nadeau, Maurice. [1946] 1993. *There's no black problem in the U.S.A., but a white problem, the black writer Richard Wright tells us.* Combat 11 May: 1.

the fore. By focusing on strengths of the past and local ancestral struggles, a pathway into the future is being revealed, and lived.

Today when I look at the social landscape that I saw through younger eyes thirty-five years ago at community meetings with my grandparents, or recall their tales of a century ago when their grandparents were young, so much has changed in the big wide world, yet not really. It seems that when I travel back down the same dirt road to the Green Corn dance grounds, and when I hear those same ancient songs on the night breeze, smell the same sofkee cooking, or see the same tired but peaceful faces in the early morning light after a night of stomp dancing, I know very little has changed. We are still here, we are still together, and we are still struggling to carry on as a people, part of a larger people scattered now but bound by a common heritage.

Before I leave our little settlement to go back to my pursuit as a graduate student, I always stop by the graves of Mary Brown, Emma Hill, Hugh Oxendine, Corvia Jacobs, Mathias Porter, Tom Scott, Sarah Scott Etheridge and the other heroes from my grandparents' stories of a darker time when the strength of heart was all that they had going for them, and I feel them riding with me into the future's unknown challenges. When I see my own son Harjo circling the Green Corn Dance fire in the moonlight I know they rest peacefully knowing we will endure. In this circle of generations I am complete. In this great wide world wherever I find myself they are with me.

Works Cited

Adolph, D. (1975). *The Only Land I Know*. Syracuse: Syracuse University Press.

Affairs, B. o. (1980). *Petition Poarch Band of Creek*.

Archives, N. C. (n.d.). PAR. *21584607*. Nacogdoches, Texas: Clounty Clerk.

Callahan, S. (1891). *A Child of the Forest*. Univ. of Nebraska Press. XVII.

Chaudhuri, J. H. (2001). *A Sacred Path: The Way of the Muscogee Creeks*. Los Angeles: UCLA American Indian Studies Center.

Cherokee Phoenix. (n.d.). Retrieved from Library Digital Collections: http://www.wcu.edu/library/DigitalCollections/CherokeeP hoenix/

Church, A. H. (n.d.). *excerpted from Asbury Manual Labor School and Mission Fort Mitchell*. Alabama Heritage Landmark of The United Methodist Church.

Clarence Edward Carter, J. P. (1938). *The Territorial Papers of the United States* (Vol. Volume 6). U.S. Government Printing Office.

Commission, H. C. (n.d.). *Chatahoochee Trace Historic Markers, Alabama*.

Crediford, G. (2009). *Those Who Remain; A Photographers Memoir of South Carolina Indians*.

Crevecoeur, J. H. (1957). *Letters from an American Farmer*. New York: E. P. Dutton.

Ellisor, J. (2010). *The Second Creek War: Interethnic Conflict and Collusion on a Collapsing Frontier*. Lincoln: University of Nebraska Press.

Fabre, G. (1994). *History and Memory in African-American Culture*. Oxford: Oxford University Press, Incorporated.

Foreman, G. (1945). *Muskogee: The Biography of an Oklahoma Town*. St. Louis: privately printed.

Works Cited

Frank, A. (1970). *Creeks & Southerners.* Lincoln and London: University of Nebraska Press.

Frank, A. (2005). *Creeks & Southerners.* Lincoln and London: University of Nebraska Press.

Frank, A. (2010). *A Peculiar breed of whites: race, culture, and identity in the Creek Confederacy.* University of Florida.

Frank, A. K. (2002). "The Rise and Fall of William McIntosh: Authority and Identity On the Early American Frontier.". *Georgia Historical Quarterly.*

Frizzell, G. (n.d.). Hunter Library. *28723.* Special Collections, Western Carolina University, Cullowhee, North Carolina.

Galloway, C. (2008). *White People, Indians, and Highlanders: Tribal People and Colonial Encounters in Scotland and America.* Onford University Press.

Gazette, T. L. (1500-1926). Journal of Criticism, Science, and the Arts. *Volume 1.*

Genealogy, A. (n.d.). *1832 Creek Census.* Retrieved from Cussetaw Town: http://www.accessgenealogy.com/native/1832-creek-census-cussetaw-town.htm

Genweb, U. (n.d.). *Archives.* Retrieved from Special Native American : http://www.usgwarchives.net/special/native_american/

Green, M. D. (1982). *Politics of Indian Removal:Creek Government and Society in Crisis.* Lincoln, Neb.

Hawkins, B. (1980). Letters, Journals, and Writings of Benjamin Hawkins:1802-1816. *Beehive Press.*

Hill, R. M. (1829). *Missionary Institute near Fort Mitchell Creek Nation.*

Howell, R. (1972). Dominicker: A Regional Racial Term. *American Speech,* 305-306.

Littlefield, D. F. (1984). *American Indian and Alaska Native Newspapers and Periodicals 1826-1924.* Westport Connecticutt: Greenwood.

Lowery, M. (n.d.). Volume 29, Issue 1-2. *American Indian Culture and Research Journal,* 41.

Nation, R. o.-I. (1870).

NPR. (2014, 4 1). *Native Americans Losing Tribal Membership: DNA Tests Identity.* Retrieved from National Press Report: http://www.npr.org/sections/codeswitch/2014/04/01/2957

98832/for-native-americans-losing-tribal-membership-tests-
identity

Paredes, J. (1974). *The Emergency of Contemporary Eastern Creek
Indentity. Social and cultural Identity: Problems of Persistence and
Change.*

Phoenix, M. (1902, June 1). p. Front Page.

Rogers, W. (1995). *The Papers of WIll Rogers: The early years, November
1879-April 1904.* Oklahoma: University of Oklahoma Press.

Ryan, M. (2007). The Indian Problem as a Womens Question: S. Alice
Callahan's "Wynema: A Child of the Forest". *Atq,* 23-45.

Ryan, M. (n.d.). *The Indian Problems as a Woman's Question:* (Vol. 21.1).
American Transendental Quarterly.

Sider, G. (1994). *Lumbee Indian Histories: Race, Ethnicity, and Indian
Identity in the Southern United States.* CUP Archive.

Society, A. H. (1879). *Quarterly.*

Society, A. H. (1879). Alabama Historical Reporter.

Sparks, W. (1870). *Memories of Fifty Years: Containing Brief Biographical
Notices of Distinguished Americans and Anecdotes of Remarkable
Men in 1872.*

Speck, F. (1947). *Notes on Social and Ecenomic Conditions among the Creek
Indians of Alabama in941.* America Indigena.

Sykes, B. (2012). *DNA USA: A genetic portrait of America.* New York:
Liveright Publishers.

Taylor, A. (2002). *American colonies; Volume 1.* NY: Penguin.

Webb, S. (2005). GTT: Redbones Gone to Texas. *1st Annual Conference
of the People Known as Redbones* (p. 76). Alexandria: Redboone
Heritage Foundation.

White, K. (1930). JOHN CHISOLM, A SOLDIER OF FORTUNE.
Chronicles of Oklahoma, Volume 8(No. 2), 75.

Woodward, T. (1859). *Woodward's Reminiscences of the Creek: Or
Miscogee Indians, Contained in Letters to Friends in Georgia and
Alabama.* Alabama Book Store.

FIGURE 69ARTWORK: ORIGINAL BY AUTHOR SCOTT SEWELL,
TITLED: TEJANA